Praise for *The Salmon Capital of Michigan*

"The story of Lake Huron's sudden food web change is a cautionary tale for other Great Lakes. Carson Prichard takes the reader on a fascinating journey into the homes of those who witnessed the meteoric rise and decline of the Chinook salmon fishery in the 'Salmon Capital of Michigan.' But, at the end of the day, those who stayed in Rogers City continue to enjoy a new fishery, one with more diversity of species, and a wonderful part of the Great Lakes."

—Titus Seilheimer, fisheries specialist, Wisconsin Sea Grant

"Prichard provides the reader with a look back at a time when salmon fishing was all anyone could talk about within Great Lakes communities. The size of the fish and the numbers taken were truly astonishing! He does an exceptional job of capturing the essence of what it felt like to experience the dramatic rise as well as the sudden collapse of the fish that put port communities such as Rogers City on the map."

—Scott McLennan, mayor, City of Rogers City

"Carson Prichard is the conductor of a symphony of voices in a groundbreaking oral history turned ethnography that explores the personal, scientific, and community dimensions of the Lake Huron alewife and Chinook salmon fisheries crashes. Exploring the humble beginnings of Rogers City to its rise and fall as 'The Salmon Capital,' Prichard's work is a reminder of the fragile ecosystems *Homo sapiens* inhabit and upon which they depend. *The Salmon Capital of Michigan* should be a staple read for fisheries managers and coastal community leaders, residents, researchers, and anglers."

—Brittany Fremion, professor of environmental and
oral history, Central Michigan University

"I have over thirty years of experience as a student and professional with Great Lakes ecosystem changes. What you don't usually learn from books or experience is how changes in the fisheries affect people in coastal communities. Carson Prichard captures the social and economic aspects of the Lake Huron fishery through his interviews with anglers, business owners, and community leaders."

—Jay Wesley, Lake Michigan Basin Coordinator,
Michigan Department of Natural Resources

THE SALMON CAPITAL OF MICHIGAN

GREAT LAKES BOOKS

A complete listing of the books in this series can be found online at
wsupress.wayne.edu.

Editor
Thomas Klug
Sterling Heights, Michigan

THE SALMON CAPITAL OF MICHIGAN

The Rise and Fall of a Great Lakes Fishery

CARSON PRICHARD

Wayne State University Press
Detroit

ISBN 9780814351130 (paperback)
ISBN 9780814351147 (e-book)

Library of Congress Control Number: 2023940084

Cover images © Alamy / © Shutterstock. Cover design by Laura Klynstra.

Publication of this book was made possible through the generosity of the Friends of the Great Lakes Books Series Fund.

Wayne State University Press rests on Waawiyaataanong, also referred to as Detroit, the ancestral and contemporary homeland of the Three Fires Confederacy. These sovereign lands were granted by the Ojibwe, Odawa, Potawatomi, and Wyandot Nations, in 1807, through the Treaty of Detroit. Wayne State University Press affirms Indigenous sovereignty and honors all tribes with a connection to Detroit. With our Native neighbors, the press works to advance educational equity and promote a better future for the earth and all people.

Wayne State University Press
Leonard N. Simons Building
4809 Woodward Avenue
Detroit, Michigan 48201-1309

Visit us online at wsupress.wayne.edu.

CONTENTS

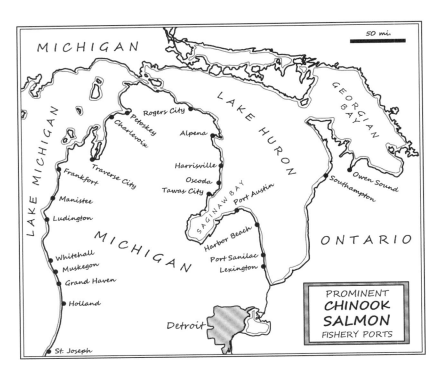

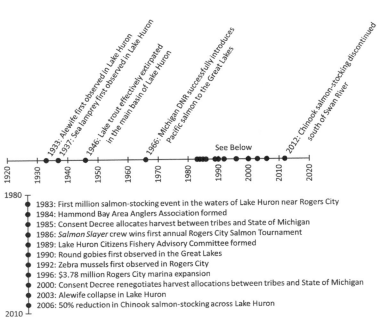

1933: Alewife first observed in Lake Huron
1937: Sea lamprey first observed in Lake Huron
1946: Lake trout effectively extirpated in the main basin of Lake Huron
1966: Michigan DNR successfully introduces Pacific salmon to the Great Lakes
2012: Chinook salmon stocking discontinued south of Swan River

See Below

1920 1930 1940 1950 1960 1970 1980 1990 2000 2010 2020

1980
1983: First million salmon-stocking event in the waters of Lake Huron near Rogers City
1984: Hammond Bay Area Anglers Association formed
1985: Consent Decree allocates harvest between tribes and State of Michigan
1986: *Salmon Slayer* crew wins first annual Rogers City Salmon Tournament
1989: Lake Huron Citizens Fishery Advisory Committee formed
1990: Round gobies first observed in the Great Lakes
1992: Zebra mussels first observed in Rogers City
1996: $3.78 million Rogers City marina expansion
2000: Consent Decree renegotiates harvest allocations between tribes and State of Michigan
2003: Alewife collapse in Lake Huron
2006: 50% reduction in Chinook salmon-stocking across Lake Huron
2010

Timeline of major events related to the ecology of Lake Huron and the Chinook salmon fishery in Rogers City.

ACKNOWLEDGMENTS

This book would not have been possible without the guidance and support of Frank Krist and Brittany Fremion. Frank recognized that fishery impacts can extend far into the community, and he helped me connect with many of the Rogers City residents whom I interviewed. Dr. Fremion provided the encouragement I needed to develop my original ideas into a proper research project, and her mentoring helped ensure the project's professionalism and credibility.

Funding for the original interviews was provided by a Great Lakes Fishery Commission pilot project grant.

Special thanks also to Leslie Edwards (Archives of Michigan), Kevin Pangle (Central Michigan University), Mike Belitz (Michigan State University), and three anonymous reviewers.

PROLOGUE

Fall was well underway in Michigan's Upper Peninsula on Monday, October 31, 1994. The air in Detour Village was a brisk forty degrees. Winds off the shores of northern Lake Huron were out of the northeast at about eight miles an hour, making for relatively calm seas. At precisely 2:34 p.m., about two miles offshore, the crew of the seventy-five-foot RV *Grayling* was just beginning to lower back its sampling gear for—fingers crossed—the final tow of the day. I say "fingers crossed" because there's always a chance of the net getting fouled, or of the knot that cinches up the back of the net, called the "cod end," failing to hold. And such errors would be all the more likely on this, the twelfth day of the sampling voyage.

You see, the "RV" in RV *Grayling* stands for "research vessel," this ship being part of the U.S. Geological Survey's fleet for sampling the prey fish populations in each of the Great Lakes. Each fall, a crew of four or five fisheries biologists and technicians is assembled to perform the USGS Great Lakes Science Center's annual bottom trawl survey on Lake Huron. Working together with the boat's own captain and crew, the fisheries biologists and techs perform net tows, called trawls, all throughout Lake Huron in a standardized manner, counting, measuring, and taking samples from the fish they catch. "Standardized" means that every year sampling is conducted out of the same ports and at the same depths. In this way, trends over time in fish populations can be revealed. The annual survey was begun in 1973, and in most years since then the Michigan waters outside of the ports of Detour, Hammond Bay, Alpena, Oscoda, and Harbor Beach have been sampled at eleven specific depths, ranging from about 30 feet to about 360 feet of water, and as far offshore as twenty miles.

This final tow on October 31, 1994, was at the twenty-seven-meter depth contour (roughly ninety feet of water). To lower the net all the way to the lake bottom, however, takes much more than ninety feet of steel cable, since the drag of the net in the water causes it to angle far behind the stern of the boat. But that drag is also what opens the net so that as it descends to the bottom, its mouth will expand to a width of thirty to forty feet.[1] For each sample, a broad swath of the Lake Huron floor, otherwise concealed from anglers and biologists above, is swept for a full ten minutes before the hydraulic winches begin to slowly rewind, pulling the net back on board and revealing some of the mystery from below.

Taken together, between all the sampling days, driving days, and "blow days" during which the weather is too rough for either driving or sampling, the annual endeavor is an arduous, multi-week venture. At this point in the survey, having spent eleven nights sleeping, eating, and everything else on board, you can bet the biological crew was ready for a break. After this tow—which would be the thirty-second of the survey so far—they'd be given a rest on land as the RV *Grayling* would be piloted roughly 140 miles all the way down the west coast of Lake Huron to the port town of Harbor Beach for the final leg of the survey.

The survey had started on Thursday, October 20, when the crew first wetted their gear off the shores of Oscoda and Au Sable Point. The next day, Friday, was spent motoring fifty miles up to Alpena in order to sample the waters in and outside of Thunder Bay Saturday through Monday. By Thursday the 27th, the *Grayling* had made it up to Hammond Bay, where the crew began sampling the waters there before making their way up to Detour Village by the morning of Sunday, October 30.

For this final tow outside of Detour Village, just as with every other tow up to that point, the crew was well aware that whatever fish might be hauled on board would have to be sorted, counted, and measured. Some would need to be kept and frozen for subsequent analyses to be performed back in the lab throughout much of the rest of the year. But I wouldn't be surprised if the crewmembers were thinking, *Wouldn't it be nice if, just this once, the net came up empty? For pity's sake?*

Well, despite what their wishes may have been, such would not be the case. Maybe the gravelly crunching of the steel cable winding the net back in sounded more labored than usual, or perhaps the winch motor's whine pierced more shrilly. Maybe the boat strained more than it had on previous passes to maintain proper sampling speed. Or maybe half a ton is nothing for a boat that big—I can only imagine. Whatever the case, whether the gear had performed properly was certainly no longer in question as the crew was made aware of their catch: a silvery, shimmering haul just shy of nine hundred pounds sagged weightily in the back of the net as it slowly emerged. At final count, it would be revealed that that single ten-minute trawl pulled up 8,933 fish.[2] So much for an empty net.

The detailed records of the survey database show that it would be one of the heaviest hauls in the entire history of the Lake Huron bottom trawl survey. Just to manage such a mass on the back of a boat must have been difficult, if not downright dangerous, especially at that stage of the sampling tour. Combatting the constant, rhythmic heaving of the boat among the waves over the course of several days is more taxing on the mind and body than life on land. I know from experience, having participated in the 2015 fall bottom trawl survey.

What I don't know from experience, however, is what it must have been like to see such quantities of fish, and that's what makes the scene I'm imagining based on the data collected from the 1994 survey so remarkable. In the 2015 survey, when the crew that I was a part of sampled that same twenty-seven-meter depth contour out of Detour, we caught far, far fewer fish. Most notably, we didn't catch a single adult alewife. Alewives are a small, silvery herring species, with adults typically ranging from about four to seven inches long. For about half a century, they were usually the most abundant prey fish species throughout Lake Huron. That single tow in 1994 in which nine hundred pounds of fish were hauled up contained, among everything else, 7,556 adult alewives. In fact, among the forty-one sample tows performed throughout the entire 1994 survey, a whopping 55,025 adult alewives would be caught—an average of 1,342 per sample. And while 1994 was a prolific year for alewives in Lake Huron, it wasn't outside the realm of normal from the mid-1970s to the early 2000s.

But in 2015, among all forty-three ten-minute trawl samples performed that year, not only were no adult alewives caught in twenty-seven meters of water off the shores of Detour, *not a single adult alewife was caught during the entire survey.*[3] They had effectively been extirpated from Lake Huron. But by 2015, this was old news; the bulk of the alewife collapse happened in 2003 and 2004.

It was surreal—examining the full dataset from earlier decades and comparing the sheer numbers of fish that had been collected in the years before the collapse with the paucity I personally observed in 2015. If memory serves, I was on board for about fifteen of the trawl tows in the 2015 survey—those off the shores of Detour and Hammond Bay. I was relieving one of the technicians who'd helped sample the more southerly Lake Huron ports. But I don't remember anything remarkable about the fish we caught. To be honest, while on board the new multimillion-dollar vessel, doing trawl after trawl with all this immense gear but catching only small smatterings of small fish, my thoughts were, "Why are we going through all this effort?" I had hoped to be proud to be part of such a long-standing Great Lakes fisheries survey, but at the end of my time on board, I really just felt bummed out. The prey fish bottom trawl survey no longer seemed necessary at this point. It was merely a formality—an antiquated remnant of an earlier era.

That earlier era in Lake Huron was the era of alewives—alewives and the Chinook salmon that ate them.

TOO MANY SALMON

Alewives formed the basis of the diet of Chinook salmon—one of the most popular Great Lakes sportfish species—and with the collapse of alewives in Lake Huron came the crash of the Chinook salmon fishery.[4] I remember where I was when I first learned of the Lake Huron Chinook salmon fishery crash. I had just finished my bachelor's degree and gotten my first full-time fisheries gig. That job found me in the basement of an old Coast Guard station, situated on the channel that connects Muskegon Lake to

The RV *Arcticus* replaced the RV *Grayling* in 2015 as the USGS's research vessel for surveying Lake Huron. Carson Prichard was on board the *Arcticus* in 2015 as a crew member for the fall bottom trawl survey. (Source: www.usgs.gov/media/images/rv-arcticus-0)

Lake Michigan. It was a pretty tedious job. The bulk of my time was spent thawing out bags of frozen fish and then, one by one, measuring their lengths, dissecting their stomachs, and getting a real close look at what they had been eating. I stared into a dissecting scope for hours on end, identifying and counting the organisms that were in those fish stomachs. It was mostly tiny zooplankton, but occasionally I'd have to pick through partially digested fish remains to find a diagnostic cleithrum (jawbone) or otolith ("ear stone"), which allowed me to identify the species of the fish that had been eaten. The scope sat on a lab bench between a pair of fish-drying ovens and a piece of equipment called a bomb calorimeter. The bomb calorimeter was used to measure a fish's "energy density," while the drying ovens were set just below cooking temperature in order to evaporate off all the water within a biological sample—often fish tissue or the "gut contents" I was sorting through—in order to obtain a "dry weight." For three months, I bathed in that warm, thick, pervasive fishy fragrance, which by some perverse primal instinct made me either hungry or nauseous, depending on the time of day.

Most days I was in that basement by myself, but one day, for whatever reason, the fisheries biologist I worked for was down there with another researcher—I don't remember who. I just knew that whatever they were talking about was going to be a welcome distraction so, discreetly maintaining my position at the scope, I listened in. They were talking about Lake Huron and salmon.

"—yeah, they really underestimated how many wild salmon were coming out of Canada—," I overheard. My ears perked.

I gleaned from their conversation that there had gotten to be so many Chinook salmon in Lake Huron that the alewife population had collapsed. The predation pressure got too high. But having cut my teeth salmon fishing on the west side of Michigan, it had never occurred to me there could be such a thing as *too many salmon*. Of course I knew what alewives were because, beginning around Labor Day weekend, my friends and I and all the people who fished Lake Michigan from the Grand Haven pier would throw cast nets in the channel to catch alewives for bait. If you had a live alewife, you were going to catch a king salmon (back then, no one I fished with called them "Chinook" salmon).[5] I looked forward to Labor Day weekend because it marked the start of the salmon run. By October, the salmon would be well up the rivers, and each fall I'd transition from fishing for them at the piers on Lake Michigan upstream to where they'd spawn in rivers like the Grand, Manistee, Pere Marquette, and Betsie.

That was in 2010, over thirteen years ago, and I've never stopped being intrigued by the Lake Huron salmon story. And so in 2015, when I actually worked as part of the federal government research crew that performs the annual prey fish bottom trawl surveys on Lake Huron, I gained an invaluable experience. Being on the boat and witnessing the process that used to sample alewives in Lake Huron, and imagining the exact same scene playing out twenty to thirty years prior, spilling thousands of fish on board, each haul weighing hundreds of pounds, tow after tow after tow . . . it's almost unbelievable that there could have been so many fish, given how few there are now. In seeing it firsthand, the reality of the magnitude of the loss became undeniable. And that's when I realized that the meaning and impact of the joint alewife collapse and Chinook salmon fishery crash in Lake Huron was not well represented in the textbooks and scientific literature that I had been reading as a student and in my early years as a Great Lakes fisheries professional.

What, I wondered, happened to all the people who used to fish for Chinook salmon in Lake Huron? What happened in all the port towns dotting the Lake Huron shoreline when the salmon fishery crashed? Having grown up on the west side of Michigan, fishing in coastal towns like Grand Haven and Frankfort on Lake Michigan where Chinook salmon fishing is still a thriving activity, I thought about what it might mean for those places if all of a sudden salmon fishing were to disappear.

ROGERS CITY: THE CONTEXT FOR A CASE STUDY

Lake Huron is the third-largest freshwater lake in the world by surface area. It's bisected by the border between Ontario, Canada, to the north and east, and the state of Michigan to the south and west. But despite Lake Huron's vast size, its shoreline in Michigan is relatively sparsely populated. As a result, all the salmon anglers who used to head out onto Lake Huron had to funnel through a limited number of port towns whose marinas and boat launches granted them access. Michigan Department of Natural Resources (DNR) fisheries management biologist Mark Tonello remembers the scene:

> So one of the things I grew up doing was fishing for salmon. Coming from Sterling Heights, the easiest places to fish salmon were the Lake Huron ports in the thumb [the state of Michigan resembles a hand wearing a mitten] and also Oscoda. And so that's where we'd go on

weekends, and in fact, I literally turned sixteen on Wednesday, got my driver's license, and Friday night me and a buddy were driving my dad's van up to Port Sanilac to go salmon fishing. It pains me to this day to know that that fishery that I grew up fishing basically doesn't exist anymore. I sucked at it too, man, I hardly ever caught any—but you know the parking lots'd be full, there'd be people filling both piers and the docks and it would just be an awesome scene. People out there all night with lanterns, just a fun, awesome time. It's gone. It's—it's gone. And to know we had these ports that were phenomenal salmon ports in the late '80s and '90s but aren't anymore is painful. And I remember fishing there one morning with my dad and we had fished all night, and we counted boats heading out in the morning and we decided when, when we got to a hundred boats, that's when we were going to quit, and we did, and it was like 8 a.m. By 8 a.m. there were a hundred boats that had gone out! And now there's no fishery. It's gone. Back in the early 2000s you had fifty charter boats in Harrisville and fifty in Oscoda. And now there's just one or two in each port, and they're typically retired guys that are just doing it for fun and don't need to make money at it. So, economically, you know what that did to that, that side of the [state].[6]

Port Sanilac's population according to the 2020 census was 567. Harrisville's was 437. Oscoda's was 916. For a hundred boats to descend on such places any given weekend, July through September, would have been—what, exactly? A calamity? A bonanza? Dangerous? Exciting? And for whom? At the very least, it would have been impossible to ignore. For these modest places and the people who lived there, what did it feel like to experience the buildup of the Lake Huron Chinook salmon fishery, and then its crash?

In investigating the human aspect of the loss of the Lake Huron Chinook salmon fishery, what better place to start than the town that, once upon a time, called itself the Salmon Capital of Michigan? Rogers City is nestled up on the northeastern shoulder of Michigan's Lower Peninsula, right on the shores of Lake Huron. On sunny days, stunning aquamarine water meets picturesque, pebbly beaches. In 1983, the State of Michigan began annually stocking roughly a million juvenile Chinook salmon there, making it the most abundantly stocked site in the entire state. Soon after, in 1986, Rogers City hosted the inaugural Rogers City Salmon Tournament, which by its sixth iteration in 1991 had become the largest salmon-fishing tournament in Michigan.[7] When salmon fishing was really hot in

Rogers City, recalled resort owner and charter fishing guide Bruce Grant, trucks and trailers would be "lined up all the way out of the harbor, all the way back to the streetlight in town at 5 o'clock in the morning to unload boats to come in and go fishing. Three hundred boats was nothing." That streetlight of which he speaks was a good half mile from the marina. "This time of year back in the '90s," recalled resident and angler Frank Krist on a pleasant, mid-May evening, "there would be eighty, ninety boats out there in the middle of the week."

Well, flash-forward a few decades and the streetlight that Bruce described has been reduced to a four-way stop sign. And when I walked the break-wall of the harbor the morning before my interview with Frank on May 18, 2021, there were no boats out fishing as far as the eye could see, despite crystal-clear skies and unseasonably warm weather that would see Rogers City reach a high of seventy-nine degrees that day. Of the 158 extended truck and trailer spots in the marina parking lot, only two were occupied. In terms of the bigger picture, Rogers City has seen its population drop by 45 percent since 1960. What role did the Chinook salmon recreational fishery play with respect to the dynamics and culture of the people of Rogers City, and what was the impact when the fishery took a big downturn in the mid-2000s?

ORAL HISTORY

This book arose from an oral history project. The goal of the original research was to create a new primary information source to help document the subjective human component of the Lake Huron Chinook salmon recreational fishery as experienced in Rogers City. The term *oral history* describes two things. First, in the most straightforward sense, it encapsulates the product of the original research, which is a collection of interview audio recordings and their corresponding transcripts. That oral history collection is being maintained in perpetuity by the Archives of Michigan, and it is freely available online, where the audio recordings in their entirety can be downloaded or played right in the browser—much the same as a podcast. The participant-reviewed transcripts are also available to read online or to download.[8] The transcripts are fully time-stamped and have word-search capabilities, so the savvy reader intent on digging deeper could easily find (and listen to) any interview excerpt in this book in the corresponding recording.

"Oral history" also describes the methodology undertaken in creating such a collection—that is, the *practice* of oral history. Now, I am not an oral historian but rather someone who has adopted oral history as the best tool for performing the task in which I was interested. I'll admit that I still feel very much like a novice in the practice. In undertaking this project, I had concerns about whether I could record and share interviews in an ethically sound manner, and whether a collection of interviews could be academically rigorous enough to be of use to future researchers. I consulted textbooks and the best-practices guidance materials produced by the leading oral history professional societies and academic institutions. Most important, I received valuable guidance from Dr. Brittany Bayless Fremion, professor of history at Central Michigan University. Brittany is an accomplished environmental and oral historian. She was generous enough to offer an online one-on-one crash course in oral history for me in June 2020, right in the midst of the COVID-19 pandemic. What I gathered from all the instruction is that at its core, the practice of oral history is primarily interested in capturing *that which is important to the person being interviewed*. As such, oral history is about creating an environment conducive to the sharing of such information comfortably, genuinely, and fully.

I viewed my role as an oral history interviewer as simply to facilitate a comfortable conversation around a topic of interest. Identifying potential interview candidates and vetting their suitability for participation in the project were processes that had as much or more to do with the participants' willingness and desire to share their stories than anything else. I began by talking with current members of the Fisheries Division of the Michigan Department of Natural Resources and inquiring about important points of contact. I then built a list of interview candidates based upon researching the local history in Rogers City from roughly 1982 to 2007 as well as through "snowball sampling," meaning the people I contacted or subsequently interviewed suggested further candidate participants whose stories and experiences might be relevant. Ultimately, though, the goal was to document what the Rogers City salmon fishery was like from the perspectives of the people whose livelihoods were shaped by it, and whose experiences might otherwise go undocumented (that is, not fisheries professionals, not journalists, not people with a "voice," so to speak). Several people who contributed interviews to the project had little or no experience salmon angling but were no less eager to share their stories about the salmon fishery's influence on the town and their own lives.

Well before doing any actual recording, I tried my best to build rapport with each interview candidate through phone calls and emails. During this pre-interview phase, I told each person:

I am doing a research project to document the impact of the rise and decline of Lake Huron's Chinook salmon fishery on Michigan's coastal communities. Your experience regarding the development of the Chinook salmon fishery in Rogers City, and how that changed over time, from the early 1980s through the major decline in the mid-2000s, and continuing to now, would be a very valuable contribution to this project.

For the project I am recording long-form oral history interviews that would allow you to tell your story and what you think is important. Potential questions would be:

What was it like in Rogers City during the peak of salmon fishing?
What did it feel like to experience the sudden downturn of the fishery?
What is the legacy of the Chinook salmon fishery in Rogers City?

My agenda, if it could be construed as such, was to learn. After all, it was the lack of anything written or recorded about the local human aspects of the fishery crash that made me interested in doing the research. I explained that the interview could last anywhere from thirty to ninety minutes. I also ensured that each person who agreed to an interview fully understood what would happen next. Participants signed two forms: a consent form granting me permission to record their story, and a deed of gift form allowing me to donate the transcript and audio recording of their interview to the Archives of Michigan for long-term preservation in the public domain.

By the time of the actual interview, I trusted that the participants understood the purpose of the interview. During the interview itself, I tried to impose as little as possible on each person's story. Except when an interviewee came charging from the gate right after I hit "Record," I started each interview with the same question: "Can you tell me a little bit about yourself?"—a little piece of advice I'd learned from Brittany. And while I did arrive to each interview prepared with a list of questions and prompts that I'd written to help stimulate discussion, I tried to keep my intervention to a minimum. When I did intervene, it was mostly to encourage participants to elaborate on feelings instead of facts. Generally, the conversation continued until it meandered off topic, or until *I* was asked, "What else can I tell you?" That question signaled to me that we had essentially covered everything the interviewee thought was important. Still, I finished each interview with the same question: "Is there anything you would like to add about the story or legacy of the Rogers City Chinook salmon fishery?"

The pages that follow contain the reminiscences of nineteen people who were there during the rise and fall of the recreational Chinook salmon fishery in Lake Huron, and who wanted to speak to the experience in Rogers City. The experiences I draw from are diverse. You'll see that I layer interview excerpts among several different conversations, one upon another. In some cases, this helps build a story along a shared timeline. In others, it serves as an engaging call-and-response. I present the respondents' stories this way in order not to intervene narratively. I want it to be as clear as possible whose ideas are whose, avoiding imposing my own interpretations on the words of others. Therefore, I wrote introductions to each chapter that stand apart from and contextualize the oral history sections, which contain solely direct quotations from the interviews.

I realize that nineteen storytellers is a lot to keep straight! I hear the actual voices of those with whom I spoke when I read their words, but to the reader, many or all of these characters will be new and unfamiliar. However, I do not think it imperative that each person has a well-delineated and distinguishable voice—especially in the earlier chapters. On the contrary, I think it might be appropriate that the lines between people blur, thereby emphasizing the collective narrative rather than the more personal. Not to mention that I feel uncomfortable trying to distill the lives and character of the people I interviewed into short biographical blurbs. Nonetheless, for those who feature as primary protagonists at various points, I do provide context and backstory to prepare the reader appropriately.

ON FORMATTING, GRAMMAR, AND PUNCTUATION

"There is no such thing as a neutral transcript: each comma is an act of interpretation," wrote Alessandro Portelli in the introduction to his book *They Say in Harlan County—An Oral History*, a work that has greatly influenced me.[9] Transcription is the process of turning the performance of the spoken word into text. In transcribing the interviews, I retained the grammar and syntax of the speaker. However, punctuation is, at best, an imperfect aid in approximating all that exists in speech beyond the words themselves. For one thing, the idea of what punctuation conveys differs among readers. My use of punctuation is intended to improve readability as well as to portray common speech phenomena similarly among the multiple people quoted. False starts, interjections, and long pauses are represented by long dashes (—); vocal emphasis is denoted by italics; and transitions between statements are marked with periods. Laughter and any words not actually spoken appear in square brackets.

Lastly, in order to present the many voices as a coherent symphony, I took liberties regarding which material I selected and omitted, as well as the order in which I arranged the excerpted text. However, in all instances I strove to remain true to my perception of the speakers' original meaning.

INTERVIEWS

The following list describes the people whose interviews are quoted in this book. Names are followed by year of birth, primary occupation and/or orientation to the fishery, and the location and date of the interview.

Thomas H. (Tom) Allum: 1942 (d. 2023); Rogers City family doctor, 1970–2014, recreational angler, Rogers City Harbor Advisory Commission member; Dave Nadolsky residence, Rogers City; May 18, 2021

John Bruning: 1968; recreational angler, former charter fishing guide, and former Rogers City city manager; Bruning residence, Rogers City; April 23, 2021

Bruce Grant: 1942; recreational angler, retired charter fishing guide, Hammond Bay Area Anglers Association member, and resort owner; Manitou Shores Resort, Rogers City; March 29, 2021

Joseph (Joe) Hefele: 1971; Rogers City city manager; teleconference; May 25, 2021

Mary Ann Heidemann: 1950; community planner and former Presque Isle County board member; Lakeside Park pavilion, Rogers City; June 15, 2021

Matthew (Matt) Hollabaugh: 1954; recreational angler and retired former Calcite (Rogers City) and LaFarge (Alpena) employee; Hollabaugh residence, Rogers City; June 16, 2021

James E. (Jim) Johnson: 1946; Michigan Department of Natural Resources fisheries research biologist and Alpena Fisheries Research Station director, 1989–2014; Besser Museum for Northeast Michigan, Alpena; May 19, 2021

Robert C. (Rob) Kortman: 1967; Rogers City Waterwaste Treatment Plant employee; Rogers City Waterwaste Treatment Plant, Rogers City; March 29, 2021

Frank Krist: 1947; retired environmental health officer, Hammond Bay Area Anglers Association member, chair of the Lake Huron Citizens Fishery Advisory Committee, and recreational angler; Krist residence, Rogers City; May 18, 2021

Scott McLennan: 1954; Rogers City mayor and former nurse; teleconference; April 13, 2021

David (Dave) Nadolsky: 1940; retired pharmacist, Rogers City City Council member, 1986–2000, Rogers City mayor, 2000–2002; Nadolsky residence, Rogers City; May 18, 2021

Amanda (Mandy) Partyka: 1951; recreational angler and wife of Ken Partyka; Partyka residence; June 15, 2021

Kenneth E. (Ken) Partyka: 1952; Rogers City Salmon Tournament winning captain, 1986 and 1987; Partyka residence, Rogers City; June 15, 2021

Myron (Mike) Peltz: 1931 (d. 2022); Consumers Power Company employee, Rogers City Police Department officer, and Presque Isle County Sheriff's Department sheriff, retired 1984; Peltz residence, Rogers City; May 18, 2021

Kenneth R. (Ken) Rasche: 1944; Rogers City harbormaster, 1989–2006; Rasche residence, Rogers City; April 23, 2021

Edward F. (Ed) Roseman: 1961; research fisheries biologist for the U.S. Geological Survey's Great Lakes Science Center; teleconference; March 11, 2021

David (Dave) Smrchek: 1948; retired speech therapist, recreational angler, and Hammond Bay Area Anglers Association member; Smrchek residence, Rogers City; April 23, 2021

Jayme Warwick: 1969; recreational angler; Warwick residence, Rogers City; March 29, 2021

Ivan J. Wirgau: 1953; retired Stoneport limestone quarry employee, recreational angler, Rogers City Salmon Tournament winning crew member, 1986 and 1987; Wirgau residence, Rogers City; June 16, 2021

1

"A DARN COLD SWIM"

When I began this project, I suspected I'd hear tales of sadness and despair, or perhaps resentment and regret. But I soon learned that rather than just a story of loss, that which could be called the "Rogers City salmon story" was as much or more about the creation and building up of a world-class fishery. It was about the recognition by outdoors-minded people of the hints of a potential salmon fishery and the pursuit of turning dreams and hopes into reality. Actually, the Rogers City salmon story has all the elements of an epic journey: an upward struggle motivated by humble beginnings; hard work and good fortune met justly with success; chaos, then loss; and finally resiliency, lessons learned, and memories to last a lifetime. The story features colorful characters. It plays out in an inspiring and beautiful setting. And it is not without its share of conflict. I so enjoyed listening to the stories people shared with me that many times I found myself wondering if I didn't want to relocate to Rogers City myself!

This chapter is about those humble beginnings. Not all that long ago, recreational offshore fisheries in the Great Lakes really didn't exist. In the 1950s, there was hardly an offshore top-predator species to even fish *for* in Lakes Michigan and Huron. Lake trout, the native predator species that might have fulfilled such a role, were essentially extirpated from Lake Michigan, and were nearly so in Lake Huron. Several decades of commercial fishing, followed by the invasion of parasitic sea lamprey in the late 1930s, wiped out the vast majority of those game-fish species.[1] Steelhead had been around since the early twentieth century, and they generated some fishing interest during their spawning runs up the rivers, but even steelhead were severely negatively impacted by sea lamprey and they weren't being fished for in the Great Lakes proper.[2]

The most telling evidence of the lack of predatory game fish out in the lakes was the proliferation of a non-native herring species called alewives, which rose to nuisance-level abundances. Because the alewives had little commercial value and were subject to massive post-winter die-offs that spoiled the beautiful beaches with piles of their rotting bodies, a desperate (albeit well-conceived) initiative to introduce Pacific salmon to the Great Lakes was undertaken by the Michigan DNR in the mid-1960s. I say "desperate" because it's clear how much of a nuisance the alewives had become, and how very depleted the desirable fish species were.

"The superabundant populations of alewife in the Great Lakes would be a blessing rather than a curse if they could be utilized on a wide scale as forage for high value species," wrote Wayne Tody and Howard Tanner in a Michigan DNR report in February 1966 called "Coho Salmon for the Great Lakes." This report describes the underpinnings for and the very start of the Pacific salmon program undertaken in Michigan. In the fall of 1965, Tody and Tanner obtained coho salmon eggs from the Oregon Fish Commission—eggs from fish that had matured thousands of miles west in the Pacific Ocean. Coho salmon are a closely related sister species to the Chinook salmon for which Rogers City would later be known. Chinook salmon were successfully introduced in 1967. It was hoped that the introduced salmon would take advantage of the alewives as a food source, thus reducing their abundances to non-nuisance levels, and as an additional benefit also create recreational fishing opportunities.[3]

By many accounts, the initiative was a success, and it set the stage for what continues to be the primarily recreational fisheries-based management paradigm of the Great Lakes. Before then, if someone asked, "You wanna go fishing?" they almost certainly were not talking about taking a boat out into the "big lake." But that soon changed, and today each of the Great Lakes supports recreational offshore trolling fisheries for a variety of species. For the uninitiated, it will be helpful for me to paint a picture of what this type of fishing entails because it is largely the type of fishery that developed in Rogers City and elsewhere for those targeting salmon and lake trout. Trolling is a method of fishing that involves driving a boat to pull fishing lines through the water at a desired speed and depth wherever the fish that an angler desires to catch are suspected to be. Nowadays, sonar "graphs"—real-time graphical sonar displays on an onboard monitor—inform the angler of the water depth and produce "pings" that reveal the presence of baitfish, game fish, bottom "structure," or any other feature of the substrate or any entity suspended in the water. Sonar is even used in conjunction with other instrumentation to provide information on the temperature profile of the water, and this is helpful because certain fish species—both predator and prey—orient to specific water temperature ranges. And since water density varies by temperature, areas where warm and cold water meet (called the thermocline, or temperature break, such as can happen in the heat of summer) create somewhat of a barrier to water movement. This can congregate materials suspended in the water such as plankton and other small organisms that attract prey fish, which therefore are patrolled by game species such as salmon and lake trout.

The sophistication of offshore fishing deepens—as does the jargon that needs introducing. Heavy weights, called "cannonballs," that are attached to wire cables are used to lower fishing lines and maintain them at a desired depth while trolling. The apparatus used to lower these cannonballs is called a downrigger. Fishing lines are clipped to the downrigger cables or cannonballs just securely enough to keep them in place, while the driving of the boat imparts movement to the lure. The lure is often a "spoon" (a spoon-shaped metal blade with a hook), a "fly" (a tuft of tinsel with a hook), a "plug" (a tubular, tapered hunk of plastic with a painted eye, and a hook), or some similar artificial bait designed to trigger a salmon or desired game fish to bite. Sometimes reflective boards or paddles, several inches long, called "dodgers," "flashers," or "dipsy-divers," are attached ahead of the lure to impart even more flash and more erratic movement ("action") to the lure to further entice a fish to bite. The boat is driven slowly while the passengers on board face backward toward the stern. All eyes scan left to right, right to left upon the rod tips, which are angled up so as to provide a visual cue of what's going on down below, at the end of the line. A subtle tick-tick-tick at the rod tip indicates the lure is fishing properly, while a lively stuttering pulse—or a deep downward bend—alerts the angler to a fish strike. Should it all go to plan, someone announces "Fish!" as the force of the scaly brute frees the line from the downrigger clip, and the rod-and-reel battle between angler and fish ensues.

Then there are the boats themselves. Nowadays, the typical Great Lakes trolling boat might be anywhere from eighteen to thirty feet in length, accommodating four to six people. In the Great Lakes, the rules have varied over time and differ by state, but typically two or three lines can be legally fished per licensed angler. However, I know from experience that it's pretty rare for more than ten lines to be run at a time—and often many fewer when the fishing's good! Such a setup lends itself well to charter guide services that can take a party of people out fishing, usually with the help of a first mate who sets lines, nets fish, and generally tends to the gear and guests.[4] It's a worthwhile expense for those who might not otherwise be able to afford the gear, much less the years of time on the water acquiring the expertise, to experience a successful day of salmon fishing on their own.

But before the successful introduction of Pacific salmon, none of what I just described about trolling existed in Rogers City or anywhere else on Lakes Michigan and Huron. When I think back on the history of the development of the recreational salmon fisheries in the Great Lakes, I'm amazed at how quickly things progressed—from both an angler perspective and a fisheries management perspective. What the fish populations themselves might do, what they might be capable of, was conceptually a new frontier. Just in terms of Chinook salmon, they went from nonexistent in the mid-1960s to an estimated population size of tens of millions in Lake Huron just a few decades later. In chapter 4 retired Michigan Department of Natural Resources fisheries biologist Jim Johnson relays his story of how he and his colleagues were finally able to assess the salmon population abundance in the early 2000s. Altogether, the biologists and fishery managers, the towns like Rogers City that would become fishing communities, and the people who would become anglers were watching an unprecedented fishery develop and flourish. Each contingent and each individual person observed, learned, and made progress through trial and error.

In much their own way, salmon evoke emotion. On one end of the emotional spectrum, many tribes throughout Chinook salmon's native range revere the species collectively as a cultural and spiritual deity—an honor held by few fishes. The word *Chinook* is literally derived from the native Chinookan peoples who fished for them on the lower and middle reaches of the Columbia River in the Pacific Northwest. Fittingly, Chinook salmon are also called king salmon. On the other end, in modern times, spawning runs of Chinook salmon have been known to invoke a type of sociocultural degeneracy among anglers disparagingly called "salmon fever"—madness induced by the ephemeral abundance characterized by senseless acts such as trespassing, poaching, littering, and a general disregard for the sanctity of nature.

With this in mind, I was curious about the evolution of the sociocultural role that salmon played in Rogers City. I asked those I interviewed to relate their earliest memories regarding salmon in Rogers City—how the Rogers City salmon narrative began. For many, their first experiences were at the Ocqueoc River (pronounced OCK-ee-ock), a half-hour drive north of Rogers City. Often the scenes depicted anglers "snagging" salmon—a method of fishing that involves inelegantly yanking a hook somewhere into the body of a fish (often a fin or the point of attachment of a fin) and catching it that way, rather than the more sporting practice of enticing a fish to bite. In those early years it was largely people who fished that were first to observe salmon in the area, and so it is predominantly angler accounts that reveal the beginnings of the Rogers City salmon narrative. As I listen again to those interviews, I imagine myself seeing and experiencing, for the first time, salmon and salmon fishing where such things hadn't existed before.

JOHN BRUNING: I happened to grow up about a block from our small boat harbor, so—and I fished—so we were on the lake. Up until that point there wasn't a whole lot of big sportfishing in the big lake. My dad always said when he was a kid, which of course was many years before that, "The lake wasn't good for anything more than a darn cold swim." And that was just—nobody really fished it. There were lake trout and things out there. Of course the salmon population came in later. So I saw that evolve.

SCOTT McLENNAN: And so Rogers City was initially a lumbering- and fisheries-type community. So we—I remember as a young man—and I say young man, probably more as a youth; probably junior high–high school-ish—I remember the fish docks, and there's a little harbor where just the fishing fleet would operate out of, and they had two or three fishing boats that would go out and net fish. And they had a pretty thriving business down at the Vogelheim Lumber Company yard-ish, down near the lake, near what is currently the marina. So it was—we always saw that. And as a boy, in terms of the beaches, we have beautiful beaches here. But every year there would be an issue with alewife die-off and washing up. So the city work crews would have to come along with their payloaders and—literally, with the payloaders and dump trucks—and load up the back of these dump trucks with the alewife that had washed up on our nice pristine beaches.

Tom Allum: That's kind of what prompted it. We had so many ale-wives. I can remember when I was going to school in Chicago, every morning there'd be windrows two feet deep of dead alewives for five hundred feet down the beach, and they'd come in with big front-end loaders and scoop them up and carry them away.

Ivan Wirgau: Well, I can remember when they first planted cohos back in the '60s. My dad took me out there [to Ocqueoc Falls]—my dad's name was Ivan Wirgau as well. He introduced me to fishing, up here on Trout River where I live. And I was really young at that time. I was very impressionable and the first time [that I hooked a trout above the Sportsmen's Dam]—the mystique of the Trout [River] just cooked me, you know, some people get hooked on fishing, some don't. But anyway, he always made sure that I kept my interest in fishing but he really didn't have to because my interest was always there and still is—I'm passionate about it. But he took me to the Ocqueoc River up by the falls, and you could see the coho spawning there, which was a big deal, I mean, that's the first time salmon were ever seen by people [in this area].

Dave Smrchek: Okay. Well, I moved—I came to Rogers City in 1970. I graduated from Michigan State [University] and I was [a] speech therapist. I came up here. It kept me out of Vietnam. I got the last of the occupation deferments. So that's how I ended up here. I didn't know what a salmon was in 1970. I moved into an apartment in town, and that fall the DNR was giving away salmon that they had taken from a weir somewhere. Show your hunting—fishing license and they would give you a salmon. So I went to the boat harbor and got a salmon. Probably twenty pounds or so, and blacker than your tape recorder, and I thought that I had just died and gone to heaven. I had no idea. Took it home, cut it up in steaks. The meat was white and so forth. But anyway, that was my first exposure to salmon.

John Bruning: So I saw a lot of—in the early days there were people that would get fish in the river by whatever means they would—however they got them. And people would can them and that would help sustain them through the winter because it was, you know, in a rural area, in a community like this—and I don't think you see it quite as much, although maybe a little bit more of a resurgence in the home-prepared, home-preserved foods, and things like that. So people would use it for a food source.

Tom Allum: Nobody knew the techniques, how to fish for them. And they'd only been around, what, probably five or ten years? I don't know when [Howard] Tanner—

Carson: '67 was—

Tom: '67?

Carson: —or '66, yeah, was when they were first stocked. Yeah.

Tom: Okay, so they were out there and people knew how to catch lake trout because we had been doing that. Lake trout was easy, you lowered your cannonball to the bottom, raised it two turns with your hand-operated thing, and you just trolled around, because the lake trout are always on the bottom wherever it's cold, forty-five degrees of water. These salmon were swimming on the surface in higher levels, but that's when they're getting ready to spawn, and their appetite diminishes then. And you'd see them jumping out there and some of the guys said, "I'm going to bring my shotgun out there with some buckshot. Maybe I can get one that way." Because they would jump right next to your boat.

Dave Nadolsky: The local boys snagged them out of the rivers, and when I first came here, the fellow that I bought the store from lived on Linden, which is a street that the Trout River runs next to out to the lake, and I saw three boys on bikes and they had two salmon on each handlebar, and the fish were dragging on the street and they were riding home.

Tom: It was quite a problem with the salmon running up the Ocqueoc River. Swan River, where they plant them, is inaccessible, you can't get there, because it's in the plant. But they would go up the Ocqueoc as well, and up this Trout River. And they were just there and they were going to die anyway, and people would go out and snag them with what they called the Ocqueoc—the Ocqueoc some kind of lure, I can't think of it right now—Ocqueoc Wobbler or something like that—which is a giant treble hook with a big chunk of lead [*Dave laughs*] welded around it, fifty-pound test line, and they'd throw these things. And I went out there one time with them just to see what was going on. It's exciting to catch a thirty-pound fish, but that's not really sport, that's—. One time my partner Jack McNeil and I, it was at lunchtime on a workday, we heard that they were running so he and I went down to the mouth of the Trout River, and we're standing on the beach there and watching these salmon come running up, and the Trout River's only about that deep in the fall, well, they—

DAVE: They looked like *Jaws*, their dorsal fins sticking—.

TOM: —they run up there, and it was just fun to watch them. And we were standing side by side like this in our suits and ties, and one of the things ran up right on the beach between us. I reached down, picked it up, and threw it into the river. You could catch them by hand.

MIKE PELTZ: And I did catch—I have to admit I did catch some salmon illegally. [*laughs*] But it was—

CARSON: In the early days?

MIKE: I don't know if you have the time for that. I was actually working, city police, and one night I went down there, I don't know what time it was, I went down to the mouth of the river and no one was down there and I just had my flashlight, and here's all these nice salmon coming into the mouth of the river. And I'm looking at them and I said, "*What—?*" And of course I had a pretty good flashlight. And I shined a light on one of those salmon and it made a quick turn and went right up on the bank. And I said, "*Wah*—," and I had to jump across the mouth of the river which was about twelve inches wider than I could jump, so I kept getting my feet wet. But that fish was up on the beach and so I jumped over there and kind of, with my boots, just kept it there long enough so it quit struggling. And then I turned around and I shined my flashlight on another one and that one went up on the beach on the other side, so I had to jump across again, and like I say, I couldn't quite jump it without getting wet. I think I had ten or twelve nice big salmon, with the flashlight, and [*laughs*] I had to call my brother in the middle of the night to come down and get them. [*laughs*] And they were big salmon. I mean, there's a picture someplace of those. They were big salmon. And then one other night I was down and just looking at the bridge, which is three hundred yards upstream, and some guy stopped and said, "You catch any fish?" and I said, "No, I'm not a fisherman." And he handed me a gaff hook. Just a small gaff hook that I know was made at the local plant down here, they made thousands of them. And he said, "I got a bunch. I'm leaving. Here, I got—here's a gaff hook." And I didn't have any way of getting in the river and I could see salmon going up, coming up, going under the bridge. My brother-in-law lived just, quite close by. So I went and walked over there and found a pair of boots—this is 2:30 in the morning, I'm not sure. But I put those boots on and I went in the river, and I couldn't catch those fish. I had that gaff hook but they were quicker than I was, I couldn't get the timing to catch any. And so I went back to his house and I saw a net, about a three-foot square—it wasn't a minnow net because I remember it had maybe like two-inch net. And I looked at that and I says, "That'll work." So I took it off the garage wall and went back there and went in the river, and then as those salmon came up to me I'd drop the net over the top of them. I missed the first one, I still remember that because he was quick. But then I had the timing right so that I'd drop that net over top of them and then stood on the net and then I got ahold of them with the gaff hook and took them up on the bank. And then again. I don't know how many I had but I had to call my brother [*both laugh*], my brother again to come and get them. And he did. And I remember it was kind of funny because he asks, "How'd you catch those?" and I told him and he wouldn't believe me. So the next night he went with me and we took—my son was—he had a son about the same age as my oldest son, they might have been twelve, I'm not sure what it was, but anyway, the two boys came along. So I showed them how we did it and we caught another bunch of salmon that night, which was illegal, but it was just kind of a—nobody cared, until it got to be a serious problem. I'll admit it. I signed a waiver here but, no, I don't think they're going to prosecute me now. [*laughs*] But it was just a common practice. And it was the people that abused that that made it bad, but the people that were using—taking the fish, nobody seemed to care how they caught them, there were so many. And I would say I was an amateur, I didn't know anything about fishing and I was able to catch them. So, it was just that many fish. It was fun.

Scott McLennan: —it was essentially 1970, I would say, about, before we, being my buddies and I—local amateur fishermen—we liked to fish the inland lakes, always, and that sort of thing—well, right around 1970, give or take, the salmon started really being a thing in this area. And the salmon would be in the rivers. And we would spend many a Saturday, Sunday, et cetera, going up into the rivers and pulling out large salmon. Now, I will tell you that we would have fishing licenses, but I'm not sure we always abided by the rules when it came to salmon. The salmon were so, so plentiful in those days. Large salmon. And the rivers were full of them. The only time we'd ever get in trouble is if we were trespassing on someone's property we would get chased off, that sort of thing [*laughs*], but they—you didn't want to break that—you knew enough—we knew, anyway, our group—not to break the banks down, that sort of thing. Try to be careful. But there were just plentiful salmon in the rivers.

John Bruning: But I remember, I started fishing out here when I was too young to fish. I mean, we would go out—my dad had—this was probably in the early '70s, mid-'70s, there was a handful, literally a handful of people that fished out here. And my dad, a couple of his cousins—well, maybe more than a handful now that I'm thinking back to some of the old-timers. But a really small group of people. And as I recall, my dad's first—he first fished, I think, as far as like lake trout in the deep water, big-lake fish, with a cousin—maybe they did some here, but I remember they had gone over to the west side of the state and Lake Michigan and trolled with wire line, which was just an unbelievable amount of work compared to the advances with downriggers and things like that. If anybody's familiar with that at all it's just a completely different ball game. But in the early days I can remember going out with my dad and he had, I think, one downrigger, it might have been a purchased one, it might have been one that he built. I think he maybe bought one and then he built one. And he would run one of those lines and then wire, you know, I don't know how many yards out. It was just out forever. I was way too little. I would go along and watch and try to stay out of his way, for the most part. But it was mostly lake trout fishing. And then as things evolved and the salmon got more plentiful, then it ended up more of a combined fishery.

Matt Hollabaugh: Yeah, because—but see, we didn't realize that—we didn't even know where the salmon came from or anything, that they were out there. It was just, we would wait until September to snag them in the river mouths and stuff. Because we didn't realize that they would hang along shore and on the drop-offs and stuff. Even like the big lake, we didn't have good graphs or anything. We didn't have the bottom that we could see, or the GPS [global positioning system] or anything then. So we really—it was kind of a mystery out there on the big lake. I know, my father-in-law, we'd go out and we'd troll for lake trout, and we would just go out to a point, and then we'd troll to the next point, like three to four miles, and we would just troll the bottom. And we didn't even have rods, we just used wire line with leather gloves and we'd feel the bottom and you'd feel the lake trout hit that way. But we didn't know what we were going over. We'd lose a lot of weight and stuff. Break a lot of cables. We couldn't even tell what the bottom was. But yeah, that was, back then we did a lot of it. There was a lot of snagging going on then. It was enjoyable to snag them. [*laughs*] And my dad—that was before they had Cabela's, and we couldn't find any big hooks, and he ended up in Herter's, and he bought a gross of these big snagging hooks. And I still actually have—and now I use them on my big lake trout lures, and I have a couple of those left. [*laughs*] They don't have any weight on them. There was a guy—it was hard to get weight, hard to get lead after a while, because so many people were doing it—and somebody might have already told you about this guy, but at Calcite, he would, at night he worked in the boat-loading operation, and he would take lead off the cables, and he'd just shave a little off. One night he hit the power and he's lucky he didn't kill himself—

CARSON: Oh, my god.

MATT: —but he knocked the whole plant out.

CARSON: Geez. [*both laugh*]

MATT: So people got kind of crazy about it. Just doing stuff just to get those fish, you know?

CARSON: You were sheriff in the early '80s when they were—

MIKE PELTZ: Right. When this fishing phenomenon [*laughs*] took place. It was kind of an explosion when it happened. Most people weren't ready for it. I'll tell you—add to that, when I worked for Consumers Power over at the Traverse City area, it was big there, that's where it started. Platte River. And we drove over there, some of my friends that were working with me, had time off. We drove over to watch that and that was almost like a circus. These people—I never saw people so reckless in my life as those fishermen over there at that time. It was just crazy.⁵ You couldn't get near the beach because of the cars that were parked, the traffic. The little stores were completely sold out of [*laughs*] anything that they had that the fishermen—snacks, anything—they just couldn't get enough to keep it. And these people were so reckless. Those little boats going out into Lake Michigan. I watched heavy, oversize people in rowboats get out of the boat to push it out of the river into the lake, to go out into Lake Michigan. Rowboats. It was just unreal. And of course then as the salmon spread, came around to this side of the state, and then we saw that here. But not to that extreme. It was not like that here. People were more prepared for it. In fact a lot of people from here started their salmon fishing over in the

Traverse City area because that's where it was to begin with. But then it spread over here and it got really big here because of the spawning and where they planted them, and the reproduction, and the food. So that's when I was working and that's what I saw.

Matt Hollabaugh: We had a guy that—I won't say any names, but he fished in like a ten-foot boat out there. And it was like, well, they say "salmon fever," he must have had it because he was out there and he'd be trolling and we thought he'd never make it back but he did, every time. And he was a bit of a big guy, too, and it was like, wow.

Bruce Grant: And before the boat fishery got here, . . . when they planted some fish in the Ocqueoc—I lived downstate then, I brought my sixteen-foot wood boat up—when they—because I just went through some old pictures of—I had a one-and-a-half-ton stake truck—and a half a dozen of us came from Onaway, and we went down there, and at that time everybody snagged, that's how you got fish, you snagged them—and we had that truck with one-foot sideboards level with salmon, took them back to Onaway, gave them to all the old people, some to churches, and then what we wanted for—. Black, nasty fish you wouldn't even think of. After that run started—and you learned that you go down there—there was still people snagging all over—all you had to do was go out by the mouth and fish with some salmon eggs. But more people got here that knew how to do that, and then a fishery started. But most of it was in the river snagging in the fall. I went out in the lake—I would say it would have been '69 up to about '75—with my old wood Thompson boat, and we would troll with pike lures. And to this day I could never—and what would you fish with back then? Daredevles. Could never catch a fish on a Daredevle. Never. Because they were red and white. You get in the river and you catch a pike right away in the Ocqueoc. And there's some big pike in the Ocqueoc. Salmon don't bite red and white. I don't know what it is.

Matt Hollabaugh: I kind of wanted to let you know like how, at first, the way the fishing was here. The first fish I ever caught, I snagged in Ocqueoc. And that was in October because we figured salmon just came in the river and that's where you fished them. We didn't know anything about the big lake. I mean we fished, like, perch and pike out there and stuff like that. And we dipped smelt. And then the alewives, of course they came and were dying on the beaches and stuff. But we thought they wouldn't bite. So for those first few years, that would have been in the '70s, snagging was legal too. And I look back on it now, it was a bad thing to do, but everybody did it, and it was enjoyable, actually, to snag, and you'd get a lot of fish. I mean there was times in Ocqueoc River when there'd be a hundred people out there and everybody would be getting fish. So as we got into that we—my father-in-law, he was quite a character. He ended up, like when we were deer hunting and stuff, we would see fish in the rivers and stuff, and he built his own—like these big hooks and stuff that he would bring them out with. But nobody wasted the fish. They all ate them all. But it was a totally different idea—it wasn't sporting, when you think back, but that's the way we thought it was with salmon. And actually even to eat them, because normally you wouldn't be getting fish until September and October, and we thought they were only good for smoking. Nothing fresh, you know. Very rarely would you even see a silver salmon. And then as we started to fish a little more—well we all had fourteen-footers, most of us, just small boats, just tiller mount. And we would go out on the big lake, in maybe like the end of August, and you'd see them jumping out there. And there was times when my buddy and I that fished a lot, that we would go out off of Nagels or Smith Creek, and there would be a hundred fish in the air at one time, in twenty feet of water, and you could just see clouds of dark fish moving through the water, and nobody out there. We'd just take our boat, we'd row—we'd get up close to them and then we'd start rowing into them so we wouldn't scare them, you know? And we didn't know how to even—we'd cast red and white Daredevles to them because that's how we fished for pike. And we'd get some, but that's not what they were—. So eventually then when they got the Little Cleos, they started inventing those, that's when we really started catching that way.

KEN PARTYKA: —so we're doing that. And the next year rolls around and we're doing and okay. Now people are around and they're doing that. Not so many boat fishermen, but they're still back in the area. And one day I was in to Clem's Bait Shop, Sonny's Bait Shop, whatever, in Alpena by the Ninth Street Dam, they had this three-quarter-ounce glow-in-the-dark Cleo—not Cleo, it was a—

CARSON: K.O. Wobbler?

KEN: —it was a—Krocodile. Okay. A glow-in-the-dark Krocodile, okay? So I'm out there—we're out there fishing before daybreak. We're out there fishing before the sun comes up. And that's [*laughs*] what so many people never did. So many people *never* did that. We're out there before—so I'm out there. I give this Krocodile a shot. Fling that baby out there. Three-quarter-ouncer goes out there—.

MANDY PARTYKA: A shot of light. We had flashlights at the time, shine up that glow.

KEN: Anyway, I fling that—

MANDY: I'll fill in—fill in—[*Carson and Mandy laugh*]

KEN: —I fling that baby out there. Hits the water.

MANDY: —gave it a shot with a flashlight.

KEN: Crank it. Bingo, right off the get-go. For two years people were like, and then all of the sudden they're realizing, Okay, he's got a light. Now he's throwing this lure out there. I can see it go out, you know? Pretty soon now there's other people. But we were just casting. And it was kind of funny because, you know, I'd go out there, I'd have waders. My brother, always a little bit radical, had—he was a diver, so he had a wetsuit.

CARSON: Chuck?

KEN: Yeah.

CARSON: Is he [an] older brother?

KEN: He's younger.

CARSON: Oh, he's younger. Okay.

KEN: Four years younger than I am. But anyway, he had a wetsuit. So he'd put on his wetsuit, and he'd put on a pair of bib coveralls and a flannel shirt [*Carson and Mandy laugh*], and out he is in the water like this here, and people are looking at him like, Holy Cuh-rist that guy really wants fish. *Jesus Christ*, you know? And there he is, just, you know? And we'd lose some lures. I'd take his other suit and we would go out snorkeling for lures later on in the day. But oh, yeah, it was like, you know, people go, Them guys are crazy, you know?

MANDY: Tell him the size of the fish back then when they first planted them.

KEN: They—yeah, they were all—they were all nice. They were nice fish. I mean even—I mean—I mean we were catching forty-pound fish.

CARSON: Really?

KEN: My mother—I mean, you would catch fish and you would just stop because your arms were sore. We were catching very big fish, back early, early. Not a lot of plants, but we were catching—my mother caught—some big fish. We caught big fish. Big fish.

MATT HOLLABAUGH: Yeah, some of the things, like back then when we were, essentially we were casting Cleos to the big schools of fish in the fall, we didn't carry nets in the boats. We all had gaffs because it was quicker. You would get them up by the boat and gaff them. Or, I know Kenny [Partyka], he would tail them, and he'd pull them up by the tail.
CARSON: That's scary. You get a hook in the eye. [*laughs*]
MATT: Yeah. Yeah, but see those are the things—yeah, they would never—because the gaffs were legal in the big lake. You couldn't take a gaff on the trout stream, but you could use them on the big lake. So we just, every boat would have a gaff. Why would you waste time with a net? It's just a salmon, you know?

KEN PARTYKA: I had a time, I had a time—I just got off on vacation. I just got off on vacation—it was another one of these things. I just got off on vacation, I'm on the 12 to 4. It's 4 o'clock in the morning. I got my bags packed, I'm off. I'm off the boat, I'm on vacation. I come home, it's a full moon. It's like a full moon, and it's like, I'm howling, I'm going [*howls, then laughs*]. It is a full moon. And I [*laughs*] turn around, and I come home, I grab my fish poles, throw them together, and I'm out on the breakwall of the boat harbor. By daybreak I had five salmon and three lake trout, and I was like—hey! [*laughs*]
CARSON: Were you the only guy out there?
KEN: No, there was two other people out there, if I'm not mistaken. But you know, there you are, got a flashlight in your mouth, you've got a pole here, you've got a net here—because we never used to use nets back in the day.

CARSON: This made me start to recall myself fishing off piers on the west side of the state and we fished a lot at night. Was there a night-casting fishery here?
ROB KORTMAN: Oh, yeah. The people were down—we'd go down. I mean, used to [*laughs*]—we had a signal, my buddy and I, because he lived just kind of across, kitty-corner across from each other. And we'd be up 4 o'clock in the morning to get down there to go fishing on the weekend. And we'd have our alarm set. You look—oh, yeah, his light's on, my light's on. We'd meet, or—we'd get, or you know we'd

have curf[ew]—[*laughs*] we'd have to—You guys have got to be home by a certain time. But we were lots of times between 11, 12, midnight, fishing, trying to get that nighttime fishing in. There was people down there. I don't know—trying to gauge how many now is a little rough. But there was always someone trying. I mean, it's fun. That's a thrill at night, to have a fish on. Can't really see. We didn't have the head lights we've got now, that they make, on your head. But one buddy's holding a flashlight while you're trying to—

CARSON: It feels like you're casting a million miles.

ROB: Yeah. Yeah. It's a different feel at night, that's for sure.

JOHN BRUNING: There was some sportfishing when I was in probably junior high to high school. . . . I think the boat harbor, our small boat harbor—and it's evolved a little bit; there's been some breakwalls added on and so forth, but—about Labor Day weekend, we couldn't wait for—it was bad because we had to go back to school, but it was great because the salmon would be close to shore, and I would spend every waking minute that I could, and I'd come home—the rule was come home, get your homework done, then you could go to the harbor, [as] long as you wear your life vest. I was a twelve-, fourteen-year-old kid or whatever. And there were days when the breakwall, the outside of the breakwall would be lined, we would say "shoulder to shoulder," but within a rod's length away so that you weren't bashing your neighbor in the face with the end of your fishing rod, all the way down the whole breakwall. Casting. As the fish would get closer to shore they'd start coming into the harbor. People would be fishing off the docks inside. And it would be busy. You'd have to get down there pretty early to find that spot on the wall that you wanted because—oh, you took—it was better on one end than it was on the other and as it filled up you ended up getting down towards the not so desirable end.

FRANK KRIST: But when the salmon fishery started here—I moved up here in '74, and we got up here in June and went down to Seagull Point—that's the point just on the edge of town there; and this was in August—we're sitting on the bank there and we're seeing these boats out there. They were small boats back then, you know. People were out in fourteen-footers and stuff. And salmon jumping everywhere. That's when we got initiated to it, really. We did a little bit of [fishing] inland on the rivers when they were running when we were—I was in graduate school at Central [Michigan University]. And anyway, we started fishing. And, you know, we didn't know much. And then I'm hearing, "Oh, the DNR—they're going to stop the salmon plants at Rogers City." And they only planted fifty thousand as opposed to the million they stocked originally up here. And it was a tremendous fishery. We actually caught more fish then by shore, by far. They were going to stop it. So I said, "I've got to get my information together," and that's when I got involved in fishery issues.

2

A MILLION FISH

BECOMING THE SALMON CAPITAL

To this day, a defining characteristic of Rogers City is that it sits just north of the largest limestone quarry in the world: Calcite. Ground was first struck at Calcite in 1912, before which the major industries in Rogers City were forestry and commercial fishing. Operations at the quarry and the shipping fleet associated with the quarry quickly became the primary socioeconomic influence on Rogers City. However, it wasn't long before technological advances in automation saw labor at the quarry become increasingly mechanized, and jobs were lost. The town that had grown rapidly into a city through the first half of the twentieth century was almost as rapidly shrinking by the 1960s. In 1950, the population in Rogers City was 3,873. It swelled to 4,722 in 1960 but then began steadily declining: 4,275 in 1970, 3,923 in 1980.[1] The situation worsened further. By the early 1980s, unemployment in Rogers City and Presque Isle County exceeded 30 percent, portending further population decreases that have extended to the present day.[2] The most recent census, in 2020, revealed a population of just 2,581.

In the early 1980s, in the midst of the employment crisis, many people who were keyed into the area's burgeoning salmon fishery were growing increasingly concerned about the effect of Native American gillnet fishing on Great Lakes sportfish populations. The 1836 Treaty of Washington guaranteed to Native American tribes rights to fish for commercial and subsistence purposes, and it was the U.S. federal government's role to establish regulations for such tribal fishing. In the waters around Hammond Bay and in the general vicinity of Rogers City, where tribal fishing was occurring, many community members were observing negative effects of gillnet fishing on lake trout and brown trout.

A gillnet is simple to operate and very effective for catching fish. But gillnet fishing poses many potential problems. A gillnet consists of a mesh of monofilament fishing line, typically several hundred feet long and several feet from top to bottom. It is stretched out in a straight line and suspended vertically in the water. It's designed to entangle unsuspecting fish as they swim into the "windows," which are the diamond-shaped openings between the crosshatches of the mesh. As a fish enters, the mesh stretches and slides over its gills and perhaps some of its fins, but the circumference of the fish's widest point keeps it from being able to swim all the way through. Unable to push forward or slide out in reverse, the fish is trapped.

One problem that gillnets pose is that they fish indiscriminately with respect to species. Generally speaking, the goal of tribal gillnetting is to catch whitefish. Non-target species such as lake trout and brown trout cannot be sold and therefore must be discarded when incidentally caught in a gillnet. But a second problem with gillnets is that they are often fatal to fish. Because fish become wrapped as they struggle to free themselves, their gills and mouths may be squeezed shut so that they suffocate and die. And if that doesn't kill them, it's not an easy chore to free a fish from a gillnet without injuring it. Rogers City resident Ralph Dashner described some particularly sad scenes in a letter to the editor of the local newspaper: "If you'd like to lose your lunch someday go up to Hammond Bay and watch the area residents recover the bodies of loons killed by Indian gill nets. Or even worse, go out with the DNR or BIA [Bureau of Indian Affairs] when they recover Indian-abandoned gill nets with hundreds of pounds of decayed fish trapped in the net."[3]

Concerned sportsmen banded together in the early 1980s to form the Hammond Bay Area Anglers Association with the goal of developing "an Agreement that would allow the commercial and recreational fisheries to effectively coexist."[4] Among its earliest members were Frank Krist and Bruce Grant, whom I interviewed as part of this project. The Hammond Bay Anglers were vital in negotiating the 1985 Consent Agreement that established rules designed to reduce conflicts between commercial tribal fishing and recreational sportfishing in order to promote the sustainability of the interests of both parties.[5] The agreement had tremendous positive impacts on sportfishing in northern Lake Huron and, importantly for the future salmon fishery in Rogers City, the negotiation process was a key unifier of people interested in the area's fisheries. Relationships and a collaborative framework were developed that, in addition to dealing with the gillnetting issue, also helped promote the prospects of an enhanced Rogers City salmon fishery.

Meanwhile, in 1982, members of the Presque Isle Sportsmen's Club proposed to ask the State to stock more fish in the Lake Huron waters of Rogers City. In the absence of an established procedure for making such a request, the hope was that if the plan was well founded and had enough community support, that could increase the chances of the DNR adopting the club's idea. Early arguments focused on the habitat features of Lake Huron near Rogers City. It was deep nearshore, and the prevailing westerly offshore winds meant the waters out of Rogers City were usually not too riled up to take boats out on the water—even small fourteen-footers. In other words, fishing the "big lake" for salmon is easier to do in Rogers City than in most other places. Therefore, planting fish in Rogers City would be a good return on the State's investment. The Presque Isle Sportsmen's Club passed a resolution to ask the State to plant one hundred thousand Chinook salmon there.[6]

The local salmon boosters apparently were very convincing—too convincing, some said. The DNR received the Sportsmen's Club's request and counteroffered a proposal to turn the waters of Rogers City into "a major Chinook salmon fishery"—a "bombshell" of a proposal, as one city council member put it.[7] Having recently completed major hatchery renovations, the DNR was in possession of more fish to stock than had been allocated. The mayor questioned if the city and harbor were equipped to handle such a boost.[8] Some wondered how many salmon the tribes would net. And wouldn't stocking so many fish create an uncontrollable snagging situation?

Things progressed quickly. On April 19, 1983, the plan was set: five hundred thousand Chinook salmon smolts would be planted in Swan River, the creek that runs through the Calcite limestone quarry. U.S. Steel, which owned the property, would work with the Michigan DNR to coordinate the stocking. Upon the salmons' migratory returns in the fall, a weir would be implemented to harvest the "excess" fish. Since the lower reaches of Swan River where the fish would be stocked is completely within private land, there would be no potential for a snagging fishery, and the harvest of returning fish would mitigate the problem of dead and dying salmon fouling local beaches or streams.

Early May 1983 presented a surprising twist when the Michigan DNR planted 250,000 *coho* salmon in Swan River, and announced that now

750,000 Chinook salmon would be planted—a total of a million salmon! "Every year," it was said, "beginning in 1983, some 500,000 to one million [C]hinook salmon smolts will be planted in the Swan River," which was "destined to become . . . the major planting place for all of Lake Huron and a fishery will develop from Saginaw Bay to the Straits of Mackinac."[9]

There were people within the community who didn't embrace the dream of a new fishery. Some outright opposed it. But the wheels were in motion and there was no stopping it now, warned Glen Sheppard in the *North Woods Call*, a newspaper devoted to wildlife conservation and outdoor recreation in Michigan. It was time now to prepare. "Unless Mother Nature throws a curve, Rogers City is sitting on a time bomb. The explosion can be filled with joy and gold or with confusion, disruption and lost opportunity."[10]

Would the fish return? How many? What was going to happen when they did? The first returns of big three-year-old, ten-pound-plus adults were expected to happen in the summer and fall of 1986. Experts from Michigan State University Extension advised Rogers City council members to expect two hundred boats to be launched *per day*. The small boat harbor only had two launch ramps. Rogers City needed to expand or create new boat launch facilities, but some locals didn't want angler activity near their homes. Some thought spending the city's funds on new infrastructure might be a bad investment. "What if this thing fizzles out in four or five years?" asked Rogers City resident Ed Smith. "We're stuck with another dead horse." "No matter what we do, Rogers City is going to change," city council member Chuck Dettloff said, in general agreement with others in the Rogers City government. "Everybody is going to feel the effects of it (the increased fishery) no matter where we live. It's not going to be the same working man's town it's been for all these years."[11]

It seemed that, in an ironic turn of events, Calcite's socioeconomic role in Rogers City might soon be supplanted by this new potential natural resources boon—the world's largest limestone quarry poised to become the epicenter of Michigan's biggest salmon fishery.

All told, the Rogers City recreational fishery would be bustling following the initiative to become the largest salmon-stocking site in Michigan. Hard work and dedication by the Rogers City City Council, the Presque Isle Sportsmen's Club, the Hammond Bay Area Anglers Association, the Michigan DNR, U.S. Steel, the *Presque Isle County Advance*, Representative John Pridnia, Natural Resources Commission chair Harry Whiteley, and many others coalesced such that the *Midland Daily News* announced

Rogers City as the "Salmon Capital of Michigan" in September 1987.[12] The town prepared itself, people came up to fish, and ecology, biology, weather, and climate seemed to have blended fortuitously.

SCOTT MCLENNAN: And then it was probably, oh, 1972 or so, that we, anyway, started really going out in the lake and finding out that, wow, what a great sportfish this salmon is in the lake. It was quite a bit different than just trying to haul them out of the river. I mean, that was fun, but you get out in the lake and start fishing salmon—it was terrific. So that was a real peak time, in the '70s, for salmon fishing in the Rogers City area.

CARSON: The '70s you say, then?

SCOTT: Yes, all through the '70s was really good in the Rogers City area.

CARSON: Oh, okay. So that's before, really, the major stocking.

SCOTT: We went out regularly all through the '70s, and it was a very good time for salmon fishing. And then it just kept getting better as those years went on. But yeah, we had great salmon fishing all through the '70s.

BRUCE GRANT: Well we've been here at Manitou Shores—we bought it—it had been shut down and [a] dilapidated place. And we had a business downstate in southeast Michigan. We were looking for change. That was in '83–'84. And we bought this place, completely rebuilt it, and wanted to get in on the ground floor of the salmon fishery because we knew it was a new industry coming. And we thought being on the ground floor might be the best place. And we just—for lifestyle, we wanted to live in the north anyways. And due to an industrial accident I kind of had to get out of the business I was in anyway. So this worked out very good for us, and thirty-five years later we're still happy to be here.

CARSON: So you came in '83–'84—that was right around the time where the big initiative to stock—

BRUCE: —just started. They did some Ocqueoc River stocking in, I believe, around '67. And I think it was around '68–'69 we started being able to harvest some of the jacks and the early spawners in the Ocqueoc River, and that kind of started it all. And it kind of went that way for quite a while. And then the population just kept growing and growing, and to go to the river and catch a thirty-pound fish was just—I mean that was just normal. And most of us got our limit and left and came back tomorrow, or when the weekend was over you went back downstate and lived to the next time you could get back up. And many people just harvested for waste. And then we also saw—it was—waste got to the point [that] people were coming just harvesting for eggs, for spawning. And it was really bad. Then they realized, We really have got to do some work here to clean up. And I have got to say law enforcement did a good job. I mean, they were on it all the time. And to some extent it's still an ongoing problem. And I really think going back then and knowing the people—I mean, everybody here at one time or another has been a transplant—but a big majority of the transplants here are here because of the fishery. They came up. Our business was based originally on people coming up for the fishery. And now they're our neighbors. We stand in the voting line with them. And they moved. A lot of people changed occupations. People bought small businesses. But most of them came as soon as they could retire. And a lot of early retirements. Rogers City's full of retired people that like to fish and boat. Kind of how it went.

CARSON: Yeah. So how did you—what role did you play in that early initiative to stock salmon? Or, I mean, I've talked with Frank Krist and he was a big promoter. I read back in the newspapers [that as] early as 1982 they were really pushing to make Swan River the site. And then it became, quickly, the largest plant—individual planting—the State of Michigan did. And in Lake Huron, so—.

BRUCE: Well, my involvement was once I got—I was in—I love the outdoors. Just wildlife—birds, fish, conservation issues. When I had my cabin in Onaway [Michigan] we would come over this way to smelt fish in the spring because they'd come up all the creeks real heavy, and that was a great thing. But once I moved here and then start getting around the harbor and getting in and out of hardware stores and building places for materials because we completely—we spent a year and a half completely rebuilding Manitou Shores—and I started running into people with issues. And then the Hammond Bay [Area] Anglers [Association] started. I should say, fishing issues. And the Hammond Bay Anglers started. And they'd started a month or a couple of months before I really got into it, but I got in just about on the ground floor. And then it was like, gee, we're doing full-time meetings. It's all we were doing is meetings, meetings, meetings because [we were] trying to get people together, trying to get people involved. And one of the big issues was raising money so that we could be part of the system. It was kind of like, politically. And Department of Natural Resources—every once in a while somebody would come through and tell you what was going on—but they really weren't real happy about you getting involved. Or they weren't welcoming people to get involved. They were handling it. But then the issue got pretty heavy between the tribes and the sportfishermen because you couldn't even fish out here. It was solid gillnets all the way. And the thing that upset me the most is right at that time Alpena was building a beautiful brown trout fishery. And every time you picked up the paper people were headed to Alpena to go brown trout fishing. But yet, after a few years—and that was getting really well established—I'd walk out and I'd have to go on to the beach two times a day and clean up the dead brown trout. And a lot of lake trout. It was because they were caught in gillnets and they couldn't sell them and they threw them back in and there was nothing—I mean, the beach would stink with trophy fish. I mean, nice brown trout. And decent lake trout. And that's got a lot of the shoreline people really involved and the people that would come over and see what was going on because of the waste that was going on. So, a few that got started with the Anglers, we started doing Sea Grant meetings and really getting involved and getting pushy and getting loud. We started doing newspaper articles, taking pictures. The *Detroit Free Press* and *Detroit News* put us on the map, coming up here to take pictures of [*laughs*]—and it was kind of tough for a while because the good people and the people that were willing to be in a group like the Anglers or the Steelheaders or something like that, they weren't out there for trouble, they were out there to save the fishery. And there was a couple pictures posted in the Sunday *Free Press* and *Detroit News* and after that I was threatened—a couple of us were threatened like you can't imagine. Had phone calls and, "We're going to burn your place down." And just all kinds of stuff. And then it got to the point, it was just, I'm going to stay in this to survive because it was a big issue. And then, oh, a little later on when it really got going good, then they started putting salmon nets out. And the fish were being blocked from going up and spawning. And that went on right up well into the '80s.

And so, if you didn't get involved then you really didn't care about the fishery, the community, or anything else, because this community was growing. And what it was doing, it was bringing people in here that could make it better. This community didn't have a lot of money. And this little community didn't have too many people in it that knew how to get the press so people would come. And a few of us had a few ideas and we started doing outdoors shows. Got to know the outdoor writers. They'd come up, we take them out fishing, give them a meal, maybe a night's sleep, and they start writing about Rogers City.

And then at that point—and they were also helping us with the tribal issue, which I think really helped to settle things down so that it wasn't, I want what I want, and they wanted what they wanted. It was like, Why don't we sit down together and try to work this out so we can all live with the problem? And I think that's pretty much where we've been since—at least since—the '85 [Consent] Agreement, it was tough. But when we got the 2000 [Consent] Agreement, it was tough, but it was agreeable, and it worked. And that made a big difference. But we had to get people in here to—like the *News*, the *Free Press*, and the outdoor writers, and the magazines—get them here to make an issue and to explain both sides. A lot of them were very fair and some of them were terrible. I've got some articles out there hanging on the wall that I won't let go away because I don't want people to forget. You had two sides with different attitudes and we actually had some outdoor writers that were saying, Well, hell, [the tribes] started here, let's just give them the fishery. Well, what do you do with the population that's here? And what are we supposed to do, drive to Detroit to go bowling? You know, I mean, go fish at Belle Isle when we have one of the greatest fisheries in the nation starting to establish right here? I had people out from France—on my charter boat from France, Germany—because they read about this. And Japan. Oh, my gosh, I had so many customers that came from Japan. Because usually the husband worked here as a salesman or a technician and they came back and they brought people out fishing. Families. What more could you ask for? And it was because of the help we got from the media. And we had some very wonderful people. Most of them have passed away now. But they knew what it took to get a community established. The biggest problem I've seen—our community wasn't ready to be established. And we had a serious local problem because the people that were—well, the old families, very few of them were born and raised here. They were transplants too. But their families maybe came here in the '30s or '40s or '50s. But this was their fishery. They didn't want charter boats here. They didn't want people coming here because this was their fishery. The State [of Michigan] did this for the people of Rogers City. And it was a tough go in that situation because they'd get belligerent and come to the meetings and, "We don't want these people here." You know? Which—and another thing you had—like some of the family restaurants were here for years, the grandfather started them, then the father, then the son's into them—and we'd go to them and say, "We're going to start a fishing tournament, would you open at 4:30?" They normally opened at 6 or 7. "No, I've got plenty of business. I've got all the business I need. I'm feeding my family. I ain't getting up at 4:30 to feed a bunch of fishermen." Things like that had to be overcome. Then businesses started getting bought out by other people that did open at 5 o'clock in the morning to feed the fishermen. And it got better because they had seen what it was doing for the community. I mean everything. The restaurants. The bars. Gift shops started springing up. And never had a sporting goods store in this town. All of a sudden got a sporting goods store—big one.

DAVE SMRCHEK: The community, I don't—we got the sense that the community never really embraced fishing. There was a group of people that thought that all these fishermen were a bunch of drunks that were going to rape and pillage when they weren't out fishing, and they didn't care for that. Well, probably it was the local guys that were more that way than it was the people coming from all over. And they just—I don't think that they ever appreciated how much money was there. They would come down and they'd look at all the boats and, "Oh, gee. I wish someday I could afford one of those." And probably most of the guys that were up here fishing for the weekend could buy and sell 90 percent of the people in Rogers City. They had their 150,000 dollars' worth of boat, truck, and—back in the '90s—. They didn't come just to party. They might party when they got there, but they came to fish.[13] They had a lot of money invested. But you couldn't find a place to eat after 11 o'clock, in town, during the summer, when we would be fishing until dark. You couldn't find a place to eat.

JOHN BRUNING: And that of course evolved into a much more robust recreational fishery with almost everyone having a boat, and the boats getting larger and more expensive and more sophisticated. But I remember our neighbor, because we were so close to the harbor and his wife was somewhat of an entrepreneur, and he fished some, but I think they saw an opportunity because there was discussions of increasing the plants. I think we were getting around a hundred thousand planted in the area at the time, and it was going to go to a million. And so they had a little place that they had operated—I think a child's clothing store and stuff that was on their property. So they opened a bait shop. As they were talking about that it was really exciting to me because we had one or two others in town at the time, but that was right next door. For me it was like a candy store.

CARSON: Was that Blair's?

JOHN: It was Blair's. Yeah. And I worked for them for—oh, I don't know, up through, maybe up into college. I probably started there when I was sixteen. I think I did some things for them [when I was] fifteen but I actually worked there and staffed the store—it was a little tiny store. One room. Pretty small. And very much oriented towards the salmon fishery at that—salmon and lake trout, the big-lake fishery. They had other things, too, but that was the emphasis. And so that was really exciting for me to see that because that was additional opportunity, certainly for me personally, but also for the community because it was an indicator of what was to come. Which, really—you know, I don't remember how quickly it changed, but obviously it did because in a matter of just a few years those fish that were planted were large, and pretty plentiful. And so it drew people from other areas, other ports. Especially if there was bad weather, or maybe a week of bad fishing because of previous bad weather or whatever somewhere else, people would come here.

CARSON: I was reading back through the newspapers and saw that you were working at Blair's Bait and Tackle when it opened.[14]

MATT HOLLABAUGH: Yes. Yes, I did. And that was when the harbor was really going strong. And a lot of kids would, if it wasn't during the week, if there wasn't school on, the kids they'd just go by steady riding their bikes down there to go fishing. And you don't see that nowadays, they're on their cell phones. And they'd stop by, and they'd buy hooks or whatever they needed, or Cleos or whatever from me. So that was kind of neat. That was in-between jobs. That was kind of a—I had gotten laid off from Calcite, and that was back in the recession back in there. So I needed a job. And he is—Blair, that's my wife's maiden name—that would have been her uncle. It was his shop.

Ivan Wirgau: Well, initially it came in and you started seeing, when the salmon started booming you'd see bait and tackle shops show up. I can think of three or four of them that aren't even operating anymore; they're closed. They were selling anything in the line of big-lake fishing. Of course the restaurants and the motels, they all depended on it, they got to depend on it. All summer long it would be just loaded down here with cars and trailers, people coming in for the salmon because we were the Salmon Capital of Michigan. That's what Rogers City put out there through the chamber of commerce, and so that's who we were, Salmon Capital of Michigan, so the people would come from all over, even the other side of the state; they'd come from out of state as well. I got a guy from Texas that comes up every year and he always wants me to take him out. "We don't catch fish like that down there."

Carson: Can we focus in on just the start of the initiative to stock so many salmon here? What do you remember about those initial discussions, and how did they arrive upon the number of fish that they stocked here? And what was it like being on the committee that Mayor [Fred] Lewis here appointed to the fish advisory commission to kind of think about planning for what that stocking would do to the city?[15]

Frank Krist: Well, actually, I remember that clearly because what happened—I think what I was going to tell you is the fishery was different here because the other places on Lake Michigan, they're migrating up. Well, back in the early '80s—probably '81–'82—we'd go out here end of June and we'd start catching immature salmon. And they'd be anywhere from a couple pounds up to maybe eight, nine, ten pounds. And thought, Well, okay. Maybe they're coming from Oscoda. Maybe they're coming—well, what we learned later, they were probably coming from Georgian Bay, the rivers up there. Nottawasaga River's a big one. And so we're catching these salmon. I mean, we're going out there catching salmon every trip. And that would start at the end of June, usually about the third week of June, and we caught them all the way up through the summer and into October. In fact, we—you get into October the wind is really bad out here. But you can get out maybe once or twice a week, and we were catching them all the way up to deer season. By then you start getting snow and it's hard to get in the harbor. And so we kept saying to the DNR, "You know, you're planting fifty thousand—you need to plant more so we can really get a good fishery." Well, they always brought up, when they first started stocking salmon—I think it was in '69 in the Ocqueoc River—if you've ever been up there to look at it, and you can—if you go to the access site, and park your car there in the access site you can get up on a platform and you can see the lake right there—right at the mouth of the river is privately owned. Well, they planted the salmon and next thing they noticed is when they came back, people got crazy. They trespassed. They were breaking the guy's trees down. Damaging his property and everything else. So, anyway, the point was, How can you plant more? You can't control the return. Your harbor's not big enough. You can't do this. So we argued. Steve Swan, have you ever talked to him?

JIM JOHNSON: —there's, of course, always been Swan weir. Steve Swan [retired Michigan DNR fisheries biologist] set it up, but Swan weir wasn't named for Steve Swan, it was already called Swan weir. But that was at the urging of the Hammond Bay Anglers. I'm not—I'm sure Frank has that story, but it's my understanding that the Anglers urged Steve to try something there. And it worked so well that they ended up setting up an egg-taking station there. It's a very secure location where just anybody can't go in there. It's on private property, and the quarry's been super good to work with, and seems to be proud to be helping the DNR get eggs there. So that was a wonderful idea that they came up with.

FRANK KRIST: But we were going back and forth with Steve Swan; he was the area biologist. And Myrl Keller, he was a Lansing guy that kind of oversaw stuff, and fishery chief down there, John Robertson. And we just kept harping on them and taking all these pictures. Okay, so then about 1983 or so, "We've got to come over and meet with you." This was after about three years of just pestering them. "Okay. Come on over." And we sat down, and they said, "We've been thinking of a way of dealing with this is to—," and apparently they talked to Calcite to see if they would go along with it, "—well, we'll put a weir on private land and we'll just control the access from shore in the fall." Worked great. And that's what really got that going is we were just constantly persistent. And been real involved—we got real involved with the tribal issues back then. In '79, that's when Judge Fox made his ruling and there was a lot of tribal fishings, so we were communicating a lot with the DNR and the other parties. So we were real visible in the community. And so okay, we got them convinced, and of course when that happened—you probably read that article I sent you that Glen Shep[pard] wrote, and that kind of summarizes: okay, the community took it seriously and they got ready. And I give them credit, they did a great job on the harbor. And to this day it's a great harbor.

Matt Hollabaugh: Oh, I was going to tell you about, back then too, the families would buy boats—bigger boats. See, Partykas bought that Pro-Line down in Florida, I think.
Carson: The *Salmon Slayer*?
Matt: Yeah, and they brought it up here. Because you couldn't get a boat like that in Michigan yet. There was nothing—you know, like I said, we were using mostly fourteen-footers with tiller mounts. And so the families would start buying—they'd go together and buy a boat, and I knew quite a few that did that.

John Bruning: When the big plants came and we had—the fishery itself was evolving. People were learning. Downriggers and bigger boats and stuff was much more the norm, I guess. In those early days, I can still remember, I was thinking yesterday, we were out, and now you go out and you put whatever lines out, whether it's lead or copper or downriggers, and you put a spoon or a plug or something on and you just run it back. In those early days we were learning a lot. The lake trout, typically you'd use something like a herring dodger with some kind of a bait behind it to attract them. And when we first started fishing salmon, at least out of here, we almost always ran some sort of a herring dodger, even a six-inch dodger ahead of a spoon, because we didn't really fully understand how effective it could be to just run the spoon. And maybe it was—maybe the water clarity—there might have been some other variables. Maybe it helped, maybe it didn't. But things really evolved and people started—you know, they weren't terribly difficult to catch. I mean, certainly some fishermen were better than others. And time on the water and tracking, like with any fishing opportunity, being aware of where the fish are or where they weren't yesterday so you avoid that and go somewhere else. You increase your odds of success. But people were catching fish. And they were coming. There was—the little bait shop I worked at, we'd get constant calls from people, either trying to plan their stay, or maybe make a decision as to what port they were going to go to. Because when you're—a lot of the people from here, since we're up north and rural, there's certainly a core of local fishermen, but a lot of the folks were coming from the Detroit area. And I don't know so much about the southwest part of the state, but certainly on this side, the Detroit area and the [Saginaw] Bay area and those guys would come up here. And for some of them it wasn't a whole lot different to go to Pentwater or wherever than it was here, it just—did they veer right or did they veer left? And so they would call. We would provide reasonably accurate reports. As good as you can—how they did that morning or whatever. And we started to build a pretty good reputation. I think it flourished. I don't know, because I was in a different segment, I would assume that the restaurants and the hospitality, the lodging and so forth, industries did fairly well, as well, because people had to stay somewhere. Short-term rentals or whatever. Because some people would take their vacation and they'd come up and they'd fish salmon. That's what they did. And it was, it was pretty good. And I'm thinking, those were probably—I would think those were probably the years I'm thinking of that were the best were the late, mid- to late '80s. I don't remember exactly when the first big plants came. I think they were probably in the early—

CARSON: '83.

JOHN: —yeah. Yeah. So three years after that. And for a time period it was really good.

BRUCE GRANT: I've got a magazine here—goes back to I think '86. And before you leave I just want you to read something—a paragraph in here.[16] And this was the biggest, hottest magazine going here on the Great Lakes when the salmon thing started. And by accident—back then we had the East Michigan Tourist Association—and they had a weekend setup in Oscoda for the editor and a group for this magazine. And I don't remember what it was—oh, their boat broke down. When they got here their boat broke down. And it was a major breakdown. So they went back to Ohio and came back a couple weeks later. Well, it was right in the heat of the season, but we'd just opened. I mean, we'd just opened the doors. And the tourist association came and said, "Is there any way you can put these people up?" Well, sure. We did. And it worked out so well because in this editorial that he wrote—it's a whole-page editorial—but one of the paragraphs in here he said a very important thing is that it happened in the past and it's going to happen in the future—hopefully something that you're writing will tell people ahead of time to have a work plan. Have a plan together so when these kind of things happen. But just think like what he said, they fished Lake Michigan right from when the salmon bonanza started right up until Rogers City started hitting the newspapers, and they love fishing in Lake Michigan, and the fishing was good. But they got tired of the way they were treated in the restaurants. They got tired of the way they were treated in the marinas because there was so much business, the people forgot about what it was like before they had this business, and then they built an attitude because they had too much business. And his thing in there that just touched my heart—I've never forgot it—he says, "The experience we had in Rogers City was like none we've ever had. We just hope that the people don't change like they have on Lake Michigan. But I'm afraid it's going to happen because that's history." And what he said—to me, there's an awful lesson in what he says there because if you don't have a plan—and we have a wonderful city here, but we're going back—this was a commercial fishing town and a lumbering town, it wasn't a tourist town.

3

SALMON SLAYER AND THE ROGERS CITY SALMON TOURNAMENT

Salmon Slayer is what Ken Partyka named his twenty-four-foot Pro-Line, Florida flats boat. Whereas boat names are typically displayed discreetly on the stern, "SALMON SLAYER" was emblazoned in big, black, sans serif letters against the white fiberglass sidewalls of the boat. A profile view of the boat positioned the moniker below and in the foreground of the center console helm. In an imagined scene, I picture Ken standing behind the wheel, in Swan Bay in late August, "SALMON SLAYER" appropriately positioned below him and his determined gaze. Of course, that simple scene played out in reality many, many times.

Coming out of the Rogers City marina, a three-mile boat ride due east past the entrance to Calcite puts you in the middle of the entrance to Swan Bay. "Swan Bay is not that big," as Ken would tell me; the expanse it covers is less than one square mile. If you entered at a southeasterly angle, the major features would be Quarry Point on your right, and Adams Point extending out in the distance to your left. *Salmon Slayer* would have made that trek countless times—a mere ten-minute drive on a calm day.

The relatively shallow and protected waters of Swan Bay must have had excellent salmon fishing before the major Chinook salmon–stocking initiative in Swan River, but I struggle to understand how or why. After all, Swan Bay comprises just one of the twenty-three thousand square miles of Lake Huron—the third-largest body of freshwater in the world—and Swan River, as retired biologist Jim Johnson would tell me, "is really a creek that

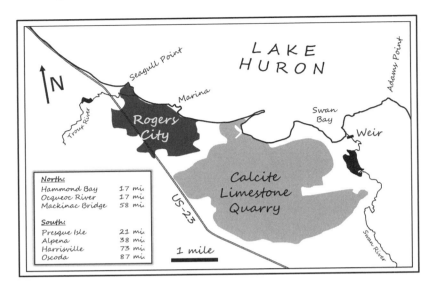

Geographic features in the greater Rogers City area, including the man-made weir on Swan River where the Michigan Department of Natural Resources stocked nearly a million Chinook salmon annually beginning in the mid-1980s. Driving distances from Rogers City to other prominent coastal destinations on the Lake Huron shoreline are also shown.

drains a limestone quarry, and no self-respecting salmon would try to reproduce there"—except, of course, for the salmon that had imprinted there because that's where they had been stocked. So it makes sense to me that beginning in 1986, the year of the inaugural Rogers City Salmon Tournament, many large, mature Chinook salmon should have returned to Swan Bay beginning in late summer. That would have been the run of the first cohort of three-year-old adult salmon corresponding to the major stocking events that began there in 1983. And so it also makes sense to me that Ken and his crew could have slayed salmon in Swan Bay, as they did, en route to near domination of the '86 and '87 tournaments. But in the years prior to the arrival of those millions of stocked fish, how had the Partykas—Ken and his younger brother Chuck—seemingly perfected the salmon fishery microcosm that was Swan Bay before the tournaments had begun? It makes me wonder.

Each year, the biggest prize in the Rogers City Salmon Tournament was awarded for simply the largest fish caught over the two or three days of the event. So, as Dave Smrchek would tell me, it only took "*one good fish.*" This format helped generate suspense at the weigh-ins—the true spectacle of the event for the community—because it was largely anybody's game. Mere fractions of an ounce influenced how anglers placed, and the public watched intently as the leaderboard kept shuffling. The largest-fish format also catered to smaller boats and smaller crews. And so while technically the angler who reeled in the biggest fish was crowned champion, the truest measure of salmon-fishing aptitude was inferred from the tournament's "boat division." Each day, the heaviest total "captain's catch" was awarded a relatively nominal prize, but it conferred the real bragging rights. The *Salmon Slayer* crew dominated the boat division, and coincidentally Ken even happened to haul in the largest salmon of the 1986 tourney. At twenty-five pounds, eight ounces, its size was "no big deal," but Ken won a fourteen-foot Starcraft boat because of it. Altogether, the *Salmon Slayer* crew amassed roughly $6,000 worth of cash and prizes in those first two tournaments.

You might think, *Not bad for four days of fishing!* But the stories I heard conjured a risk-reward image much more like that of *Deadliest Catch* than anything else. Lifetime angler Ivan Wirgau was a crew member aboard Ken's boat each of those years. He and Ken related to me their experiences fishing through highly inclement weather conditions, the likes of which I hope I *never* find myself in, on their path to tournament success.

The Rogers City Salmon Tournament became a local fixture, and by my estimation grew to be largely embraced by the community. It brought "an energy," as City Manager Joe Hefele described. Each year, more and more people signed up for the tournament, so that participation was eventually capped at 350 boats. At the tournament's height in the 1990s, about eleven hundred anglers, not to mention other family and friends who might have accompanied them, descended upon Rogers City, whose population then ranged from just three thousand to four thousand residents. The hubbub of the tournament would have been prominent, to say the least.

Each successive iteration of the tournament is truly indebted to the groundwork laid by the organizers of that first go-round in 1986, as well as the exuberant anticipation sparked by the collaborative efforts to stock a million salmon each year in Swan River. It actually is remarkable how well the 1986 tournament played out. It was proposed to city council only eleven weeks before the target weekend of August 23–24.[1] Terry Fitzwater, Mike Modrzynski (muh-DRINZ-kee), and Mike's brother Ron were the three directors of the first Rogers City Salmon Tournament. Fitzwater, who had been the general manager and editor of the *Presque Isle County Advance* since the early '80s, wrote articles covering sports and the outdoors. He promoted the tournament locally and secured sponsors, while Mike Modrzynski, a member of the Michigan Outdoor Writers Association, helped the fledgling tournament garner enthusiastic praise from those who wrote for bigger media outlets, both downstate and throughout the Great Lakes region. In that short eleven-week span, the tournament directors secured thousands of dollars of sponsorships and prizes, ultimately prompting 443 anglers to sign up in hopes of cashing in.[2]

With Fitzwater at the editorial helm, updates regarding the impending salmon tournament were front-page news. As I dug into Fitzwater's articles in the archives of the *Advance* from June through mid-August 1986, I found myself riveted with anticipation for an event long past. Scheduling that tournament right on the heels of the state's largest salmon-stocking venture was a true test of the program's success—and it passed. Rogers City, and Lake Huron in general, became a Chinook salmon–fishing mecca.

But in order for Rogers City to become a destination, many would-be anglers from downstate metropolitan areas would have to drive past other salmon-fishing hotspots on either side of the state. From Detroit, anglers might drive to Port Sanilac (90 miles), Oscoda (200 miles), or Harrisville (200 miles) on the Lake Huron side. Or they could drive 250 miles to Rogers City—which happens also to be the same distance to the major salmon-fishing ports of Ludington, Manistee, and Frankfort on the Lake Michigan side. For my and subsequent generations, it's difficult to comprehend the importance of Detroit on things such as fishing and boating tourism because Detroit's population—especially the number of would-be vacationers there with expendable income—has declined so much since the automotive industry's heyday in southeast Michigan.[3] But back then, it was a big deal that Dave Richey, the outdoors editor for the *Detroit News*, marshalled the first several tournaments.[4] And it often made the local news when the Detroit Area Steelheaders came up for salmon-fishing outings in Rogers City.[5] As resort owner and charter fishing guide Bruce Grant implied, those Detroit connections were instrumental in putting Rogers City "on the map" as a salmon-fishing destination, and those relationships were largely fostered in the formation of the Rogers City Salmon Tournament.

MARY ANN HEIDEMANN: So I wanted to talk a little bit about the salmon tournaments themselves, because again we were coming into—might as well have landed on Mars as far as we were concerned. Local festivals were something new to us. And the salmon tournament certainly took on all the aspects of a local festival. And it's really unbelievable how much fun people had at the tournament, and it was kind of a whole weeklong thing, because fishermen would come in and it was—the fishing itself was Friday, Saturday, Sunday, and Friday and Saturday were all day and Sunday you had to bring them in earlier to wrap it up, award their prizes. But Thursday night was the captains' meeting where all the rules were laid out and all the registration was confirmed. And this town was just overrun with people. And you can understand that there is not a single business here that runs all night, but during the salmon tournament they did. So they had special hours, especially the restaurants, they'd have breakfast at whatever, but down here in the park they had a food tent, and the food tent ran 24/7 from Thursday on. And the food tent was staffed by a couple—local sausage shop, Nowicki's, had a booth in there. But again, here's a German tradition, all the Lutheran churches tend to fight with each other, and the biggest Lutheran church here in town, Peace—pardon me, St. John's Lutheran Church, had a pastor who was very opinionated, and had problems with women's participating in services. And so he laid down a bunch of rules which some people thought went against Lutheran theology and organizational principles. So long story short—and I didn't belong to that church—but that was a huge congregation and it split in half. So half the people left to start a new church, and the ones that left needed money to build a church, so they had a food booth at the salmon festival.[6] And they would cook fantastic meals, all day, all night, and drinks, and all the fixings, you name it, you know, breakfast, lunch, dinner. And they were able to pay off their mortgage with the tent proceeds at the salmon tournament.

CARSON: That's interesting, yeah.

MARY ANN: Really funny. So that was the shortest time period to burning the mortgage known to man. And in fact they got the mortgage paid off before the fish stopped biting [*laughs*], so that was good for them. But the tournament brought a lot of cash into town.

CARSON: So what was that like when the tournament was getting started? And because—I've read that it just got bigger and bigger with participation, the fish got bigger every year through the early '90s and, kind of, what was that like?

BRUCE GRANT: Yeah, well, I think '86 is when it started. And we had a resident here, his name was Mike Modrzynski, and Mike was in the air force, and he was stationed in Oscoda, but he was from Rogers City. And he wrote a couple books on steelhead fishing in the rivers. And when this hit in his hometown he was excited. But he was an intelligence officer down in Oscoda. He'd run up here for the weekends. But he was part of the Michigan Outdoor Writers Association. And I give Mike all the credit for the tournament here because he had the experience—how to build one. But his experience came from all the outdoor writers he knew in the Michigan Outdoor Writers organization, and he communicated with them. Well, at that time the people had bought our newspaper out here, the *Presque Isle Advance*. The guy that bought it—his name was [Richard L.] Milliman from Lansing—he sent his son-in-law up here to run the new newspaper—or that they'd just bought. And Mike wrote articles for them. And Mike was still heavy in the air force. Well, Mike and his brother and this Terry Fitzwater started the first one, but Mike did press releases, he did all the stuff you have to do to let people know something's going on. And the word was already out how good fishing was and—but they weren't prepared for it. I'm telling you, they were lined almost out to 23 [U.S. 23 N]. What do we do with all these boats?

DAVE NADOLSKY: Yeah. In the old days they used to do a Le Mans start.[7] A running start. And they'd fire off this—
CARSON: Well, Mike [Peltz] said he was the one who fired the shotgun.
DAVE: Yeah, he used to be down there officiating. And that was quite a—you know, nothing but assholes and elbows, and people running all over the place.
TOM ALLUM: It's a miracle nobody drowned, you know?
DAVE: Yeah. Yeah.

MIKE PELTZ: I—several times, I'm not sure, two or three times I did the shotgun start. Get out on the breakwall, and I think it was 6:30, I'm not sure now the time, but when the time came, fired that shotgun and [*laughs*] it was unreal to hear those engines roar up. I mean, you could hear it all over Rogers City, those engines. There were so many boats. And they were fighting to get out of the harbor, which was dangerous at the time because there was too many boats for the harbor. So eventually, they moved the starting point into the lake so they didn't have to compete with that entrance to get—exit to get out of that harbor. It was actually—the small boats were in danger, no question about it. But fortunately we never had any incidents. But it was hazardous, to say the least, for all those boats to get moving at one time. But when they fired up all of those engines it was a roar. [*laughs*]

CARSON: So you were the one who fired the gun to start it all off?

MIKE: Several times. Yeah. Yeah. Yeah, oh, yeah, we were down there. We had a patrol boat. I don't remember now if we had the patrol—I think we had the patrol boat out on the lake, ready to help anybody [who] got into trouble. But I never went out in the boat, I was on the breakwall to fire the shotgun. But I didn't do that every year—I did it several times. It was a big show. Half the town got up early just to go watch those boats head out into the lake. It was quite a sight. [*laughs*] Something you couldn't plan ahead of time, when you get that many people out that early in the morning to do that. And the breakwall was a perfect place to watch it because when the boats get ready to leave they're on your right, when they got out into the lake they were on your left. You couldn't miss anything, it was the perfect place. Kind of, spectators were right in the middle of the action. But it was a big thing. . . . I'm sorry some of my friends aren't here to tell you the story because they were out there in the boats, and I was not. We didn't have any real incidents that I can recall. The biggest problem was fishermen out there getting lines tangled up because there were so many boats. And these boats were all in a big hurry when they left to get to a certain spot. I don't know how they found a certain spot, they didn't have the equipment they've got now. But they all had a favorite place to fish out there. And they were all in a big hurry, they wanted to be there first. But then they got there and everybody was dragging four or five lines, and somebody didn't make the right turn, the right place, they were snagging other people's lines. That was the problem. But I don't recall any serious—you know, it caused friction. I'm sure there was some name-calling, and some choice words, but—[*laughs*] especially with guys out there that weren't experienced fishermen that were probably causing most of the problem. But it was nothing serious. And I don't recall ever having any injuries or altercations. I'm sure there were a few; I'm not aware of them.

DAVE SMRCHEK: In the meantime, the friend that had gotten me involved in Ducks Unlimited had fished in Lake Michigan. He lived in Charlevoix for a while. And he said—and they had started the salmon tournament; that was going—and he said, "Well we can win that tournament. We only need to catch *one good fish*. There's nothing *to it*!" So we got in his fourteen-foot boat and went out here and went fishing. Well, there was a few more boats around in the '80s. The first time we went out in the evening, we pulled out of the harbor, and everybody made a left turn out of the harbor, they trolled down to Seagull Point, went out to about a hundred feet, and went back around, trolled over to Adam's Point, and then came back up along the shoreline to the harbor. And that was the pattern. It was like a big parade out there that night. And when it got dark, here was this whole line of lights on the boats. Well, that was my first experience out there. We didn't catch a fish. But we learned real quickly you didn't want to go the opposite direction of anybody—everybody was mad at you. So anyway, we caught a couple of fish that—but then that was kind of—it was expensive, and I didn't really care that much.

CARSON: Did you used to go down and watch the weigh-in, when the boats would come—?

MIKE PELTZ: Oh, yeah. Yeah. Oh, that was a huge crowd. That was a big thing. They had a good setup. They had—they used the local band shell, which is almost perfect for that. They had the sound system, and the park right in front, and park benches, and a big parking lot. Yeah, it was great. People couldn't wait. They had concession stands there, they sold lunch for people, for—the fishermen really loved it. Just hamburgers and hotdogs, stuff like that. Cold drinks. The fishermen had their own—beverages, we'll put it that way. But it was an annual event, no question about it. It was big. Locally, as far as economics it was a huge impact on that. There was a lot of people. But we'd go down.

KEN PARTYKA: You know, I mean, we came in on that salmon tournament and we quit at nineteen because I knew we had nineteen, but I didn't want to make a mistake. So we're going to quit one short. And we came in and it was getting close to quitting time anyway because I think that was a Sunday 1 o'clock cutoff, and we had to get back. But we came in. People asked, "What did you catch them on?" I show them this little chrome Grizzly. I said, "Eighteen of our nineteen fish came on this." "Bullshit. [*Carson laughs*] Bullshit." You look—I says, "This was a brand-new lure. I took it out of the package this morning. Brand-new lure. Look at it—," it is just carved up with teeth marks, "—look at it.

This was a brand-new lure this morning." "Bullshit." "Um, what can I tell you? [*laughs*] What can I tell you?"

Dave Smrchek: Anybody would tell you anything, *except during the tournament.* Then everybody had all these codes and got competitive and nobody would share anything about how they were catching fish. But wave a net, and here would come everybody. You could be five miles away from the closest boat and if you got a net out you'd have twenty-five boats around you before you got the fish netted. It was just—people following around that way. And the poor charters, it's like they had a magnet on the transom of their boat. Everywhere they went there was a parade following them because they were supposed to know where the fish were.

Carson: When did the crew come together for the first—
Ivan Wirgau: Salmon tournament?
Carson: —salmon tournament? How did that all begin?
Ivan: Well, we were all steelhead fishermen, and we knew each other through that. And lake trout, and then salmon, too. Jeff Heward was part of that crew. But the Partyka brothers—and Partyka brothers always used to go and fish in the bay all the time. They found these Grizzly plugs. They're really small, they're like, maybe a third the size of a J-Plug, and they were using them a lot on the west side of the state, so they were using those. And I always remember, whether it would be if we were out socializing at the bar, Chuck would always go, "Well, I'm going fishing tomorrow, so I've got to go home." Never paid a lot of attention to it. Well, they locked onto the deal, when you had some rough weather, you'd get in there the next day when the lake's calming down and get in there with those Grizzlys and they just beat the heck out of those fish. But they were looking to put together a salmon crew. So, of course, Chuck and Ken were brothers and they'd fished a lot using that technique, for long-lining them in the bay. And they knew Jeff Heward, because we were all part of that same—and they asked me if I wanted to, if—"[Would you] be interested in getting in on this with me?" I said, "Yeah, sure. That's cool." So we drew straws. I remember the tournament we drew straws to see who's going to catch the first fish. Well, it was calm that day in the morning. Glass, just like glass, offshore wind. We got into Swan Bay, and I had drew the first straw so I'm catching the first fish, and I don't know, it was like a twelve-,

fourteen-pounder. Nice silver fish. Okay, got it. So I don't remember who was up next for whatever reason. It was slow, we weren't catching much, and we got behind in the leaderboard, and we weren't doing much. We stayed out there and the weather got really bad. [Wind] started coming out of the north, northeast, and waves got really high. There was six- to eight-foot waves out there.

CARSON: That first tournament, were you the only boat that was in Swan Bay, doing what you were doing?

KEN PARTYKA: Oh, god, there was, there was—there was so many boats in there that it was unbelievable. You would not believe—there had to be—I couldn't even—I mean, that's a long time ago, okay. That's a long time ago. There was so many boats, I've never seen so many boats. Okay? There was so many boats, there was thirty-five, forty boats anyway, anyway. And they had spotter boats out, because I knew—I talked to one guy that was in a spotter boat. They're just checking to make sure nobody's doing anything wrong and they're going, "Wow. You guys are catching fish like crazy." And the funny thing was it was an onshore wind, it was windier than a bugger, and everything was riled up. And prior to that I was doing good like on—not a Bomber, but a something like a Bomber that was a firetiger. And I caught one fish right off the get-go on this firetiger.[8] But we ended up going to—I had these little teeny Grizzly plugs, little J-Plugs, Grizzlys. Just like a J-Plug, but a small, little—. And the four of us went to that. And we're just—I mean, we're running right up on—we're dragging these through sand, they're bouncing, and we are just—. And there's so many fish, I mean, we landed fish that I can't even imagine how it happened because I know we landed fish that were on and it's past that boat [*Carson laughs*] and it's past that boat. And there's—Swan Bay is not that big. Anymore like when we go out, hey, there's like three or four people in Swan Bay, half a dozen, it's like really crowded. It was like, there's I think forty boats in there.

IVAN WIRGAU: So we were in the bay, and we didn't want to make the trek to go across, in front of Calcite to go back to the [boat harbor] because we'd be going right into the teeth of the waves. So we decided to put the boat in Calcite. And we tied it up there near the old BT [Bradley Transportation] building where they used to do winter work on the boats when they owned their own fleet here at Calcite. And we got out, we got picked up there, and we had the boat tied off on the dock. Well, we told the tournament that's what we were going to do, we weren't going to make the trek across. Okay. So we were just going to call it quits, and we weren't even on the board.

CARSON: Tomorrow I'm interviewing with Matt Hollabaugh and Ivan Wirgau. And Matt told me that he sees you on Swan Bay every fall. And then I know Ivan was part of the *Salmon Slayer* crew.
KEN PARTYKA: Oh, he freaked out. He freaked out.
CARSON: During the tournament?
KEN: Yeah. Oh, that was—I don't know whether it was the first day or the second day. It was really rough. And we're out there—
MANDY PARTYKA: Poor Ivan.
KEN: —he was, he was a good fisherman. He was a good fisherman. But he didn't like the weather we were in. I was in waves where I drop down, drop down in the waves, I'm standing, steering the boat, coming into the bay, the waves are so big I'm dropping down and I can't hardly see the top of the trees in front of me. I come up, and I take water over the bow. Pushes all the tackle boxes and everything to the back of the boat. But it's a self-bailing cockpit, you know, these center console things bail themselves. They all go this way, as you're going up, as you're coming down, wave comes over the back [*laughs*], all the tackle boxes go forward [*laughs*], all the tackle boxes go back, all the tackle boxes go forward. I've got water in the boat this deep [he held his hands about eight inches apart], all over. I mean, it's like—and we're to the point where, okay, this is too much. We can't really do this, okay, so we're going to go, and we're going to go back. We're going to head back. And we head back inside the breakwall of Calcite. And we head back inside the breakwall of Calcite, and Ivan's father-in-law was up on Harbor View, used to have an access road up onto Harbor View. We came inside the breakwall, he saw his father-in-law up there. We pulled up, dropped him off at a wall. Boom—he's up, he's out of the boat. Because we were deciding whether we were going to attempt to come around the breakwall of Calcite and make it back to the harbor. And it was like really bad. There was big, big seas. Big seas. Somebody said ten-footers, I don't—you know.[9] Big seas. So we pulled around, we came up, we took a look. Got out, took a look at things. Called tournament control and says, "I don't know that I can safely make it out." My brother, hey, he's always, "Eh, we can—," you know? His buddy Jeffy Heward says,

"Mort," he says, "hey—I say you got a 90 percent chance of making it back." And I'm going [*laughs*], 90—? I think we could have made it, but it was like I called tournament control. I said, "I'm going to tie up inside of here, inside of Calcite, and bring my catch in, and I'm going to leave my boat here. I don't know that I can safely make it back." And they were cool with that. But, yeah, Ivan—yeah.

IVAN WIRGAU: And it came in the afternoon where Chuck called, and Ken, and said, "Well, we're going to go back out at 3." Well, I called Jeff, and he lived down the river from here, and he said, "No, I think I'm just going to sleep in. I don't think it's worth it, it's too rough out there." The waves were still rough. It was building, actually, even more yet. So I said, "I'll go with you." So we put in the boat and we thought, well, our deal was to troll around in the bay where we were protected from the wind, on the backside of the breakwall. So we're trolling around in there. Their dad was a captain of the boats, and he was down there—he had access in back of Calcite, he could go down there by Swan Bay. And he was parked there down at the bay, by the river mouth, and he said, "Paul Durecki just made two passes in front of the river and he hooked two fish." We picked up our lines and we headed for there. And there were a lot of waves and we came out of that breakwall and we had to time it to get into the waves, follow the waves in there. And it was rough. I mean, there were waves splashing right up in the boat. And you had to time your turn. And you really had to watch so you didn't get thrown out of the boat, because the *Salmon Slayer* was like a big cedar log floating in the water, it didn't have real high sides on it. So you had to kind of be careful you didn't get knocked out of the boat. It was a big, steady boat. And it was a self-bailing bilge on it. Water'd come in and wash right out the back. So we made a pass in there and we nailed two fish, right off the gate, you know? One time, that guy that was in there came up on a wave and when he came down he bottomed out right on the—.

CARSON: Really?

IVAN: Oh, yeah. It was bad. Those waves were huge. There were waves big as this ceiling in here. [*laughs*] Big waves *crashing* in there. So it was really crazy. But we made, I don't remember how many passes. I don't remember if we had five or six fish. I don't remember what it was off the top of my head. And then we made the long trek to go—because we had to weigh those fish in, so we had to go back to the harbor. We couldn't stay and then carry our fish over there. So it was kind of an interesting ride back going over those waves. But we got back there and then all of a sudden we take the leader. Now we're head of the game. We got the first-place fish. We're in first place in the boat tournament. Well, everyone took off, got off the lake, see. So the next day, the lake was coming down. It was still riled up out there, but the winds were starting to subside some. So everybody goes, everyone's going out there. They didn't come out right away, but close to it. We got in there and every time we made a pass we had doubleheaders. Right in—we were only in, I don't know, probably eight to ten feet of water. But we were long-lining with those Grizzly plugs. Sometimes we had three lines out. What we would do was go parallel to Swan Bay near where the river mouth is, and pull all our lines up, turn around 180, and then just let all the lines out and go back the other way. And every time we'd do that, *tt-tt*. So we caught a pile of fish. And we went back and we did well. So that's how that all evolved, that particular first trip. They knew the bay because they'd been fishing it for years, Chuck and Ken. Nobody was really in there doing much of that stuff. But that all changed. [*laughs*] Yeah. Everyone got the idea, then, that maybe that's a pretty good time to be going in there after these storms, and going after these fish. It was insane. It was just, the fishing was fabulous. Nice fish. Fighters. Screamers. Lot of fun.

FRANK KRIST: As far as—I didn't get into the promotion end too much. I was more into getting the fishery here, concentrating on the biology, and making sure things are running smoothly. But, I mean, it was a big event. Not only did the harbor fill up with boats, but we had cars and that parked on the street. And then the sewage plant, they had a lot of overflow parking, people were parking down there.

TOM ALLUM: Yeah, it was overwhelming on a weekend, or during the salmon festival. There was no place to park. I remember when—if I wanted to go down to the harbor I had a little two-cycle motorcycle I would ride down there, because you couldn't take your car down. Remember, I had a boat there now. I'm paying 1,500 dollars a year to keep my boat there, and it would be nice to be able to go down and see it [*laughs*], but you couldn't even get down there.

DAVE NADOLSKY: But the kids made a little money off it. The wrestling team used to go down and check the coolers and stuff on board. And then the cheerleaders handled the weigh-ins and so forth. And it was a big deal. The community came down. We had a portable trailer there. The parking lot was full. The food concessions were all making money, and Kiwanis was selling donuts, and so on and so forth. Good times, you know?

CARSON: That was for the tournament—the Rogers City Salmon Tournament?

DAVE: Yeah, they've got a couple tournaments now, but they aren't anything like it. Although they still do the portable trailer and weigh-in, so people come down and watch for a little while.

TOM: The tournaments were—it's interesting, I can tell you a bit about that. The tournament back in the day was a big money-making operation. I don't know how many—five hundred boats?

CARSON: Three-fifty was how much [all three talking at once]—yeah.

TOM: —and was more than the city could handle, really. But there was a lot of money to be made there. And if you recall, whenever there's more money than people are accounting for, sometimes it disappears into the cracks, and I think that happened on a couple of occasions.[10]

BRUCE GRANT: First couple of years it was just out of Rogers City. Then we decided—well, first it went for a few years—there were some—eh, I say financial problems—it didn't work out with the three guys that started it. And they—Mike stayed clean; the other two guys didn't—so Mike said—he came to the Hammond Bay Anglers and said, "Why don't we set this up through the Hammond Bay Anglers—the other two guys are gone—it's over with—and the Anglers run it for a fundraiser for these—help us raise money for the issues we're going—for our fishery?" So then we opened up the Hammond Bay Harbor and went down to Presque Isle and offered them to open up their harbor. Now, man, we got boats coming, every year it's getting bigger and bigger and bigger. And we got a real education. The problem was a couple of us that run charter boats, we had to park our boats when fishing was good, and some guys were taking—well, I had a lot of legal firms and insurance companies, and they'd pay 2,000 bucks to take their customers out to let them fish the tournament. A few of us had to park our boats to help keep it going. But it was so good for my business. It was good for the community. And we did it. But it just kept growing, growing, growing.

KEN PARTYKA: But this was Rogers City, this was going to be a small boat tournament, okay. Small boats. Hey, this is not all about big boats.

All of a sudden, in two years, Oh, you can't go in a line from here to there. You can't go anywhere over there. You can't—I just quit fishing, I mean, they put so many rules in, in my opinion [*laughs*], the anti–*Salmon Slayer* fishing rules to—you can't go—. But there was a lot of—

CARSON: What were the rules? I'm curious now.

KEN: Well, you could just go anywhere from here to here and you could fish anywhere. Now after that they changed the rules and they says, "Okay, you cannot fish inside of a line from the breakwall to Swan Point or Quarry Point over there. You can't fish any—"

MANDY PARTYKA: Inside. Yeah, you can't go in the bay, where people were catching fish. [*laughs*]

KEN: You know, there was forty-some boats in there, there was.

CARSON: Huh, I didn't know that.

KEN: Yeah.

MANDY: It wasn't fun anymore.

KEN: You know, okay, you can only—like I think I told you, I says, "Hey, catching the big fish is just luck," okay? We were out for the daily boat captain's catch. Three times a day they take the most—now they're down to three fish. Well, one good fish—it's not right. We came in that day that we had the big one, and it wasn't that big, whatever it was, twenty-five pounds or some god-darn thing, it was nothing. No big deal. But we won every daily captain's catch. That's what we were looking for. Cash money. Just cash money. That's what you could talk smart about. Yeah, we kicked ass. We took every—

MANDY: That's why they changed the rules because they wanted it to be fair for everybody. [*Ken laughs*] But when you're just on top of the game, and you fished all your life and your family fished all your life, and you know what's going on—you kick ass.

CARSON: Right. [*laughs*] Yeah.

MANDY: And when it's not fun anymore you go and you just have fun with other tournaments. There were other tournaments going on.

KEN: Oh, we had fun.

IVAN WIRGAU: There were times in those tournaments where some family members were down here by Seagull Point and those big clouds of alewives would be coming in nearshore and the salmon were right on shore slashing into them. Just crazy. There was a lot of fish around. You had the alewives and that's what they wanted. They're tearing into them babies. And my wife, she caught big fish: twenty-eight-pounders,

Left to right: Ken Partyka, fellow crew member Doc Ryan, Ken's wife, Mandy, and Ken's brother Chuck pose in front of Ken's boat *Salmon Slayer* following the Northeast Michigan Steelheaders' win of one of the "other tournaments going on" that Mandy spoke of. (Source: "Will You Make the Leader Board?" *Presque Isle County Advance*, August 20, 1987)

twenty-seven-pounders. There were some years that were better than others for whatever reason.

KEN PARTYKA: So here's the other story I ought to tell you. This was—this was so cool. "Them guys are such assholes," okay? But anyway [*laughs*], they had a salmon tournament, it might have been the third, might have been the fourth, might have been the fifth. Whatever. At that point in time I could still get in back of Calcite and there was a little launch ramp back there, and I launched the *Salmon Slayer* in back of Calcite early in the morning. My brother and I, our take was we're going to come out here and we're going to kick ass at daybreak. We're going to kick ass at daybreak before anybody gets out here. Because the launch time, flare up in the air is 6 o'clock. Whatever the case is. So we launch in back of Calcite, there's nobody around, so we come out of Calcite back in—there's a boat launch way back in the corner in Swan Bay—come out of Swan Bay. Come across. Come across the breakwall of Calcite, we're coming across, and you see all these boats. All these boats with all the lights on, all their running lights, all floating, all floating, all floating. And we're coming by, I don't have my running lights on. I'm coming by. Pitch black, coming by, coming by. [*laughs*] I turn on my running lights, hit the throttle, and go full-speed heading this way. And I got, like, I don't know how many Q-Beam lights, mega-thousand-watt candlepower lights, we are lit up like daytime. [*laughs*] We are lit up like every—"Tournament Control! Tournament Control! *Salmon Slayer*'s taking off early! *Salmon Slayer*'s—*" "Uh, boys [*laughs*], they're not in the tournament." [*Carson and Ken laugh*] And we are lit up like, we are lit up like—

MANDY PARTYKA: Fun. It was all about fun. [*laughs*]

KEN: Oh, geez. [*laughs*] Just come by, just come by, just come by. I said, "Okay, Chuck, I'm going to turn the lights on and throttle up!" Turned the lights on and just go. [*Mandy and Carson laugh*] "*Salmon Slayer*! *Salmon Slayer*'s taking off early!" Yeah, well, hey. "Boys—uh, nobody likes them guys." [*laughs*] Just play around. I mean, that's what we do. I mean, you want to know where we're from, or what we're at? We're just different. We just do what we do. It's like, I'm not hurting anybody. Just a few things.

CARSON: I've had a great time talking with you, or listening. [*laughs*]

KEN: I mean, I don't, I don't, honestly, I just don't generally say much. I'm a pretty quiet person, but—[*laughs*]

CARSON: Well, I love to fish and it's always fun to hear from people that are hardcore about it. [*Ken laughs*]

MANDY: Oh, we are that. But we like to have fun too.

BRUCE GRANT: —it grew too big too fast. Growing pains actually killed it. And the fishermen killed it. If you drive through our town it's clean. The houses are clean and painted. You don't see too much trash laying around. And I—you haven't even brought the guy's name up yet because it hadn't got into it—we had a gold mine here with one man, his name was Harry Whiteley. He used to own the [*Presque Isle County*] *Advance*. He was the longest-serving—still on record the longest-serving DNR commissioner and chairman. And when we had a problem that we couldn't get through, you called Harry. Harry took care of it. And he took care of it well. Because you went to Lansing with Harry and you walked down the halls with a hero. I mean, everybody, "Harry, come on in my office," you know. Didn't matter who it was. Senators, representatives, and the DNR loved the old guy. And they really did the right thing at the—Higgins Lake there at the center there [the Ralph A. MacMullen Conference Center, Roscommon, Michigan]—made a Harry Whiteley building. Harry just passed away, couple months ago. But Harry was good at keeping things in control too. And he warned us, This is growing too fast. Get some more rules. Get things settled down. And we fought real hard. And I'm probably the one behind it—that pushed it too hard. It's my fault. We said, "We've got to cut this thing down," because a fisherman could come in and register—it cost a boatload of people maybe a hundred bucks. Or you could fish all by yourself for 35 [dollars], by yourself in one boat, which is fine. It's a good thing for a family. But when you get too many people you can't control them. When you get people that go out there at 6 o'clock in the morning and come in at 8 o'clock at night and they've been drinking all day, you've got a serious problem. And when we tried to cut the hours—when it got to the Hammond Bay Anglers—from 6 o'clock in the morning to 2 in the afternoon, before they'd had so much to drink and the sun bleached them out. Volunteers—you can't run something that big without volunteers. And then when you make money, you give it back to organizations like 4-H, the school groups, and things like that. Well, when we get the cheerleaders, or the girls' basketball team and the coach to agree to come down and weigh fish, you can't have a bunch of drunks out there cussing and swearing and slobbering. And then they'd come up, and they'd pick their fish up, and they'd dump them down in the tubs you weigh them in, and here's a little seventeen-, eighteen-year-old girl, or guy—or anybody—gets all splattered with fish slime and fish stuff, and this guy's stumbling all over. It got out of hand. It got out of the hand where, you know, we complained to the—and our local police department wasn't bad, it was the state police—well they'd sit out like predators and hammer everybody after they leave the harbor because they knew half of them were half screwed up on beer and drinking all—that's not good. You're out of control. If a guy goes out there and drinks a little bit and he can handle himself or if somebody else drives—but this is what they were doing. Even had conservation officers here doing traffic patrol after dark, getting—they didn't—not in the morning coming in—at night going out. You lose control when it gets too big. So how are we going to shrink it down? Well, I got to talking with some of the other outdoor—or we—a couple of us did—other outdoor writers and said, "Hey, the problem is your tournament is too cheap." You're not—because we never got big boats. We might give a sixteen-foot boat away with a twenty-five-horse motor on it. Or then we got to the point we'd just give you half of what we collected and pay for the first fifty slots. And somebody might walk away with 4 to 5,000 dollars, which is a lot of money. But as other tournaments are run, that's no money at all. I said, "You've got to get up—[if] you want the big boats to come in, and you want the big-money supporters—the advertisers—to come in, you've got to give away some money." But Starcraft isn't going to come in. Mercury or Evinrude isn't going to come in. Jay's Sporting Goods isn't going to come in, or Cabela's, unless you've got the big guns here because that's where they get their coverage. And we tried to do that. We did it one year, and we did it that you could have as many boats as you wanted—or you could have like six people on your boat—but it was a thousand bucks. So if you had four people each guy paid 250. And you got 50 percent of the take. So if you've got three hundred boats, they're going to walk out of here with a lot of money. And then we went from fifty prizes, I think, to maybe twenty prizes. But they were much better. You didn't walk away with a six-pack of Pabst. You could walk away with a few hundred bucks. The lowest prize would have paid everybody back that paid 250 bucks. And do you see the boats that come in here? Two hundred and fifty bucks is nothing, you know. Anyways, it dwindled down—and it started dwindling down—and then the Anglers got—they—it just got—it was so hard to get the volunteers.

CARSON: Well, I guess I'm trying to think about how much the fishery became a part of the community of Rogers City itself versus the fishery just kind of was imposed on the city—I don't know if I'm asking that, kind of, the way I want to.

JOE HEFELE: Well, I see what—I think I know where you're going, and my recollection, again, having pretty much grown up here, is that the fishery was in no way a burden at all on the community. And I know when you have any type of a large influx of people from out of town, whether it's a festival or a tournament like this, some folks would just as soon have it be quiet and peaceful and not have all those people, but I honestly—I think the community welcomed and was excited about that tournament every year. Again, a big part of that tournament was the weigh-in of the fish. And so I just remember, even being a young person, we were all down there, and as the boaters and fishermen came in at dusk, or somewhere near 10 o'clock to get in on time, and were waiting in line to weigh those fish. We were all sitting there and waiting to see because inevitably there was going to be multiple twenty-pounders and some thirty-pound Chinook salmon brought in literally every weigh-in. It was just cool to see that. And again, on top of that it was just the energy that everybody was having fun, they'd hop off the boat, and talking about how they did, and there was fish stories being told, and there were some cocktails, and it was just a lot of fun. And I honestly think the community looked forward to it and embraced it, which is interesting because the big tournament that's literally every year right after our big Nautical Festival, which also brought tons of people into town. I think it turned what was kind of a one-week party into in essence a two-week party. And I think for the most part most of the community at least were good with that. And it definitely was a huge boost to the local economy and very welcome.

4

"A S***LOAD OF SALMON"

The early to mid-1980s saw the wheels put into motion for the Swan River Chinook salmon–stocking program and the annual Rogers City Salmon Tournament. By most accounts, the salmon fishing in Lake Huron, and especially in Rogers City, continued to be exceptional through the early 2000s. But that span of unparalleled fishing and its origins are now decades old. And no matter how gloried in its time, that which was commonplace, or that which slowly phases out, can slip unceremoniously into the past.

But the benefit of hindsight, it seems, is that the tremendous Lake Huron Chinook salmon fishery, which had become routine as it was playing out, is now reflected upon fondly, with awe and appreciation. When I first spoke with local resident Ken Rasche on the phone in hopes of hearing his version of the Rogers City salmon story, he told me, "I always said, I should've written a book. I should've written a book." I know that salmon fishing was only part of what he envisioned in saying that, but I can't help but ponder the overlap between his hypothetical book and this one. I wish he had written his.

Ken retired from his seventeen-year appointment as harbormaster in Rogers City in 2006. In terms of salmon fishing, he figures Rogers City "was probably the hotspot on the Great Lakes for ten [of those] years." But as I listened to his and others' recollections, I can't imagine the salmon fishing being any better *at all*, let alone better somewhere else. For example, in the middle of Rasche's tenure, the *Presque Isle County Advance*'s front-page feature article on August 14, 1997, began: "Imagine 1,548 salmon weighing in excess of 20,000 pounds. That is how much fish was pulled out of Presque Isle County waters over the weekend by participants in the 12th annual Rogers City Salmon Tournament."[1] With 337 boats participating, that was 60 pounds of salmon hauled in *per boat*.

But in 2003 and 2004, alewife populations in Lake Huron suffered a near-total collapse from which they have not since recovered. With that collapse came the crash of the Chinook salmon fishery. In 2010, just as I was beginning what I thought might be my career as a fisheries scientist, the cadre of Great Lakes fishery professionals was just beginning to publish the "official" account of how such a thing had happened. In essence, the predator demand grew to exceed the prey fish base. The annual Lake Huron fish surveys conducted by government agencies documented the sharp declines in alewife and rainbow smelt—the two prey species on which Chinook salmon in the Great Lakes are almost solely dependent. It was reasoned that the cause of this was essentially twofold.

First, a study led by biologist Jim Johnson assessed just how many of the Chinook salmon being caught in Lake Huron had been stocked, as opposed to those that were the product of natural reproduction. The working assumption among many if not most anglers, as biologist Ed Roseman told me, was that "it seemed like the more fish you put in, the more the anglers were harvesting out." But since the mid-1980s, Great Lakes fishery biologists expressed concern regarding the balance of predators and prey in Lake Huron.[2] Michigan's hatchery capacities were limited, so Johnson was continually working on ways to improve the survival of the fish that were stocked to *effectively* increase the amount of fish put in. What he discovered in that study closes out this chapter, and lends it its colorful name. As it would turn out, there were far more wild, naturally reproduced Chinook salmon in Lake Huron than stocked Chinook salmon.

The other major influence on the collapse of alewife in Lake Huron has taken biologists longer to understand. Zebra and quagga mussels are invasive phytoplankton-filtering mollusks, the former first observed in Rogers City in 1992, attached to the water intake pipes at Calcite.[3] Quagga mussels came shortly thereafter. These two penny-sized, closely related species, native to the Black and Caspian Seas, gained access to the Great Lakes via the ballast of transatlantic freighters. Ever since their arrival, they have competed for the phytoplankton (the single-celled algae suspended in the upper layer of the water into which sunlight reaches) that the zooplankton and small invertebrates in Lake Huron relied upon, and which in turn were the prey of alewife and smelt. In terms of the food chain, alewife and smelt were the middle links, and they were getting squeezed from both the top (too many salmon eating them) and the bottom (too many zebra and quagga mussels eating the phytoplankton that the zooplankton—alewife's and smelt's food—relied on). The personal narratives of Lake Huron fisheries biologists Johnson and Roseman regarding the ecology of the Chinook salmon fishery crash are presented in the next chapter.

In order to understand and appreciate what was lost with the salmon fishery crash, it's necessary to know what *was*. Overall, the biology and ecology of the ecosystem changes that occurred in Lake Huron regarding the Chinook salmon fishery collapse are now well documented and scientifically explained. But the social aspects of the fishery in its prime and through the crash, which extend far beyond the fish, and even beyond the anglers, are grossly underrepresented. This chapter is meant to encapsulate what was great about the Rogers City Chinook salmon fishery during its prime—specifically but not solely the fishing.

My motivation to present this chapter is as that of an angler, specifically a salmon and steelhead angler, because I believe that Chinook salmon evoke something deep, almost inaccessible, that has to be experienced to appreciate. It borders on the metaphysical and spiritual. I hope this chapter will help convey the value of salmon fishing in the Great Lakes to those not familiar with it. I hope this because fervent anglers will tell you that the activity is not really about things that can be measured—quantities that are accessible to science. It's about experiencing moments. It's about hope, and memory, and passion. Certain settings, certain species, and certain techniques lend themselves to instantiating such moments. I hope this chapter helps reveal and document the answer to the following question: What is, was, and could be the value—specifically to an angler—of the Great Lakes Chinook salmon trolling fishery?

CARSON: Do you think kids today that are in junior high, high school have any idea of the salmon fishery that existed in the '80s and '90s?
MATT HOLLABAUGH: No. No I don't think they have a clue. [*laughs*]

KEN PARTYKA: Matt's been around, Matt's been around pretty much as long as it's been going on.

SCOTT MCLENNAN: You know, it's interesting to look back on those years because what happened when I moved away, it was also a time that I was preparing to be married and starting a family. And in the mid-'80s—I married in '86—so, raised a family, and jobs, commitments, those kind of things, became the priority, so I lost track. I would hear from my friends, "Yeah, boy, come on out. We're slaying them out here." But my life took a real busy turn. But they were—my friends who had boats in the Rogers City area—were out on a regular basis. And the other thing that I would see in visiting Rogers City is that there was a pretty thriving charter boat service as well, taking people out. What was interesting was in the '80s, we have a marina, a marina that is very popular in the area, and it has a very large parking lot, relatively speaking, and that parking lot—I remember in the '80s—that parking lot would be full with boats and trailers and vehicles. And cars would actually be—vehicles would be parked up on the streets because there wasn't enough room for them down by the harbor. So many folks were out taking advantage of the great salmon fishing.

FRANK KRIST: We fished early, late in the season. Fishing was just *good the entire season*. And that was true before they stocked the fish here. We're catching these immature fish and we knew they can't be all the fish that were stocked here, there weren't that many. And that's what happened.

DAVE SMRCHEK: Most of the time I fished alone. So that got to be an issue when there were lots of boats. You get a fish on, and trying to stay out of everybody's way. So I got in the habit of getting up at 4 o'clock, launching. And most of the time I would be done fishing, I'd have my limit of salmon, before the rest of the boats got out and caught up with me. I was going back in when they were all coming out. And it didn't take a lot of people that were paying attention very long to figure that out. So more and more there was this early crowd. That—people watch, the other fishermen are watching what's going on and so forth.

KEN PARTYKA: But, you know there's a—. [*laughs*] We went out—. People never went out early, okay? People never went out early. We went out early. We were out setting lines before it's breaking day, okay? We're out there setting lines before it's breaking day, setting lines with flashlights. We came in one time, Mandy and I, we came in one time, it's like 8 o'clock in the morning, come in and it's like 8 o'clock in the morning. We're done. We got our limit. Ten nice salmon. This guy meets us on the dock, he says, "You forget something?" [*Carson laughs*] Mandy goes, "No, we're boxed out. We got our limit." "Oh, bullshit," you know? [*Carson laughs; Ken laughs*] We had this twenty-four-foot center console. We didn't have no livewell or anything like that. I had a big wooden box made. Big wooden box. She lifts the cover off this wooden box and it's full of salmon. We had people lined up—I mean, you can only do so many fish, you know? Back then, there was people [who] knew we fished, and that's what we did, we fished. And they'd get on the list. You're giving fish away. And people have no problem taking fish, especially—they're fresh caught, they're cleaned, filleted [*laughs*], skinned, cleaned—you got them. We never really had a problem getting rid of fish. There's always somebody [who] wanted fish. So yeah, we had some pretty good times there for a while.

CARSON: How did the fishery—can you describe how the fishery really changed once they started planting nine hundred thousand to a million a year?

IVAN WIRGAU: Yeah, you could go out there anytime, go out there anytime, and a lot of people fished early—salmon of course are really active early in the morning before sunup and then last light of the day, that's a very active time for salmon. But there were so many salmon out here I would go in the middle of the day and catch them. People were coming off when I was going—I'd be going out there 11 o'clock in the morning. People were coming off from fishing because they were tired. I'd catch my fish and I'd be coming back in at 3 and they'd be going back out. [*laughs*] It was great because there were hardly any boats around me. But back in those days there were boats everywhere, you had to watch where your [lines were], you know, where you're trolling, so you're not getting in front of somebody. And people didn't always know the rules of the roads. There could be some heated moments at times with people cutting across in front of you, so you pick and choose your times. You go when there's less people, it's better. But there's always—and a lot of times you would see—and you'd look around you and everyone's fighting fish in the boats. Everybody's fighting fish. Go in the bay early in the morning, catch fish. Then come out, after the sun comes up. And I was—I still am a true believer in water temperature, so I'd go out and find a water break where the temperature break was at and then I'd go and fish for the salmon in the water break. The ones that were in the bay were getting ready to spawn so water temp was not an issue with them. But your fresher, more silver fish were out deeper, so you fish the temperature and the thermocline, you're going to catch nice fresh fish, you know? And that's what I did. I mean, catch ten salmon you couldn't even hardly lift the cooler. They always said, "Well, I got three in the box. Five in the box." Well, I had a box. I actually made it out of particle board and painted it and caulked it and it was a box. Everyone else they had coolers, but I had a box. I had the true box. [*Carson laughs*] People would say, "Well, I have four in the box." Well, when I would say, "I have five in the box," I had them in a box, not in a cooler. [*laughs*] So that was kind of unique.

KEN PARTYKA: —geez o'petes. But you know that back in that time your average fish was eighteen to twenty pounds.[4] Your average fish. You caught a lot of twenty-fours. Caught a lot of twenty-twos, twenty-fours, twenty-fives. You caught thirties. You caught a lot of fish, okay? And this is when the Stroh's Tournament was going on. They had this Stroh's Tournament going on statewide. And geez, I think we won every, we won every—

MANDY PARTYKA: Every weekly—

KEN: —every weekly—once a week at the weigh-in stations, we won every—we'd go out—geez, my brother was relentless crazy. He was working, I had six weeks off. He had a two-week vacation, and when he had a two-week vacation we fished every day. I mean, I'm telling you, we went out—phew, we went out in crap that was, like, unbelievable. We fished in lightning. I hate lightning.

MANDY: Waterspouts. Three waterspouts out there. [*laughs*]

KEN: But we fished, we fished where—

MANDY: You fished.

KEN: —we came in one morning to go out, and there was like five boats sitting at the harbor. And it was ugly. It was ugly out there. Terrible. Rough. Oh, I go to the guys, I say, "A little gnarly out there, eh, boys?" "Uh, yeah. Yeah." I said [*Carson laughs*], "We're gonna go take a look at her." [*laughs*] We launch the boat and take off. It's him and I. You can't—we took time. Now, if you know I'm fishing with my brother, you know things are really bad when we're fishing two lines. We're only fishing two lines because if it's him and I, we're going to be running four, and there's going to be sliders on them, because that's the way he is. He wants the max that he can run. We're running two lines. The passenger can't sit in the seat and watch the lines because it's too rough. It's too rough. It's too rough. The driver can hang onto the steering wheel, so we'd take turns catching fish. I don't know that I've fished in any worse weather than that. It was horrible.

MANDY: Kneeling in—

KEN: But you had to kneel, you had to kneel on the deck between the two downriggers, and then grab it, and it's a miracle if you land it or not. You try to turn into the waves, try to hold your own and get the fish.

CARSON: You just get beat up out there.

KEN: Holy *Christmas*.

CARSON: [*laughs*] God.

MANDY: That's where you have the experience and the knowledge and you do good [*Ken laughs*], because you have the hours on the water catching fish.

KEN: But there was three boats that left after we left that day, and one made it as far as the breakwall at Calcite, and that's as far as I saw any of them go. And we were down off of Adams Point at the end of the bluffs, and catching fish, because that's what we did. That's what we did. But that was back in the day when—that's what I lived for, you know? That's what I lived for. Now it's like, I live for a limit catch of walleye and a forty-two-inch northern [pike], and it is like, My god, nothing gets any better than this. But we still do our salmon fishing.

CARSON: Yeah, [Ken Partyka] must be—well, when he was salmon fishing in the '80s and '90s he must have been just the most hardcore salmon fisherman.

MATT HOLLABAUGH: He was, and we all kind of were. But yes, he was. Their family was. Yes, they were really very much. But you know, wherever we were they were too. We'd see them. But yeah, you just had, I don't know, it's like a drive, you know, like a feeling that you've got to get out there. You've got to get out there again, you know. You've got to get out there, you've got to get as many as you can, got to find out who's getting them where. It's kind of weird because as you get older you don't worry about that anymore.

KEN PARTYKA: Matt Hollabaugh is a heckuva fisherman—heckuva good fisherman, heckuva good guy. He's a good, good guy.

CARSON: —do you have any remarkable or memorable trips or a series of events or experience that really sticks in your mind or that is something that you always go back to?

JAYME WARWICK: Yeah, a lot of—I think about—of course, me and my dad out fishing—he isn't here anymore—but in that small fourteen-foot boat. There's times in the fall we would anchor out and cast for them instead of troll. I mean, we're catching twenty-five-, thirty-pound fish that—thirty-pounder was always a big fish; to this day it still is, but—and actually literally pulling up the anchor because we couldn't—it was so big we had to follow it around, and it would actually pull the boat around a little bit in the water. Just those times. So many that I think of with friends and tournaments. And the ladies' tournament—my wife and her friends get into it. But my dad catching his thirty-pound salmon was probably the biggest memory I have.

CARSON: When was that?

JAYME: You know, it was probably back in 1984. Or '85. Yeah. It was exciting. We had come back in and of course a small boat like that, you don't have livewells or anything. If anything you have a stringer over the side of the boat, and hopefully you remember to bring the stringer in when you take off—that's some of the other memories. We'd go and they're flopping around and some of them were getting off. But the bottom of the boat just full of salmon. I mean, you couldn't even step. The slime and everything was there. Yeah, it was just great times.

KEN PARTYKA: So, go in the shed, grab the motor, push it [fourteen-foot Starcraft] out. And that's a little teeny-tiny boat, but okay, so you know what you got out here, this is like—oh, yeah, I've got another story for you too.[5] But anyway, you go out here and it goes sixty feet—boom. From the fire pit to the water, you're in sixty feet, you're in eighty feet [a distance of less than twenty yards]. So I go out there in the morning, pop a couple salmon! *Ain't anybody* out—there ain't *anybody* fished out here. *Nobody* fished out here, okay? [referring to Lake Huron directly off his property on 40 Mile Point] I just go [*laughs*] out there and catch a couple fish.

MIKE PELTZ: And you know, the thing about it, my son-in-law—my daughter lives in Ludington, and they had good fishing there, but they had to go out ten to twelve miles to catch fish. Here you catch them on the beach. It was that much different. The boats would go out maybe a half a mile. It wasn't a big thing to go out. But I know in Ludington it took a long time to get there and get back, and the weather was a factor, when you're out that far on the lake. And here, I think that's probably what made it so popular here is that it was so close, and it wasn't a big risk to get out on that lake. But yeah, it was just—and you know, I don't think about it often, I haven't thought about—but the more I sit and think about it, it was quite a thing. Almost unreal. And something you couldn't plan.

Frank Krist: [It] brought a lot of—two things: it brought a lot of people to the community at the time—although I could go out, like today, this time of year back in the '90s, and there would be eighty-ninety boats out there in the middle of the week. That's how much. So not only did it bring people to the community during the tournament, but it brought them back several times a year. They liked it here because you can go out a mile or less and start fishing for salmon. You don't have to go out there five, ten miles. And plus the wind here, especially like now through mid-August, you can fish here almost every day. And so it brought a lot of people into the community, and kept them coming. Not only did they come to fish, but they came, like I said, a lot of them bought lots and property. Some of them moved in. The president of our Hammond Bay [Area] Anglers [Association] that were the ones that have been involved with all this, his dad and mother moved here because he liked to salmon fish. And they still live here in town.

Ken Partyka: —back in the day when there was like eighty boats coming out of Rogers City every day it was like, you know, we were averaging—oh, geez, we were averaging eighteen to twenty pounds. Now you get an eighteen-pound salmon it's like, Holy shit, there's a dandy. There's a dandy. Eighteen pounds. It's like, shoot. You'd go out and you'd catch—okay, you'd catch one twenty-seven, a thirty-one, a thirty-three, for your bigger ones you were catching. But you were averaging back then eighteen-, twenty-pound fish, average.

Matt Hollabaugh: And another one—I don't know if anybody told you about this—was when a lot of the trolling—it would have been after Ken's; that would have been—if his was '80-, what'd you say, '80-?
Carson: '86.
Matt: '86. So this would have been probably like the mid-'90s, was we always called it the "mafia boat." There was a boat from Detroit that came up and this guy is well known—I think he's passed away

now—but the name is very well known with the Jimmy Hoffa and everything. And they could fish. And we would always laugh because there would go the mafia boat. And they loved to fish, they'd be up here all the time. It was really interesting, you know? Yeah, it was kind of neat. Just, some crazy stuff you'd see.

KEN PARTYKA: But we used to do this—I had fishermen, I had charter fishermen and—oh, god. I was down one time with a friend of mine and we popped a limit in the afternoon, him and I, in that little boat right there with a six-horse motor. We're coming up between a charter fisherman and another big boat. And we come in between these two boats and we're just hanging on [to fishing rods]. Buh-boom! Buh-boom! [*Carson and Ken laugh*] We got doubles. We got doubles. [*laughs*] And these guys are going by and they're going, *What? What?*

MANDY PARTYKA: We had fun.

CARSON: That sounds like a fun way to fish too.

KEN: We had a big Bose stereo system, a Bose stereo system—[*laughs*]

MANDY: In that little tiny boat. [*laughs*]

KEN: —in the front end, just a'cranking, and we're just out there, yeah. Yeah, he was a good friend, he happened to be a first mate at the time on the boat I was on. And hey, you talk smart. Talk smart at the fish-cleaning station.

BRUCE GRANT: I ran a charter boat for over fifteen years. The first five years, people were so grateful. As you went down the road—and I just quit when I was sixty-five, because I got so fed up of people getting on the boat and saying, "We don't get our limit, we're not paying you." That's the attitude that gets created when you have too many fish. When we first started—. Fishing and hunting have their days. I don't care what you do—I don't care if it's a weather front coming in, or whatever it is—you're going to have days [that] you're going to go out there and you're not going to catch fish. You're going to have days that you're going to go hunting and not see an animal. And that happens. But it got so good here, and it was written up so much, that people just took the attitude when they stepped on the boat [that] they were going to get their limit, and that doesn't happen.

DAVE SMRCHEK: I'm on my second boat now. I wore out the first one.

CARSON: That, the first one, was the *Houndog*?

DAVE: Yeah. Yeah, that one—that hull had to have—I'm guessing it had, it was approaching ten thousand hours of fishing time on that hull when I sold it. It was on its second power, I repowered it. The second motor had twenty-five hundred hours on it. And I wore out the first set at about twenty-five hundred apiece, or five thousand hours apiece. It was just beat from hours and hours and hours. Tired of putting money back into it. [*both laugh*]

KEN PARTYKA: We would fish—I would fish—I would set lines—. There was times—because I'm taking friends, and I'm taking people, and I'm taking friends and people and relation, and friends, fishing, who never caught anything like this, okay? They never—and I'm taking them fishing. There was times when I swear I didn't hardly reel in a fish all salmon season. All I'm doing is setting lines, steering the boat. Setting lines, steering the boat. Setting lines, steering the boat, okay. And I've got to set lines. Okay, I'm going to set lines. I get somebody to steer the boat. Steer on that boat right there. Steer right on them—don't move. Steer right on them. "Oh, we're getting close." I said, "It doesn't matter. We're bigger than him, he'll move. Okay. I've got to get these lines set, and you've got to go straight while I'm getting these lines

Dave Smrchek stands in front of his boat *Houndog* in 2003. (Source: G. Maggi, "Lots of Fish . . . and the Tales That Go with Them," *Presque Isle County Advance*, August 7, 2003, 5B.)

set." But we did different things. We did different things that people didn't do. People go, and they go, and they troll, sixty-five feet of water, eighty-five feet of water, straight—

MANDY PARTYKA: For miles.

KEN: —eighty-five feet of water. You know, you just keep going.

CARSON: Contour—they just follow—

KEN: You know, they just run that, whatever. We would run, we would run, if we're running like, if we were running, like we run a lot of Grizzlys, a lot of small J-Plugs, big J—we run J-Plugs. We run spoons. We'd go no more than twenty feet in back of the ball. Twenty feet in back of the ball, and that's it. You get a fish, you spin right around. You're not tangling your lines. You're not back there a hundred feet, trolling a big dodger that's—if you're putting a dodger down, we'd go this far in back of the ball [holds out hands in front of him] with the dodger.

CARSON: Really?

KEN: That's it. That's it. Turn on a dime. [*laughs*] Turn on a dime.

MANDY: There's a school of fish, you just caught two, you'd make a circle right back through them instead of keeping on down the shoreline. Uh, what don't they get? [*laughs*] You just caught a fish here—this is where the fish are. [*Carson and Mandy laugh*] That's what happens when you come in at 8 o'clock. You got your limit because you'd be paying attention to what you're doing. You don't need to be out there wasting time. Catch your fish and come home and clean them, and be happy.

IVAN WIRGAU: But I was in a few tournaments. And I was in it with [my] father-in-law, and I had the region head wildlife biologist with me, Bob Strong. He was the region 1 wildlife biologist out of the UP [Upper Peninsula of Michigan]. And then we had a fire marshal that worked for the DNR out of Gaylord. Father-in-law was a forester. So they were all in it with me. And they were really hardcore older gentlemen. We had a lake turnover this one tournament and it was all fog. Right to the shore, pure fog. And I said, "Well, I'm not going to be out in that." People coming and going, you don't know, someone could cut you right in half with their boat. Well, they're pacing like a bunch of coyotes around a trap, on shore. Well, you know, it's going to get—it's going to cut—you know, the weather's going to break, and the sun's going to come out. And it started to, some, but that wall of fog wasn't very far offshore, I can tell you that. Okay, let's go. I said, "Well, I'm staying fairly close so I can see shore." So we got over by the breakwall and I—it was fifty degrees on the surface; that's how cold it was. I said, "Well, salmon can be right on the surface so let's just run long lines." We ran them out there by the breakwall over there and we were nailing them. There was nobody around us. Fish were there to have.

KEN RASCHE: The salmon fishing was great. I can remember out there—and I'm sure Bruce Grant and these other guys can tell it—Frank Krist—you could go out there, and when you had the electronics like we all had, you would go through these schools of alewives, I mean, it was unbelievable. It was—they'd fill the screen up with alewives.

KEN PARTYKA: Then again, every once in a while, every once in a while out there, can't get anything going. I remember being out there one time with The Dude, Eugene Modrzynski. I think he's passed away now, but—
CARSON: I tried to call his brother Mike, but I haven't gotten hold of him.
KEN: That would be his son.
CARSON: His son?
KEN: Yeah.
CARSON: Oh, okay. Okay.[6]
KEN: But anyway, The Dude was catching fish, and it was just driving me crazy because this was back in the day when, like, *I* can catch fish, anytime, anywhere. And I can't catch—and I—The Dude has popped another one. The Dude has popped another one. And you flop around and you flop around. And you can't be afraid to change lures and I put down a blue Northport Nailer with a red stripe on it and—Boom! Buh-boom! Buh-boom! Buh-boom! [*laughs*] And it was like, yes! [*laughs*] Okay. The Dude ain't got [*Carson laughs*] nothing on me, man. Hey. It just takes a while, sometimes. It just takes a while.

JIM JOHNSON: I insisted that we couldn't keep stocking Chinooks and not marking them. I needed to know what the real percentage of wild was. And the management—fishery division management team, agreed to this massive marking proposal. Dave Fielder really helped me with this because he's an OTC specialist, oxytetracycline marking specialist. He learned OTC in his work in South Dakota marking fish there. And so he guided the process to marking in the hatcheries and we managed to get three year classes in a row all marked with OTC, and a subset of them marked with coded wire tags. And then we began collecting Chinook salmon from the creel. It was very, very hard to gillnet them, we kind of gave up on that. We collected most of our salmon from the creel and from weirs. We had Canadians helping us with some of the returns from their streams. We got a few samples there. What we'd do is sample the tail sec[tion]—tail vertebrae, right underneath the adipose fin from each fish.[7] And we'd go around and sample tournaments—that was where we could really hit pay dirt. Salmon were coming in fast and furious. We'd get lengths and weights, check their stomachs, and remove the vertebrae. So we'd weigh them and take length first, give it to them to clean, then take the skeleton back and check the guts and remove the vertebrae. We collected an ample number of samples. There was no shortage there. And that was good because there was a little bit of variation north to south, and there was a lot of doubt about the OTC technology.

And I remember—the most distinct memory of that period was one afternoon I was working at the office and Steve DeWitt, who was the technician at the time, reading all the otoliths—or all the vertebrae, he was preparing the first samples from the first year of collections from the creel, and he went through, I don't know, must have gone through forty or fifty fish and hadn't seen more than one or two OTC marks. And he called me down, he said, "Jim, you've got to see this." And we looked at these things and went through some more, did another twenty or so, and I don't know if we saw even another OTC mark. They were just not marked. And Steve's immediate reaction was, It doesn't look like the mark's holding. It doesn't look it's working. But we collected Swan weir fish. Swan weir is, maybe Frank [Krist] told you, it's on Swan River, which is really a creek that drains a limestone quarry, and no self-respecting salmon would try to reproduce there, and there's where we've been stocking for years and years. That's the center of Chinook stocking for Lake Huron, it always has been, because it's an egg-taking facility. And we had a sample from there, so we thawed those out. By now it's like 7 o'clock and we're still thawing vertebrae, but neither of us wanted to go home until we got the answer. And we put some under the scope and they all just glowed beautifully. [laughs] So the marks worked. And it was really, really scary to see the low percentage of hatchery fish that were out there. And yet we were getting good returns of stocked fish to the Swan weir, so it's not like the stocked fish weren't working. And at that time we were also getting pretty good returns at—we were doing a—we had been doing cage culture and evaluating cage culture in Oscoda and Harbor Beach and getting good returns there, too, using—and been doing that for years, using adipose clips and coded wire tags.[8] And they were coming back just fine, too.

CARSON: Is that the same as net pen?

JIM: Net pens, yeah. But in the lake you put cages in the lake and hold them until they're well smolted and trying to get out and just release them from the net pens. Yeah. But we did have raceways in—we'd built raceways on the Au Sable River and they're super slick.[9] They worked great for salmon and they improved salmon-stocking survival by about 2 or 300 percent. That's published in one of the DNR research reports. "Early Life History of Chinook Salmon and the Effects of Net Pens," something like that, by Steve DeWitt and myself. John Clevenger was a coauthor too. Myself, Steve DeWitt, John Clevenger.[10] And that gave us some insight into early life history too. We knew that smaller stocked Chinooks were not making it, and that pen culture was getting around predation to a certain extent. The fish [the pen-acclimated Chinook salmon smolts] were being stocked at a size where they were ready to move [further] offshore but Chinooks don't go offshore a lot like steelhead and Atlantics would. [Atlantic salmon] just disappear, they go out into the wild blue yonder, which makes them easier to stock around walleyes. But Chinooks want to stay on the beach for their first few weeks, and they want to stay in bays and close to shore for their first few months. Makes them real vulnerable to predation. So we were able to stock around the predation problem as long as we had alewives.[11] We knew that going into this marking study. So we knew that the stocked fish were surviving, we were doing a good job getting around predators. So we knew there were quite a lot of stocked fish out there and yet they were dwarfed by the number of unmarked fish. And so I worked with Ed Rutherford at University of Michigan—he's now at NOAA [National Oceanic and Atmospheric Administration]—and the two of us did a mark-and-recapture approach on our data from vertebrae and known numbers of fish stocked and we were able to—of course we're taking vertebrae, so—the vertebrae are not a perfect bony structure for aging the fish, but you can age them. And we were pretty confident in our ages on vertebrae, and some of them we had otoliths from so we could confirm the vertebrae ages. But we kind of roughly estimated how many were from each age group, and we knew how many were stocked in each of those age groups, and came up with an estimate of the percent hatchery, percent wild. We knew how many were stocked in each age group. We just did [a] mark-and-recapture estimate for each age group, and added them all up and came up with about 14 million recruits to the lake. That's not 14 million salmon this big, but 14 million [young-of-year] salmon this big.[12] What happened to them after that point we weren't sure. But we knew that the wild fish must be surviving as well as the stocked fish at that time. And the stocked fish weren't surviving too badly, but we never knew for sure how well they were [surviving]. Norine [Dobiesz] estimated it in her model, and I think that was probably a reasonable estimate.

At that time there were, I guess, as quantitative as I can be, is there was a shitload of salmon—[*both laugh*]

5

CRASH

So, here, I mean, people just dealt with it. What else can you do?

—Frank Krist

We can. Like, okay, it's summertime. You sit down on the beach. You sit in the shade. It's a little warm, you go for a swim. You go, you talk to your people down the road that run this farmers market. Oh, boy, we've got some nice tomatoes in. You go get a couple of bushels of tomatoes and you can tomatoes for a couple of days. And we can tomatoes, can salsa, can—. Then later on, like in September, early September, then the fruit comes in. The peaches and the pears. But pickles, and salsa, and green beans. We can gobs of stuff. And we like to do that too. You don't have to fish every day. So you go and you get your canner done, and you come down to the beach and it's, ooh, let's take a little dunk, and have a little fire, and grill something up. It's not all salmon anymore, you know? It's just our bag. I mean, we played the game. I loved it. But I got—I'm not going to say bored with it, I mean, how can you get bored?

—Ken Partyka

Crash is a loaded word. Car crashes are serious. A stock market crash is serious. Serious and *negative*. *Crash* is a word prone to hyperbole, and perhaps I was exaggerating things.

When I was trying to get this research project off the ground, I focused on the negative. My working assumption had been that the crash of alewife, and subsequently of the Chinook salmon fishery in Lake Huron, had outstanding negative effects on the coastal communities and their residents. In framing my thoughts on this project, I emphasized "crash" to help convey the research's importance. So much of convincing someone that something is worth studying is describing how difficult or awful that something is or was. And the field of oral history is largely an endeavor in paying tribute and giving voice to the have-nots—victims of either circumstance or injustice.

Hesitant to begin the daunting task of cold-calling people whose contact information I'd gathered, I productively procrastinated by poring over back issues of the *Presque Isle County Advance*, Rogers City's local newspaper. While I focused on the fishery-related material, I couldn't help but be immersed in all the other goings-on in Rogers City as I perused each issue of the *Advance* at the library.

I flipped through hundreds of pages of the weekly newspaper. As I got to the later years—2004, 2005, 2006, 2007—the "crash" played out in print like the life of a tethered helium balloon. It slowly lost air; it shrank and sank to the ground. It was in full view for all to see, but it was not something the town's residents were decrying. They just had their eye on it. The tournament always got its annual article—shorter by the year—pointing out how much further the balloon had descended this year compared to last. But the newspaper didn't get any smaller. And declines in the fishery largely didn't affect the other activities in Rogers City: the announcement of the first baby of the New Year (a staple of the *Presque Isle County Advance*), high school sports and dances, and events like the Posen Potato Festival. Nor did declines in the fishery affect, as Mayor Scott McLennan told me, "the other losses in the community"—losses that included the "mechanization of the limestone quarry that provided many hundreds of jobs."

Suspecting that the newspaper was downplaying the negativity of the fishery decline, I still pursued my noble task of shedding light on the misgivings and struggles of the poor fishery plebeians in Rogers City. With the published local narrative fresh in my mind, I made those early phone calls.

But much to my surprise, folks were not hung up on the loss. They weren't overly concerned with anything negative, really. If anything, I encountered some push-back—the term *crash* seemed to be problematic—but I couldn't quite ascertain why. Nonetheless, I immediately recognized that rather than feelings, opinions, and memories regarding a crash, people were much more eager to share stories from even earlier times. My strategy evolved quickly. I began asking people to describe what they remembered during the salmon fishery heyday, rather than to tell me how awful the crash was, and how much worse things are now. I think it worked well.

It's offensive, perhaps, to presume someone's life is in a worse state now than it was in the past. People don't like to be treated that way. People don't want to have someone like me, or the supposed audience of this project, feel sorry for them. They don't feel sorry for themselves. That's the lightbulb that went off for me—these folks in Rogers City don't express feeling worse off now than at some time in the past. And why should they? They're successful people who didn't get that way by not moving toward goals. They had lived and were living where and how they wanted. Perhaps my use of "crash," and the negativity attached to it, seemed to be asking, "Why are you still here? *How?* Wouldn't it be better somewhere else?"

The Rogers City residents with whom I spoke were not have-nots. By their own assessment, they were have-plenties. They were proud. And it was remarkable to me how the experiences and observations of the majority of the people with whom I spoke were so local in perspective—as if, in many ways, their worldview was comprised only of Rogers City (or perhaps Presque Isle County). I think that's because I spoke with the people who stayed. And those people stayed for a lot of reasons. One, there's so much more than fishing to enjoy in Rogers City. Two, there's still excellent fishing to be had. In fact, Frank Krist, Tom Allum, and Dave Smrchek had each gone out and caught limits of lake trout in the morning of the days that I interviewed them. The people who stayed didn't mire themselves in the negativity of a fishery loss. As I developed the understanding that the residents of Rogers City did not consider themselves victims, I grew hesitant to impose the term *collapse* or *crash* on the person I was interviewing; I felt it assumed too much.

I now choose to use "crash" to acknowledge that there was a prior state to crash *from*, and so to study the effects of the crash is really to highlight and celebrate how great the state of things was before the crash. I feel that such is the correct framing of the Lake Huron salmon fishery crash for Rogers City and its community members. And as such, the first four chapters of this book are primarily concerned with understanding and appreciating the magnitude of the crash.

In contrast, framing the *impacts* of the fishery crash is the subject of later chapters. This chapter is focused on observations and experiences during the time of the crash itself. But the degree to which people committed such observations and experiences to memory was dependent upon the importance of the crash in their lives, then and thereafter. That is why I chose the quotes from Frank and Ken as epigraphs to this chapter. They serve to set the tone: there's more to life, more to Rogers City, than just fishing. They could just "deal with it" because it wasn't everything.

This chapter is divided into two sections. The first relates community members' observations in Rogers City. The second portrays the story at a larger, ecosystem-wide level. This larger narrative was informed by data collected throughout the Lake Huron area from annual surveys and targeted research projects, and is told primarily by fisheries biologists who did the research. While the set of observations specific to Rogers City in the first section is rather sparse, the circumstances of the crash set into motion a new, collaborative framework between the government agencies that research and manage the Lake Huron fisheries and the fishery user groups. A handful of Rogers City community members were integral to developing this framework, which consisted of Sea Grant workshops and meetings of the Lake Huron Citizens Fishery Advisory Committee. For this reason, and because Swan River was and continues to be a primary Chinook salmon–stocking site, the Rogers City narrative and the larger lake-wide narrative are intertwined.

THE ROGERS CITY STORY

Although I've admitted that "crash" is a problematic characterization, several data sources speak strongly to the presence of what I'd call a crash.

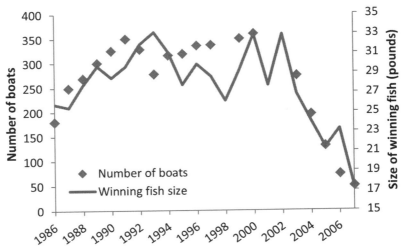

The number of boats registered for the Rogers City Salmon Tournament and the weight of the winning fish, 1986–2007. (Data source: *Presque Isle County Advance*)

The first two indicators among these lines of evidence are participation in the tournament and the size of winning fish—both of which saw sharp declines after 2003.

The declines observed at the tournament were mirrored in another peculiar data source: the poundage of fish waste hauled from the fish-cleaning station—the story of which makes for an interesting aside. When Rogers City expanded its marina, as former city planner Mary Ann Heidemann would tell me (dripping with sarcasm, I think), they "built a state-of-the-art, *beautiful* fish-cleaning station, with pulldown nozzles and all stainless steel, big grinders, and all of the top of the top—." The fish-cleaning station gets its due in the next chapter, but as Heidemann described, the whole shebang was somewhat superfluous. At the height of the fishing season, the city's wastewater treatment facility couldn't handle the additional biological oxygen demand of the ground-up fish influent. So before the years of the salmon fishery decline, the fish-cleaning station would literally be locked up, usually by sometime in August. Marina personnel would set up tables outside of the fish-cleaning station for anglers to clean their catch, and the fish entrails would be relegated to waste barrels, which would have to be carted off and emptied once or twice a day by the Rogers City Department of Public Works (DPW). Coming full circle, the offal was actually buried in pits dug on the same Calcite property through which the Swan River ran—the stream that received many of those fish when they were planted. DPW kept records of the fish waste that they hauled in order to bill the marina for their efforts. Speaking with Roger Wenzel, DPW superintendent since 2012, I obtained records of the total weight of fish waste hauled away each year from 2001 to 2007. Like the tournament statistics, these data also show a sharp decline after 2003.

The fish-waste data represent Chinook salmon as well as lake trout, steelhead, walleye, and all other species caught and cleaned by anglers. Thus, declines in fish waste depict decreases in Chinook salmon size and harvest as well as an overall decrease in fishing participation. From 2008 to 2019, the fish-cleaning station could be kept open all summer because fish waste remained below the level that could be processed by the city's wastewater treatment facility.

Among interviewees, there was much less dialogue on things negative or having to do with the crash than there was talk about all that was remarkable to see and experience and be a part of when the fishing was "booming." Overall, the crash was experienced largely as an *absence* of observations—hence, I think, the brevity of this section.

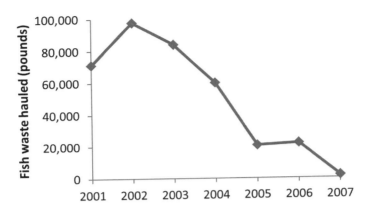

Weight of fish waste hauled from the Rogers City marina fish-cleaning station and buried at Calcite, 2001–7. (Data source: Roger Wenzel, Rogers City Department of Public Works, personal communication)

JAYME WARWICK: Yeah, never had any type of thought of it going away. I just, I planned—I could have moved out of the state. I could have took jobs other places. Family and salmon fishing kept me here. It really did. And there's a lot of other contributors. But I never [did] foresee the so-called crash of the salmon. There was no thought in my mind whatsoever. I actually wanted to charter fish, and pretty confident I could make a good living off that. But other jobs kind of sidetracked me a little bit. But then the salmon fishing started declining a little bit when I was really interested in doing that, and then there was a scare and a worry that, Wow, what's going on here?

CARSON: And I don't mean to be disparaging and call it a crash. I know that word gets thrown around and maybe I should just call it a decline or something, but you said "so-called" so it made me think, Maybe I should—

JAYME: No, it's true. Something definitely happened here.

MARY ANN HEIDEMANN: Well, first off, when you use the [word] crash, I don't think that's how it really happened. So it was a slow decline. And you never know if that's a seasonal thing. There was always a hope, you know, well, maybe it'll get better next year. So there was never a community acknowledgment of a crash. But sometimes you have a good year and a bad year and a good year, but then you just have a bad year and a worse year and a worse yet year. So you're on the downhill slide but you kind of don't know until you're down a ways. So I would be careful about using the word crash. Now, all the time there are other species that can be caught, and there's other forms of water recreation. You know a lot of people don't bother with the fishing, they're just taking their cruiser boat out. So I don't think it's so dire. But if you just look at salmon fishing, and you just are a salmon fisherman, okay, it's like you were on a six- or eight-year drunk and now you're sobering up. Again, I think people had more hopes than reality in the ideas about becoming a salmon community or salmon capital—what does that really mean? And the people here are pretty practical. They're not a bunch of nutcases. And they're used to living pretty close to the nub, and being pretty frugal, so it wasn't quite like the gold rush. So I wouldn't want to exaggerate the idea of boom and bust. If you look at the fisheries—I'm old enough to remember the rotting fish on the shore of Lake Erie, when the alewives died off, and that's really what brought the salmon fishery in, was it [Howard] Tanner or whatever, DNR, who proposed the idea? And something had to be done about the alewives. But once again, I don't think it was good ecology from the get-go, but what are you going to do? The ecosystem was disrupted.

KEN RASCHE: But I can remember—if you do go back and do a little bit of research, Carson, you're going to find there was a guy in Rogers City who worked out at the Hammond Bay Biological Station. His name was Dr. Vernon Applegate. Dr. Applegate was a guy that developed TFM [the sea lamprey larvicide 3-triflouromethyl-4-nitrophenol]. We delivered fuel to his house. He was a man of few words, but when he decided to talk to you you'd better decide you're going to sit there and listen for quite some time. Well, he gave me a lecture on salmon. And his philosophy was you would never ever introduce an exotic species to control an exotic species. He said, "We will regret the day we planted salmon in the Great Lakes." I'm not sure he was right. Okay? But they definitely were—they ate themselves out of house and home. And also with the alewives—not the alewives, but the mussels, the zebra mussels, quagga mussels. That all had a big effect on the—if they never came in, would the alewives have remained a food source for the salmon? I don't know. I guess nobody knows for sure. Yeah, so, I don't know. But

I did enjoy it, you know, fished. We had friends from down below, we had friends from out west, we had—everybody came to Rogers City.

CARSON: I tried to get as much background history as I could before I started approaching people and I read through the back issues of *Presque Isle County Advance* and I saw that you covered the tournament for them in the late '90s and I just wondered if you had any memorable experiences from that.

JOE HEFELE: You know, I don't. You're right, though, before I became a city manager, in my former life I did work for them. That was probably at the tail end of the fishery—was beginning the declines. We weren't seeing the numbers of fish. We weren't seeing the size of fish, and therefore we weren't seeing quite as many that were willing to travel great distances. It was becoming a little bit more of a local tournament because in its glory years, again, we'd go down there and look at the board of the top fifty, which would be updated as fishermen were coming in, whether it was in the morning and they were taking a quick break or whether it was in the evening, and on the fifty if you saw three or four names that you recognized it was a miracle just because there was so much interest coming from those with expensive equipment and fancy boats and fancy gear from all over the place that—. And so my recollection was by the time I became involved and was covering that, it was still a lot of fun and there were still fish being caught but it wasn't quite the same as the tournament I remember from when I was ten or eleven or twelve years old.

CARSON: Oh, okay. Then going into the mid-2000s, or like 2004, 2005, 2006, is when my understanding of when the major changes happened. But you'd say even in the late '90s you could kind of see there was—moving in—

JOE: The atmosphere just wasn't quite the same, I mean. So, in my youth, I mean, literally, the winning fish was going to be thirty-plus pounds.[1] That just was the way it was, regardless of the weather or whatever circumstances happened to be there, that was it. Those that were all on the top of the board were going to be in the mid- to high twenties. And again, I'm going on memory, and maybe I'm wrong, it's been a while, but my recollection was by the time I was covering that, it was definitely still a big deal, brought people in, but there wasn't any thought that you bring in a thirty-pound Chinook salmon if you were going to win that thing.[2] That had kind of subsided a bit. I don't think at that point we knew really what we were in for. But from the stuff that Frank [Krist]'s been able to kind of describe with the changes through some of—the clean Michigan act and some of the invasive species, we didn't see that coming. But I don't ever remember it being quite the same as it was when I was a kid. And some of that, again, maybe it's being that you were a kid and look at things differently depending on your age.

CARSON: I think that that aligns with my understanding as well. It's just hard to get from newspaper articles that are also trying to promote—

JOE: You got it. Yeah. Carson, you're exactly right. So when you work for a small-town newspaper, if there's some type of a ribbon-cutting or something and eight people show up, in the headline or the first sentence it's a great success. And that's just kind of part and parcel of a small-town paper. We're there to cover the local news but we're also there to build up, as much as possible, our small community. So, yeah, there could be something to that, having not looked at those articles in quite a while.

MATT HOLLABAUGH: And those schools of fish, I mean, just amazing to see that many fish.

CARSON: The alewives or the salmon?

MATT: Well, same thing, you know, alewives too. At first, on the beaches, piled up dead. And then as we started marking them when we all got started getting graphs and stuff when we would mark the baitfish and stuff too, it would just be top to bottom alewives. And these huge balls of fish. I don't see that anymore. A couple of years ago I did lake trout fishing, but it wasn't the big schools of alewives. It was probably small smelt, and they weren't that big. Not these great big round balls of fish. Yeah, it'd be almost—those alewives were almost like, because you see those documentaries in the ocean, when you see the herring in those big balls of fish going around, that's what the alewives looked like. And the salmon would be, probably they were on the outside picking them off. It was something. And you'd even see them coming out of the water too, the alewives. Like in the fall or something we'd be out there, and they would be—you'd start seeing fish flying out—well the salmon were obviously feeding on them. You don't see that much anymore. [laughs] Maybe you would once in a while but not very often. Stuff that we'll probably never see again.

CARSON: So I kind of want to focus in on the years of where the downturn was happening. And from what I know about the surveys that were done, it was like, they had the 2003 prey fish survey, which is a bottom trawl survey, they caught very few adult alewife, but they caught quite a few young of year alewife. And then in 2004 and basically every year thereafter they haven't caught very many alewife. And so I was wondering from you, do you have memories of fishing—salmon fishing—in like 2004, 2005, and having concerns or wondering about the size of the fish, or the health of the fish that were caught? Because I have seen pictures, or there's been—I have some idea of there were fish that were long and skinny, this kind of thing, and I was just wondering if you noticed fish that seemed to be unhealthy around that time, that you were catching.

JAYME WARWICK: Yeah, but—I remember seeing a few. Some. But nothing where you're really catching a bunch of them and saying, "Wow." I remember saying, "He hasn't been eating very good." He was longer and skinnier. But not like a whole catch of them. I would still catch probably more healthy ones than I would unhealthy ones. But the numbers were going down at that time. Seems to be, for some reason like 2008 and '7, it seems like that's when it started declining. Maybe the net surveys were showing that and then the fish were finally reacting to the less amount of baitfish. And through the years you'd still catch a good number of fish, but they weren't the big twenty-five-, thirty-pounders, they were just smaller. A four-year-old fish is a mature salmon, and you were catching four-year-olds that are twelve pounds, and fifteen pounds, and ten.[3]

CARSON: What did you start to notice in the mid-2000s when, I guess—you know, I know that the survey data show that in 2003 and 2004 was kind of where you had the major declines in alewife catches in the annual survey. What were you seeing around that time and what were you thinking about the future of the salmon fishery?

MATT HOLLABAUGH: Well, to tell you the truth, I wasn't really in with the whole salmon deal to begin with, because we would catch beautiful perch out here and stuff, and there was pike too, and the lake trout were starting to come back—the native-type fish—and when they talked about a million salmon, I was like, Why not just 100,000? Maybe I was a visionary rather than just lucky thinking that because it would have worked out a lot better with less fish. Well, we just noticed we were marking less alewives and the fish started getting smaller. You noticed a lot that the fish would be like a big head, but real skinny. It was really weird looking, you know? I mean, they still tasted good and stuff but we're going, What the heck are wrong with these things? There's no gut on them anymore. And they wouldn't have anything in them. They also, you would see sometimes like how you see the bug slick out there, they would—and I swear there must have been salmon. Normally you would only see steelhead doing that, or Atlantics, but these were probably Chinook, they were trying to eat anything they could find. So that's kind of what we started noticing. Real skinny fish, not as big. But they still tasted good, we still would fish them.

CARSON: What do you remember noticing in the mid-2000s when the salmon fishery started to decline then?

IVAN WIRGAU: Just weren't catching them. Weren't marking much. The bay was almost useless. You get a few big boats in there when they ran all their planer boards in there and all their Yellow Birds and—. The fishing wasn't all that great. You would have to hit it and really watch. But during the summer months, not as good, it just kept declining. I mean, the fish would be, in the summertime, if you hit the winds right and that out there by 40 Mile Point, up here north of town, they'd catch salmon up there. And I fished up there some, but most of my fishing was out here. Adams Point, excellent fishing—just look how much structure all over the place in there, that's good fishing in there, and it's good right off town here too, surprisingly, and right over here, right off Seagull Point's very good. But a lot of people went up thataway because you have a lot of sharp drops and structure there too. And it seemed like the salmon, when they migrated around, they were concentrated more that way as they came closer. As you got closer to spawning time they came in closer this way, it seems like.

CARSON: Was it, kind of just like, all of a sudden—well—

IVAN: Oh, you mean as far as what you caught and that? Yeah, I mean, it was getting to the point where it's getting hard to catch salmon. You can still catch them out here, but you've got to stay—you've got to be totally a salmon fisherman and you've got to really focus on it. Now they're using meat rigs out here. I don't know—how necessary is that? I just kind of, myself, I kind of got more away from the salmon fishing because there's such long periods of time in between fish when you're fishing, and just wanted to get off the lake. I don't want to sit around and troll for hours and maybe get a salmon.

KEN RASCHE: And we did see—I can't tell you exactly, Carson, I can't tell you when we first noticed it. There was—even after the alewives—you knew something was happening, okay, because for a while you had a fish that was thirty inches long, thirty-five inches long, it was close to forty pounds. In three or four years that fish that was the same length was seventeen pounds. The thing that I noticed the most was the color of the flesh. When the alewives were out there—and alewives are a very fatty food—and so our salmon here were nowhere near like the salmon are in Alaska, as far as the coloration of the meat. Our salmon was yellow. I don't like it, to be honest with you. I like Alaskan salmon, but I don't like ours. Ours has changed from yellow to more like Alaskan salmon simply because [of] what they're eating out here. They're not eating alewives. You could see this happening, and again, back at the time, Carson, we didn't, I don't think any of us knew—maybe Jim Johnson and the people from Alpena, from the [Alpena] Fisheries [Research Station], maybe they knew what was happening, because of course you've always got the creel census, down there, taker, you know, maybe they saw it—but as novices we didn't see it. We just knew something was changing, but what it was we didn't know.

JOHN BRUNING: And now it's a whole different fishery, I mean, things have changed drastically on a number of fronts. Certainly, invasive species have had a big impact. The collapse of the alewife has really hampered the ability for the salmon to thrive. Lake trout have adapted to eating gobies. There's some smelt now, I think, but not—it's just completely different. In my lifetime, to see an ecological shift like that is just phenomenal.

THE ECOLOGICAL NARRATIVE

At this project's onset, I hadn't really intended to interview any fisheries professionals because I was primarily interested in the experiences of residents of Rogers City who didn't otherwise have a published narrative. But eventually, I asked Frank Krist if he had retired Michigan DNR biologist Jim Johnson's phone number. Now, Jim lives in Ossineke and he worked out of Alpena—so not a Rogers City community member—and he has no shortage of scholarly publications on the topic of Lake Huron fisheries. But so many people with whom I spoke kept asking, "Have you talked with

Jim Johnson? You should talk with Jim Johnson." It was clear—Rogers City community members felt that this project would be remiss not to include the professional fisheries research side of the story, so I dutifully obliged.

I doubt if Jim remembered, but I had met him once before, in 2015 during dinner at a restaurant in Alpena, in between days of the convening of the Lake Huron Technical Committee. At that time I was a tag-along fisheries contractor working for USGS biologist Ed Roseman out of Ann Arbor. Anyway, I called the number Frank gave me on March 23, 2021, and left a voicemail explaining my interest in potentially interviewing him. My phone call was soon returned by Jim's wife, who told me, "Jim's on a fishing trip, so I can have him call you when he gets back." That's *my kind* of retired fisheries biologist, I remember thinking.

I don't know why, but I envisioned him fishing in some far-off land—ice fishing up in remote Canada or fly fishing in the wilds of Kamchatka. But as it turned out, when he got back to me he said he'd been steelhead fishing on the Pere Marquette River—one of my absolute passions. As far as I was concerned, this made us brethren.

Jim was more than willing to share his Lake Huron Chinook salmon story with me, and so we agreed to meet at the Besser Museum for Northeast Michigan where Jim volunteers his time in retirement. I encourage you to listen to my full interview with Jim because, in my opinion, it's better than any reading of the scientific literature as far as capturing the essence of the past thirty to forty years of the fisheries ecology and management of Lake Huron. That being said, much of our conversation is presented in the following pages.

A primary hesitation I had in targeting biologists such as Jim Johnson for this project is that their stories would *not* be specific to and fully representative of a particular coastal community. "My focus in my career has been pretty much *the lake*, and the system, not any one place," Jim told me. "I was really careful to try to give every location of the lake equal attention as best I could—Rogers City just being one of them." But in Lake Huron, fish species like Chinook salmon are highly mobile. Throughout the course of the year, Chinook salmon, along with alewife, smelt, and other pelagic cold-water species, are constantly on the move, orienting toward their preferred water temperatures, spawning habitat, and so on, often traveling between Canadian and U.S. waters, and even between Lakes Michigan and Huron.[4] Chinook salmon stocked or born in tributaries all around Lake Huron are mixed during all but the later stages of the fishing season when they start staging in the vicinities of their natal streams. So I came to realize that understanding the salmon fishery dynamics in Rogers City is to also understand the larger lake-wide dynamics—that is, the purview of the biologists.

About ninety miles south down the shoreline from Rogers City, the Au Sable River empties into Lake Huron at the port town of Oscoda. The Au Sable River and Oscoda once supported a fantastic Chinook salmon fishery, and throughout his career, Jim studied Chinook salmon returns there. A primary objective of his was to assess how different rearing practices of stocked juvenile Chinook salmon affected their survival and returns to the river in the fall. In 2004, strikingly emaciated mature Chinook salmon returned to the Au Sable River.

Johnson used Fulton's condition factor, a ratio of a fish's weight to its length, to describe the poor state of these fish. Condition factor is a rough assessment of a fish's health that is useful because it can be compared across species and across fish of different lengths. In general, "healthy" fish will have a condition factor near or above 1.0. Johnson et al. wrote:

> Several Chinook salmon with condition factors less than 0.75 sampled from the Au Sable River in fall 2004 were sent to Michigan State University, College of Veterinary Medicine for analysis. These fish were deemed by fish pathologists to be in, or approaching, moribund condition as a consequence of their emaciated state and presence of high titers of opportunistic bacterial pathogens. . . . From 1996–2002, an annual average of 3.3 percent of Chinook salmon older than age 1 had condition factors less than 0.75. The percentage in such critically low condition rose to 9.6 and 28.4, in 2003 and 2004, respectively.[5]

When considered as a whole, Lake Huron is generally accepted to have experienced a "crash." Actually, it is the lake-wide nature of the crash that helped reveal some key differences between Rogers City and much of the rest of the Michigan waters of Lake Huron—differences that helped a fall Chinook salmon fishery persist there, albeit a reduced one, and supported the continuation of Swan River as a primary stocking site. I looked at the charter fishing data, for which there is a very well-maintained dataset going back to 1990. Focusing on just those ports that served as salmon-fishing ports (that is, not shallow, warm Saginaw Bay), charter fishing harvest of Chinook salmon declined 94 percent between 1990 to 2002 and 2005 to 2018, and the number of charter fishing trips declined 74 percent.

The average condition factor of the top three fish pictured was 0.63. For comparison, the bottom picture is of a large, healthy king salmon caught in Swan Bay in September 1994, whose condition factor would have been well above 1.0. (Sources: J. E. Johnson, S. P. DeWitt, and J. A. Clevenger Jr., "Causes of Variable Survival of Stocked Chinook Salmon in Lake Huron," *Michigan Department of Natural Resources, Fisheries Research Report* 2086 [2007] [top three images]; "Conrad Paquin of Coldwater Caught a 35-lb. Salmon in Swan Bay at about 6:30 p.m. on Monday," *Presque Isle County Advance*, September 15, 1994, 4B [bottom image])

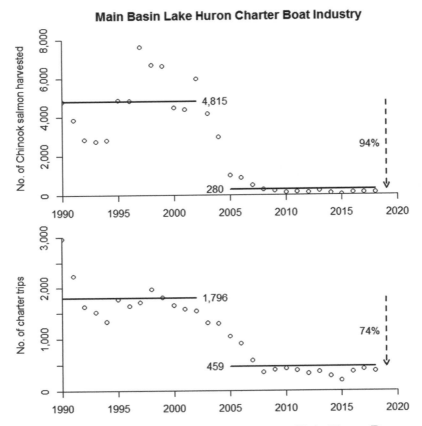

Charter boat fishery statistics for the Michigan waters of Lake Huron. Data represent fishing at ten ports outside Saginaw Bay (Lexington, Port Sanilac, Harbor Beach, Port Austin, Tawas City, Oscoda, Harrisville, Alpena, Rogers City, and Rockport). Data averages from 1990 to 2002 and 2005 to 2018, respectively, are portrayed by the solid lines. The percent decreases between time periods are described by the arrows. (Data source: Donna Wesander, Michigan DNR)

Clearly, this was a lake-wide phenomenon, and something that was not intended. A silver lining is that the major ecosystem change in Lake Huron was very influential in instigating increased collaboration between stakeholders and fisheries professionals. This section contains solely the accounts of biologists Jim Johnson and Ed Roseman, as well as those of Frank Krist, as they pertain to the lake-wide narrative and the role of the crash in that increased collaboration—of which Rogers City and some of its members were influential. I should mention that Frank is not a fisheries professional, but he takes a professional approach to the roles that he has served representing the Hammond Bay Area Anglers Association and the Lake Huron Citizens Fishery Advisory Committee. I'll get out of the way and let these three tell the story.

JIM JOHNSON: I got to come back to where I did some of my graduate work and as a kid I used to fish in Port Sanilac where my grandparents lived on Lake Huron, and my grandfather was a commercial fisherman there, for a while anyway. So I've had a long and close association with Lake Huron and it became much closer when I got the job here. So I was head of the DNR's fishery research station in Alpena from 1989 until 2014. And that station does the research and assessment work for the waters of the St. Marys River, Lake Huron, all the way down to Port Huron. So pretty good swath of water. And then, towards the end of my career, the station head position for Lake Erie, and Lake St. Clair, Detroit River, he retired and rather than fill the position they gave me that too, so for a while there I was over the research of the eastern side of the state, Great Lakes waters. Which was ridiculous, but whatever. [*both laugh*]

Anyway, what that did is place me in a position to witness some of the major changes of Lake Huron. And the changes were in about this order: the introduction of lake trout through stocking to try to restore lake trout, introduction of walleye through stocking to try to restore walleye, and then until about 2000 virtually no sign of success, other than it was basically put-grow-and-take stocking, and the system seemed to be quite stable, and based on alewives and stocking. Then the changes started to happen in rapid succession starting in 1998. 1998 there was a decline in alewives at the same time Norine Dobiesz was doing her PhD work under Jim Bence at the Quantitative Fisheries Center [Michigan State University]—got funded to look at the total consumption of alewives by Chinook salmon in Lake Huron. And she had a population model for Chinook, and she just needed to feed the Chinook in the model and needed to know what their daily consumption rates were, and I was— and for her my job was to go out and collect these salmon through the summer—you don't collect them from anglers because those are feeding fish. And she wanted to know what the ingestion rates were across the population, whether they're in feeding phase or not, she wanted a cross-section of what was in their stomachs and she needed fresh food too, she needed fresh fish. Fresh stomachs. So we thought this would work pretty well. We'd used deep, or, high gillnets. These were either sixteen to twenty foot from float line to lead line monofilament nets, larger mesh sizes. But we had a gradation of sizes because we wanted to sample two-, three-, and four-year-old Chinooks, so I think they were three- to six-inch mesh. And we'd suspend these things into the thermocline where we were marking Chinooks, and it just happened that that was the year when Norine started her work that the Chinooks didn't have anything to eat so it kind of compromised her work. [*laughs*] We had a hard time sampling fish. They weren't moving very much, they were just kind of hanging there and their stomachs were mostly empty and the fish were emaciated. And that's the first time the warning bells went off to us at the research station and to the agency that things weren't right in Lake Huron, and that the alewife population might not be so stable after all.

FRANK KRIST: We had lots of smelt and we had lots of alewives. And then when the alewives would dip a little bit the smelt were still high. I was involved with a study with Jim Diana—
CARSON: The diet study?
FRANK: —this was back in the '80s. And we turned in a lot of samples there for a couple years. And what he found is about—the statistics, anyway, were showing about almost 70 percent of the diet in Lake Huron those years back in the mid-'80s were alewi—not alewives, but smelt. So if you've got smelt you've got a pelagic species, you're still in good shape.

JIM JOHNSON: So Norine somehow managed to pull off her thesis. She got enough information on diets to show that, yeah, consumption, top-down effects were pretty serious, and the Chinook population was maybe large enough to impair alewife survival. At the time we still—her model is based upon the assumption that 20 percent of the fish were wild in Lake Huron. [*Carson laughs*][6]

ED ROSEMAN: I was hired to be a research fish biologist at the U.S. Geological Survey's Great Lakes Science Center working on Lake Huron. I started in November of 2004. And [the] 2004 survey was the first year that showed pretty much the complete collapse of the alewife population. And alewife are the main prey for Chinook salmon and a lot of other predators in Lake Huron. So I essentially came on the scene as a research scientist right after the collapse of the prey base, and have been working on Lake Huron—mostly the fish community at the prey level—for the last, what is that, seventeen years now? Yeah, since '04. And my role is to help carry out the survey on the lake using the bottom trawl equipment, and analyzing and reporting out the information that we gather in those surveys. We've done a lot of other related projects over the years related to the collapse and we'll probably talk more about those a little further into the interview, I think.

CARSON: So were you a biologist on board for the 2004 survey then?

ED: No, I got hired right after the survey completed and I think November 1st was my first day. Those surveys on Lake Huron take place in October. So they're, you know, kind of the end of the year survey for the prey fish. And for a few years our agency did do some spring surveys, typically in May. We conducted one in—I want to say 2005—more as a training exercise for the new staff—there were several of us that were new hires at that time. But also to kind of confirm or validate what we were seeing with the collapse of alewife was real, you know? That it wasn't just something that we saw in the fall and because of the distribution or something to do with their biology and behavior. But we did that spring survey and we caught very few, if any, alewife at all. So it was kind of a training exercise for new staff, but also validated what we were seeing in terms of the collapse of the prey base was real. And I've been on the fall survey every year since then.

CARSON: One of the things that I was surprised to hear different opinions on in talking with people is kind of when the peak in the fishery—the salmon fishery—was, and the chronology of what you might call the decline, and one of the first things that kind of surprised me was, reading back through the newspapers and seeing, I think it might have been as early as 1990 or '91 or '92, Jim Johnson being quoted as expressing concern about the balance of predators and prey in Lake Huron, and I thought, Well, that's a lot earlier than I thought that that was a thing that was on people's radar. Then I spoke with John Bruning, who did a lot of first-mating on charters. And then he went to college, I think around—well, the late '80s, early '90s, and he described that time period there as when things started to decline. And in my mind, my understanding of the fishery, and then reading back through tournament participation and the size of the winning fish, and it seemed like maybe the size of the winning fish started to go down in the mid- to, yeah, mid- to late '90s. And I knew of the survey showing the collapse of alewife between 2002 and 2005, and pictures of long, emaciated-looking salmon—

FRANK KRIST: That didn't happen until 2004. Go ahead, you finish, and then I'll answer.

CARSON: —but then speaking with Jayme [Warwick], he didn't recall, around the time of the alewife collapse, catching that many salmon that looked emaciated like that, so that made me think, Well, was that around the time when a lot of the salmon that you might be catching in Rogers City were the ones that had spent time in Lake Michigan and were coming back, but the more emaciated ones that were caught in that 2005–2006 period more resident to Lake Huron? And just trying to get a sense of what people were thinking about the state of the salmon and the balance between salmon and alewives in Rogers City and in Lake Huron because—and I'll speak with Jim Johnson tomorrow—

FRANK: Oh, you didn't speak with Jim today, did you?

CARSON: No, I'm meeting him down at the museum tomorrow. And he kind of told me the story about when they did the mass marking with oxytetracycline, and then he's—

FRANK: The wild fish. 90 percent.

CARSON: Yeah. Yeah, and then doing an estimate of how many wild fish there must be and how little control we have even if we do reduce stocking.

FRANK: See, the people didn't really have anything to point to. You do now, you can point to Lake Huron. Look what happens if you have too many predators.

ED ROSEMAN: Before this slips my mind you said you kind of came into this profession after the fact on the Lake Huron story. Well you're not too late, as you're probably well aware that—very similar situation in Lake Michigan and Lake Ontario right now. And the science people that have worked on the Lake Huron story are—I wouldn't say are actively involved, but very concerned and somewhat involved in communicating with the science people and the stakeholders as well on those issues. So that's just something to be aware of. It's definitely a concern to everybody that Lake Michigan's charter boat industry is just enormous. And the loss of Chinook over there would be pretty devastating as well. So they're definitely almost making daily adjustments to the science and management over there. A lot of communication between the science staff and agencies, as well as with the stakeholders. The same on Lake Ontario. It's another huge Chinook fishery. Heavily reliant on Chinook and alewife are a key player in the food webs in both of those lakes, just like they were in Lake Huron.

Frank Krist: And if you think about it, up until 2002, actually going into 2003, people were happy. There's a couple reasons fish can get smaller, right? One, there's not enough food. Well, that's a problem. Big problem. The other is density. There's just too many of them, and there's plenty around, there's just, there's only so much food, and you catch a lot of fish. In fact, they can get stunted, perch and bluegills, stuff like that. 2002 was the best harvest rate we ever had, and the fish back then weren't looking bad. 2003—we were concerned in 2002 because the smelt and alewife numbers were down and people were thinking, Well, the reason we did so well biting is because they were kind of hungry. But in 2003 we had a tremendous hatch. Better—it was at least double of what they've ever had before of alewives so we figure, Well, I guess we can relax. And so there was really no panic here. And if you go back over the years, it was kind of up and down. We weren't out of the norm or anything. And I don't know what John was thinking. Maybe the only thing he was concerned about was the size, these great—you don't need thirty-five-pound fish, you know? Or even thirty-pound fish. And so then we got into 2003 and we were feeling better. And then it didn't happen. Most of those alewives just didn't survive, whether they got eaten or they just died over the winter. That's when we saw—and people began to panic in 2004. I mean, here we're getting the big heads, skinny bodies, they're looking horrible.

Carson: Going into the 2005 fall survey, what were kind of your feelings, having gone through all of 2005, sitting on the 2004 survey? And I guess also we should talk about the 2003 survey which showed like the big decline in adult alewives, but also a big spike in age-zero alewives. So I guess, can you describe how the feelings and your thoughts—and maybe other people's feelings and thoughts—changed when you go from the 2003 to the 2004, and then to the 2005 survey?

Ed Roseman: Yeah, I've been thinking about that since we talked a few weeks ago. And I think the—there are several things that were kind of like more feeling. One was just the absolute awe and respect of nature that something so huge, at such a large ecosystem level, could happen so rapidly in one of the Great Lakes. And there were some signs that this was coming. But for the alewife to basically be extirpated from Lake Huron was unthought-of. Even though it was something that we as fishery managers have strived to do for decades because they are an invasive species—they were out of control in abundance, they were a nuisance. And they are—part of the reason that the non-native salmonids like the Chinook were put in the Great Lakes in the first place was to control the alewives. So that was—one feeling I had was just a sense of disbelief or awe that something that big could happen so quickly and so ubiquitously across the whole basin of the lake, was pretty remarkable in my perspective.

And that—I've studied recruitment of fishes for pretty much my whole career—thirty-plus years—and the fact that we have a very large young-of-the-year hatch in one year and that they didn't make it through the next year was no big surprise to me. I mean there are many factors that, Carson, I'm sure you're well aware of—environmental and biological—that influence survival of fish through time. So that wasn't a big surprise. But for it to be ubiquitous across the lake and so widespread and quick was kind of amazing, but not a total surprise.

There were signs in the fishery that something was going on with the balance between predators and prey. For—from what I understand—for a little while before that with the condition factor of some of the predators like the Chinook salmon, their weight to length ratio was kind of declining, suggesting that there was something out of balance with the predator-prey dynamics in the lake. But for a complete collapse of the alewife prey base to happen was quite surprising and unprecedented—.

There was more to your question. I'm trying to think what it was. [*both laugh*] But I think it was about the lack of survival of the alewife population. And what's even been more impressive, from a biologist perspective to me, is how the alewife have just stayed low for over a decade now, with a little bit of spotty recruitment happening. We've seen a few age-zero fish here and there in our surveys, but they really haven't bounced back to any numbers like they were in the '80s or '90s—1980s or '90s.

FRANK KRIST: I mean, a good community, really, to look at too—and maybe you've thought about it—is Harrisville. Because they had just a thriving, bouncing fishery there and it just came to a complete end.

In fact, I've been rather surprised, being on that Lake Huron Citizens [Fishery] Advisory [Committee] since 1989—that's a long time; I've seen a lot of things happen—and how they were so involved in the salmon fishery and the recreational fishery. And now they're just down to a trickle.

CARSON: You mean Harrisville? Or the—

FRANK: Harrisville. Harrisville, as far as the importance of the recreational fishery in their community. They still catch some lake trout, but not that many. And then they catch some walleye. But their focus is no longer on—more of the boaters, and other users of that facility. But, I mean, that was really, really an interesting community for several—well, it started in late August and ran all the way through into November.

CARSON: Yeah, I talked with Randy Claramunt, like, maybe a year ago, and he expressed that Harrisville was like a total collapse, whereas in Rogers City, there was still—well, the way he said it was you had more of those species that still persisted and have resulted in that there's still a fishery in Rogers City more so than there is in other places.

JIM JOHNSON: —the zebra and quagga mussel effects on the alewife population were totally unrecognized, unknowable during the 1980s and '90s. When they first showed up in—let's see, I saw my first one, I think, in '92, or '91, my first zebra mussel. And it went on for, like, six, seven, eight years and was like, What's the big deal? You know, they're a pest. They get on your stuff. They infest the beaches and all that. But the fishing just kept going great guns. I did not see an end coming. I didn't think that you could ever tap out alewives, they're so fecund. Each year-class just seemed to be bigger than the one before. The thing that concerned me was that they were younger and younger, where you didn't have as many three- and four-year-old alewives. That was the warning flag we had is that we were down to ones and twos. The bigger, older alewives had disappeared. But I don't think anybody was especially concerned about that because they seemed to compensate by just producing bigger year-classes. And there is that compensation—the older ones, obviously, feed on fry, and if you get rid of the older, bigger ones the compensation mechanism seems to be more young ones. And no, I didn't see that coming. I thought that the Chinook fishery was sustainable on the long term. In fact, I was trying to increase stocking survival using net pens to get more bang for our buck. If I had known that the alewife population was going to be limiting within a few years

I would have been reducing stocking to compensate for the increased survival that we were measuring in our net pen fish. But I didn't see that. I just, no, I thought it was sustainable.

ED ROSEMAN: I think the biggest thing was that some of the anglers, stakeholders, were upset that their area of the lake was no longer going to receive the tens of thousands of stocked salmonids like they had in the past. And this is more true for Lake Michigan than Lake Huron, I think, but it seemed like the more fish you put in, the more the anglers were harvesting out. But there's—it appears from a biological perspective that we kind of reached the threshold and broke that relationship somewhere. So there was anger and disappointment that the numbers of fish weren't getting put in like they used to. I think some people just don't like the government, especially the Michigan DNR, and that definitely came across at some of the meetings. I mean, it was like no matter what you told people or showed them as far as the science data, they just didn't want to hear it and didn't believe it. There were fishermen—there still are guys—that are like, Oh, well, I fish out here in this area, and there's bait balls out there, and the lake trout and the salmon we catch are spitting alewife up on the boat and this and that, and your surveys are all wrong. So we just were like, Well, here's the data. Here's what we do. There were people that were upset that our bottom trawl survey is a fixed-site survey and we sample the same sites across the lake every year. And we've done it that way since the early 1970s. And their thought was, Well you're not—your data don't reflect what's really going on in the lake. And then we have the newer—and the newer is, like, almost twenty years old now—is the lake-wide acoustic and midwater trawl survey that complements the bottom trawl survey. So we started combining those two datasets together and showing them that we have these two independent surveys and they're telling us the same thing, that the prey fish is in peril, and collapsed, and there are very few alewife left in the lake. And that helped with some of the stakeholders, but there are still a few very vocal people that are still angry and still say, "Well, your surveys are wrong." To me that's kind of disappointing that—I guess everybody's entitled to their own opinion—but the facts are in front of us and there's only so many ways you can explain them.

JIM JOHNSON: And then at the same time Ji [He] was measuring reproduction of lake trout and started working on his assessment of top-down effects in bioenergetics of lake trout. And Dave Fielder, who's now a damn good stock assessment biologist—he got his PhD on stock assessments of walleye and he built the walleye stock assessment models. And you put it all together with diet information and the bioenergetic knowledge of just about everybody they could scrounge up. And they estimated in Ji's paper that Lake Huron's a heavily top-down system.[7] But that was disputed in peer review. There was a lot of controversy over that. And I have to say that, yeah, the bottom-up effect—we oversimplified it. We acknowledged there was bottom-up, but we said it was primarily top-down. And I think it was primarily bottom-up, but top-down had a serious effect. But, maybe split the difference. It was both, but we had been under-assessing what the bottom-up effect was until we saw what was happening to whitefish, then we realized anything that is small is not going to find much to eat. And anything that's appealing to walleyes and lake trout is going to be fed on. So it's a double whammy. If they don't starve to death they're going to get eaten. It's that sort of thing going on. So they were working in—the two, bottom-up and top-down effects, were working collaboratively to reduce what we were seeing. But the mussel effect, especially with the later surge of quagga mussels, I think, made it mostly a bottom-up effect by maybe 2005, something like that.

ED ROSEMAN: So at one of the fish commission meetings—I forget what year it was, it might have been 2006 or 2007—some of the stakeholders were at the combined lakes meeting in Ypsilanti—I remember it very well. Frank Krist and Ken Merckel, they're—Frank is the chair of the Michigan DNR's Lake Huron [Citizens] Fishery Advisory Committee, and Doc Merckel has been a part of that group as well. And Merckel is also one of the Thumb Area Steelheader past presidents, or whatever. But they came up to Jeff Schaeffer [USGS Great Lakes Science Center] and I at one of the meetings and suggested that we take a scientific look at the diets of predators in the lake and see how they—the fish—have responded to the change in the fish community. And we were like, Well, you know, that's a pretty big undertaking. Jim Diana did a similar study, I don't know, a decade or more earlier using fish caught by anglers and pulling the stomachs out of those to see what they ate. And there's a whole bunch of bias and science stuff associated with it. But it is a very economical way to get your hands on a lot of stomachs, if your angling community is willing to participate in the study. And at that time—thanks in big part to the Michigan DNR, and Sea Grant, and all the meetings that we did, and the publicity of the story that was happening—you know, the collapse of the prey base and the effect it was having on the fishery, and subsequently the effect that it was having on the local economies that relied on those charter boats and sportfish fishing—we got tremendous buy-in on this project, for—I think we did the first one for three years. I'd have to look up the years. It might have been like 2008 through '10 or something. I can't remember.

CARSON: I think it was '9 through '11. I just reread it.

ED: There you go. Alright. Thank you. [*laughs*] And we had very little funding support for this. I think the only grant we received was like 10 grand from the fish commission or Sea Grant or somebody. But Jeff and I used the resources we had at hand to go out and get these samples. We went to fishing tournaments and we had anglers saving stomachs on trips and just kept them in the freezer. And we gave them ziplock bags and preprinted tags that they filled out and stuck in with their fish gut. And the fishing groups like the Steelheaders and some of the walleye clubs in Saginaw Bay were really instrumental in helping coordinate this and get the stomachs into freezers. And then we just traveled around and picked them up when people would call us. And we went to a lot of fishing tournaments and sat in the fish-cleaning station and pulled stomachs out of people's fish there. But the idea was to see how the predators were responding to the different prey fish community. And I think it was very helpful once we started reporting out on those data that there were some fish that were really thriving in the absence of alewife like Atlantic salmon, steelhead, coho—even though we only saw very few of those. And lake trout were really doing well thanks to round goby being in the system. But the other fish were eating a very broad diet, including a lot of invertebrates like terrestrial insects. Plankton. *Bythotrephes* was showing up in a lot of stomachs, which is another invasive species. And gobies showed up in a lot of fish diets. Particularly the lake trout were doing a lot of feeding on those. And then the walleye diets we looked at mostly came out of Saginaw Bay, but it highlighted a couple of things that we're kind of happy to see. One was the reappearance of mayflies, which had kind of been knocked down to very low abundances, if not almost completely extirpated for a time, but they were showing up in the diets, as well as showing up under streetlights and stuff like that again like they used to. But I think the management agencies used that diet information kind of to confirm some of the decisions they were making on what fish to stock into Lake Huron. So they reduced Chinook stocking because Chinook diets relied almost exclusively on alewife, and to a slightly lesser extent rainbow smelt. And the few Chinook that showed up in our study still showed that. They weren't feeding on very much else. If alewife were available, they were in their diets. If not, then rainbow smelt. But the other species, like the coho, Atlantics, steelhead, and walleye, were eating a very broad range of food items. And their condition and recruitment seemed to be doing pretty good in spite of the lack of the alewife in the system. So I think that helped confirm with the management agencies like the DNR, and the [U.S.] Fish and Wildlife Service who also plant fish in the lake, that the changes they were making in their prescriptions for stocking were justified by how the fish were responding to the prey base that was available.[8]

JIM JOHNSON: [Sea Grant workshops] used to be for charter boat captains and they'd share information and they'd learn about the latest in safety and all that stuff. And they'd be—maybe one or two speakers would come in and talk about the lake. And I'd generally go in and give an update on Lake Huron's fishery every year to the Sea Grant workshops. But there was just charter boat captains there. When Brandon Schroeder came along, he didn't see any reason to keep that template. It was amazing. He just decided to throw that right out and make the workshops open to everybody. And he invited the DNR to bring topics du jour to those meetings and use them to inform the public and inform the press of what's up, and why, and try to get the public involved early on in these decisions. The Lake Huron biologists all up and down the lake embraced this—the managers as well as the research station. And so we started setting up these annual spring Sea Grant workshops.

CARSON: I was wondering about the role that the changing fisheries and ecosystem in Lake Huron played in the bringing together of public interest groups and the Michigan Sea Grant and outreach, because I know that in, like, I think 1992 and '99 you had stocking reductions in Lake Huron, and then you had the major alewife collapse through 2002 to 2005, and having spoken with Ed Roseman and him talking about the importance of the meetings that Michigan Sea Grant held in conveying information to the stakeholders, I was wondering about your perspective on—from the—with respect to increasing communication between biologists and stakeholders, did what happened in Lake Huron with the alewife and salmon play a role in making that whole framework better, or closer to what it is now than it was before?

FRANK KRIST: Well, one of the goals of the committee, the advisory committees, DNR advisory committees—what good is it if you're just meeting amongst a few people? So we've always been real vocal about anybody that's interested can attend and so forth. And we love the idea of being able to meet during most of the year but then take those ideas out to the public. Well, when it came time to deal with the salmon issue, if you think about it, back in 2010, we're looking at the stocking in the southern part of Lake Huron, and out of the hatchery, fish that could be documented that actually showed up in the creel, it was only like fifteen-twenty—I think one port had a hundred hatchery fish that actually creeled. I mean, it was showing there was just a total collapse of that, and it didn't make sense to stock the fish south of basically Alpena, this area. So how do you get that idea across? How do you get people to wear a mask?[9] What do you do? Well, we thought—and I always liked working with Sea Grant; they're just great, great people to work with—and we said, "Hey—," we understood it because we were looking at the biology and could see it, "—we've got to take the message out to the public." And it was a tremendous success. Not only the workshops—the workshops were key because that gave us three or four meetings a year, and we already had a following, and people came to the meetings. And they were actually ahead of the DNR. When we finally explained—I say "we," the managers and that, and our group was there; I've attended, Theresa [Frank's wife] and I attended every one of these meetings over the year—and people understood it and bought into it. Then special communities that were really involved, like up in Cheboygan, we met there, and we had a couple other meetings beside the Sea Grant meetings, and the people were ahead. They were saying, "Hey, okay—," this is about 2010, "—we've got to cut them right now. And let's put the resources into looking at something else." And I know Kelley Smith—I don't know if you've talked to Kelley yet or not.

CARSON: I haven't. No. But I—

FRANK: He's fishery chief. He lives over in Charlevoix. Maybe you'd want to talk to him; maybe not. But anyway, he wanted to wait another year. But it worked extremely well.

JIM JOHNSON: But you can't help but recognize the importance of the people of Rogers City and their interest in stewardship and the leadership that the Hammond Bay Anglers have shown. That's just their doing, that's the way it is. [I] had nothing to do with that.

CARSON: I wanted to ask about—because you brought up the Hammond Bay Area Anglers and the Lake Michigan Citizens Fishery Advisory Committee—and I have kind of an understanding of the framework and what goes on with respect to meetings between policymakers and stakeholders and the researchers in recent years from having gone to Sea Grant workshops and the citizens advisory [committee] meetings—but what role did the issues like the alewife crash, and the decline in the Chinook salmon fishery, and having to abandon the brown trout stocking, those issues play in—and in your having to manage the conversations about those issues and decisions with the public—how did those issues and the history of those issues shape, kind of, the current framework we have now for meetings between the agencies, the policymakers, the researchers, the stakeholders? And how did the Chinook salmon fishery contribute, especially?

JIM:[10] Well, it's kind of changed over the years. There was like a genesis of this collaboration that happened under John Robertson's leadership when he was chief of fisheries. He set up the Lake Huron [Citizens Fishery] Advisory Committee in 1989, the same year I got here, and by 1990 we were meeting. He was a trained collaborator. He was transparent before people talked about transparency. He was a facilitator as a leader, more than an ayatollah, and he totally believed in collaborative management. Participative management was the buzzword back then. And so that's why he set up the advisory committees is to involve people that are opinion makers and opinion leaders from all the different groups up and down the lakeshore of each lake. And Frank [Krist] was appointed as the opinion leader for the Hammond Bay Anglers Association, for example. And Ed Retherford here, the charter boat captain, was appointed because he represented the charter boat fishery of central Lake Huron, and that sort of thing. And so early on we were doing that collaboration, but it changed when issues came up.

FRANK KRIST: I don't know if you know this or not, but John Pridnia really is the one that started the precursor to the advisory committees. John, he set up [an] advisory committee for Lake Huron, especially northeast Michigan because he represented this area, and we had

meetings just like the advisory where you'd have representatives, there
was about five or six of us, we had some all the way down to Hub-
bard Lake then up to the Straits [of Mackinac], and we would meet
about three times a year—this was prior to '89—with DNR people,
and we did exactly the same thing. We sat around and we talked about
our concerns and we listened to the biologists. And lo and behold, we
ended up with these advisory committees which was an expansion of
that throughout the state, and that was great. Yeah, Bill Saunders, he's
gone. But we were able to—it wasn't only the Hammond Bay Anglers,
we started with the Presque Isle County Sportsmen's Club. And then
a few years later we evolved into the Hammond Bay Area Anglers.
But, if you really think about it, it goes back to them wanting to stop
the salmon plants here and people from the community—because we
got good newspaper coverage. And Harry Whiteley was obviously an
important player just because of all the work he did over the years. And
those people jumped on and we all tried to work together, and some of
them moved or pulled out. And a lot of them died.

ED ROSEMAN: The biggest challenge I think to that, as any scientist
can probably agree to, is taking that detailed scientific data and information and making it consumable and understandable to the public.
And I think today that's easier than ever because the public is more
educated—the fishing public, anyway—seems to be more educated and
up on terminology and some of the science behind their favorite fishes.
So that was part of the reason we practiced these presentations, I think,
was to make sure we weren't just going in and talking like a bunch
of PhDs. We wanted to make sure the message was understandable.
I think the goal was an eighth-grade level, is what we were kind of
taught to do. In doing that, being the new guy on the team, and the
new guy in the Lake Huron fishing community, I was nervous. And
at a couple meetings I had people like get angry with me about stuff.
Unfortunately there was alcohol allowed at some of these meetings and
I think that exacerbated some of the emotions of people. But we were
there as a team and we stuck up for each other when we needed to,
when somebody would attack us. Credit to our training that we were
taught that this could happen at meetings, and how to kind of handle
conflict in that situation. So that was a little bit new to me but not unex-
pected, was the high level of emotion and the anger that I guess some
of the stakeholders felt with things. So being part of the team definitely

helped alleviate some of the angst and fear, and also resolved the tension in the room by helping to explain things to people that didn't quite get it, or had an opinion and weren't going to change their mind. And we had law enforcement at all these meetings, too. The environmental conservation officers were there. And they actively participated in these discussions by explaining regulations and changes in fishing zones and things like that. So I thought that was very helpful and added like some calming to the meetings.

JIM JOHNSON: The bad thing was having to cut the brown trout stocking and then having to go through the workshop process of why we can't justify stocking Chinook salmon anymore south of Rogers City.[11] And that was tough. But a lot of people were predicting that neither would succeed—that we'd never get out of stocking brown trout, never get out of stocking Chinooks because the public and the politics of it all will demand that we keep stocking regardless of what the science says. But we were able to convince the opinion leaders through the workshops and through the Lake Huron advisory committee, and the public was along with us. I remember we had one last year of hearings and discussion before we were going to actually cut the Chinook stocking, and we'd been doing this for like three years, telling them we had to cut it. And for three years back-to-back we had Chinook salmon presentations, and why the program doesn't work, and why it's crazy to keep stocking. And one guy stood up when it came to question time and said, "How many more of these meetings do we have to go through before you just cut the [*mouths 'goddamn'*] Chinooks?!" [*both laugh*] And that was really helpful. The DNR management was *very*, very antsy about the cut. I mean, the Lansing administrators. That convinced them that the public had come along enough that we could actually do this. And we made the cut with no—I mean I don't remember *any* backlash. I had some backlash from the brown trout stocking. And Ed Retherford here in town, he'll never forgive me.

CARSON: Yeah.

JIM: But, it was just—the Chinook reduction from 4.3 million a year, I think it was, to just a few hundred thousand in MH-1, that was just, Okay, let's do it.[12] No backlash. Nobody's ever said, "Can't we have our Chinook back?" Haven't had that. It was just amazing. And that was because of this whole change in the way we used the advisory committee and the spring workshops. Without the public being along with us on that we couldn't have done it. I'm worried now that that attitude isn't the same. John Robertson's been gone a long time. And I just hope the DNR doesn't lose track of how important that is: being transparent, and open, and taking your data to the public. I was amazed at how perceptive most people are if you talk to them about what your data mean in terms they can understand. They can understand it. There's some pretty complex concepts we got across, and they understood it. I think we underestimate the public too often and think, Oh, we know best. We don't need to do this. And they would never understand so let's just do it. I hope we don't go back to that way—

CARSON: Yeah.

JIM: —because it was really gratifying to me to see how that worked.

CARSON: I'm thinking of myself, or people like me who grew up or got their training kind of after the crash of alewife had happened in Lake Huron, or people that come to Michigan from outside of the Great Lakes. And you can read in the academic literature about this—and I think one of your papers describes an 87 percent decline in the biomass of prey fish in Lake Huron from the mid-'90s to the mid-2000s—and you get this sense of the awesome, drastic change that happened in the lake and with the ecosystem.[13] But then it's like, given all of the fishing that occurred out of maybe a dozen or so ports for the salmon that were really reliant on alewife and smelt, I just felt like there has to be some social component of the story of what happened in Lake Huron that just isn't available outside of the people that experienced it directly. And I was just wondering if you maybe felt the same way at all, about what exists for—in the literature for someone such as myself. And what—for someone like myself, or that person who wasn't there to experience it directly, what aspects of that social component of the story do you think are important? And then what would you recommend for somebody like that?

ED ROSEMAN: Boy, I guess from my perspective as a science guy that worked on the fishery, I kind of, like, felt responsible in some respects. And just being a fisherman and growing up relying on the environment and nature for part of my livelihood, from hunting and fishing and trapping for food and money and recreation. Empathy, I guess. You know, that I understood the magnitude of the loss. And I think we did a really good job of conveying the magnitude of the loss in terms of numbers of fish and biomass. And not having it a direct part of my job role understanding and quantifying or measuring—the social and economic impacts were kind of, in my opinion, maybe not very well documented. Although everybody had a realization that it was definitely having a big impact on local communities, as well as, like, big-level tourism for the sunrise side of the state. I have heard anecdotal stories about land and home sales prices dropping because of the fishery decline. I don't know if that's true or not. And I drive through those towns all the time and just—always go down to the marina. Like every port that I go through. Oscoda. Alpena. Rogers City. The smaller towns too. Take a walk out on the beach. And how quiet it is there was kind of a weird feeling, compared to previously. Like, I'd worked out here in the '90s, early '90s, when the salmon fishery was just going crazy. And how busy the towns were due to the fishing activity. And there'd be people lined along the banks and stuff, and that's pretty rare to see anymore. So yeah, it was definitely—like, I felt sad and sorry for what happened, and—it's hard to describe—but a certain level of responsibility for it. Like, you know, I'm one of the science people that's supposed to help manage and take care of this resource and, you know—it's *so weird with this alewife situation* in that [in] some sense it's a huge success for us because that was our goal all the time was—or one of the goals—was to, like, control these invasive species that have just caused so much trouble for our natives. But on the other hand we've built up a huge artificial ecosystem based on that invasive species using other non-native species to control it. So it was kind of a weird situation in that respect. But more contemporarily it's nice to see things have rebounded somewhat in that the current fishery is pretty viable—self-sustaining in many respects—and that the stakeholders have managed to learn how to make use of that in an economically and, I guess, satisfactorily manner. There seems to be more, in my sense and experience, just more stakeholder satisfaction than there was in 2004–2005 when the big collapse occurred.

6

TROUBLES AT THE HARBOR

Were the Rogers City marina a sentient being, I should have liked to hear its perspective on things. In terms of the Rogers City Chinook salmon fishery, the harbor was the epicenter. It was the point of interface between the angler and the fishery, and between the fishery and the community. To a large degree, it was the *face* of both the fishery and the community. The harbor had its own sights and sounds and smells. Looking at it today, it's clear it has its own timeline, its own history. It evokes memory, conjures emotion, and incites opinion. So in terms of a story, the Rogers City marina served as a character as much or more than merely as a setting. It's too bad such entities can't provide interviews.

This chapter gives voice to the marina and the adjacent Lakeside Park, telling their stories through the voices of the people who know them. The story has two primary components. The first deals with the logistical operations and sheer abundance of activity at the marina, which played out, apparently, in a spectacular fashion. It offers an entertaining respite from the seriousness of the previous chapter's focus on the fishery crash. The second section of this chapter presents perspectives on the financial implications of the massive, expensive marina expansion in 1995 and 1996. The burden of the construction costs endured long beyond the salmon fishery crash, after which marina revenue greatly decreased because anglers simply were not spending money renting slips, paying launch fees, or purchasing boat gas to the extent they had been before.

In hindsight, you might wonder whether it would have been better for Rogers City, in all those years following the salmon fishery crash, if the costly marina expansion was never undertaken. And then you might wonder if perhaps the costs of the fishery exceeded the benefits. It seems reasonable to raise such considerations, given the causative roles that the Swan River salmon-stocking initiative and the Rogers City Salmon Tournament played in the boat traffic surges that necessitated the marina expansion. What, if anything, might have been done differently to achieve a more favorable financial outcome?

SO YOU WANT TO BE A HARBORMASTER?

If the marina could be considered the face of the community, then Ken Rasche surely would have been the face of the marina. Ken served as Rogers City harbormaster from 1989 to 2006, and he was one of the first people to whom I reached out regarding the impact of the Chinook salmon fishery's collapse.[1] His supportiveness of my interests and willingness to share his story reassured me of the research's importance.

I discovered that perhaps no one participated in the Chinook salmon fishery more than Ken, albeit tangentially, as his salmon-fishing days were essentially behind him once he took over as harbormaster. When I asked him if he ever did any salmon fishing, Ken said that he *did* have a boat, but never had a chance to use it. "I was too busy down there. I worked seven days a week. It was very intense for six months."

Today, the Rogers City marina looks much the same as it did following the "marina expansion project," as it was called, that began in 1995 and finished in 1996 during the height of the Chinook salmon fishery. Ken oversaw the major upgrade in which the marina's capacity nearly doubled, increasing from 79 slips to 146.[2] In its current form, one could argue that the marina is essentially the culmination of the fishery; it endures as a conspicuous reminder of an otherwise inconspicuous salmon fishery past.

The influences of the recreational salmon fishery on the marina, and vice versa, reveal themselves in the interview excerpts that follow, which are arranged as a call-and-response between Ken and many of the others with whom I spoke. I believe Ken took pride in his abilities to perform the role of harbormaster and in the results he achieved. I feel that part of what contributed to his lengthy tenure must have been a feeling of obligation, given Ken's aptitude and diligence regarding a role that perhaps only he could have fulfilled so well. Ask yourself, without Ken Rasche, a solid, tireless, fully committed harbormaster, how much closer to disaster might the goings-on at the marina have borne out?

"We tried to run a very tight ship," Ken explained. "You know, I pissed a lot of people off. But I'm sorry, I treated everybody the same. And if I

Aerial view of the Rogers City marina at ice-out. (Source: www.rogerscitymarina .com/)

wasn't doing a decent job the city wouldn't have had me there for seventeen years."

No apologies needed, in my opinion.

KEN RASCHE: Well, I'm—everybody asked me if I lived in Rogers City all of my life, or was I born here, and I said, "No, but I got here as quick as I could." [I] was born in Detroit, actually grew up in the Hawks area, which is about eleven miles from here. Married a local girl, and went to work immediately after graduation from high school. I was going to go to CMU [Central Michigan University] and become a history teacher, but it just never worked out, I don't know why. But I went to work down at Calcite, worked there three years, and then I quit down there and I went to work for my wife's [father], who was a Standard Oil distributor. In Mount Pleasant maybe you've seen the signs [for] Coyne Oil Company.

CARSON: Mm-hm, yeah.

KEN: Okay. I know the Coynes well, and worked with them, actually. Did that for twenty-five years and I retired. Quite a few reasons. We had a good business. I didn't take any vacations. My wife refused to go on—we did take the girls to—I've got two girls, and we did take them to Florida once but my wife said that she would never go again because I spent all my time on the phone to see how the business was going.

So I sold the business and actually went to work for the people I sold it for, but I found I was working just as hard as ever but not making any money. And one day the city manager from the local city here called me and he said, "Hey, would you be interested in running the marina?" And I said, "I don't know anything about running a marina." But he said, "You do know how to run a business." I said, "Well—." So we talked about it, and for a guy that never had a—I never had a paid vacation in my life—I figured this might be a way to work for six months and have six months off, even though I didn't draw unemployment, and the six months I could do what I wanted to do, okay? And that's basically what happened. I worked there for seventeen years. And prior to working there I did have a twenty-four-foot boat and snuck out salmon fishing every chance I had. And the fishing was excellent. It really was. And then when I went to work at the marina, it was—one of the—

CARSON: You started in 1990, right? At the marina?

KEN: Oh, no. No. No, earlier than that. I have to figure it out. Probably in the mid-'80s. 1980s. Yeah. So the marina was very small at that time. We had seventy-nine boat slips. It was a real challenge. A real challenging job, to run it. When you have twice as much demand for something than you can—we constantly promoted to bring more people to Rogers City to go fishing, but we didn't have boat slips for them. And so you make some people angry. And it was a very uncomfortable job at times. Rewarding, at times.

BRUCE GRANT: And a lot of the conflict then was there was just too many boats for one little harbor. So why don't they open up more harbors? And like here, I could have put a dock in, and the State wouldn't let you. I can't put a dock in. I couldn't even—I had to send my customers to town. I could have docked them right here with a seasonal dock. You pull it out in the [fall]. You follow the rules and regulations. But, No, we don't need anybody stealing our business. Because they had people locked in. And you go back—we had ten charter boats here, and two sailing charters, all paying double dockage and paying high gas. And they drove those people out of there. They drove them—the lumberyard went and spent a lot of money to rebuild their docks and bring them in, and of course it made more room in the city. But those charter boats were bringing the business here by bringing the media in, taking them fishing, catering to them, and then they are writing all that free advertising. And I just wish we could have had a business group that could have sat down and then went to the city and the county and had a little more power to lean on them a little bit. But—and then we'd have 350 boats out there. You could hardly move. You'd catch a fish and somebody's cutting your line off. Fishing was fantastic.

KEN RASCHE: And one of the main reasons we rebuilt the marina and increased it in size—we almost doubled it in size—was the fact [that] we had so many fishermen. We had a waiting list of, I think, at one time about 120 people. I had no problem—you know, you can't fill every slip with seasonal boaters. You've got to have room for the transients coming off the lake. So the State controlled pretty much what we did down there, and it was a balancing act. Fishermen and cruising boaters really didn't get along well. A guy pulls in with his million-dollar boat, and he pulls in and he probably spends the night drinking on board, and he's staying up late and plans on getting up at 10 o'clock in the morning and taking off and going, but at 5 o'clock in the morning you've got eighteen fishermen starting up alongside of him. So there's always good and bad with both. So we enlarged the marina—and again, we still had way more boats than we could handle. We've had fishing tournaments down there—the Rogers City Salmon Tournament, at one time, I think the largest I ever saw it was 350 boats. And we actually had a waiting list of people who wanted to get in. And when you have 350 boats, you don't have 350 spots to put them. So you're going to make some people—some people are going to be unhappy. But we ended up having a lottery system—a drawing, okay? If you get drawn you get a boat slip, if you don't, I'm sorry, you've got to use the trailer. And there were days during that tournament, Carson, there were days more than just during those times—if you know where the red light used to be in downtown Rogers City; it's now a four-way, okay—at 4 o'clock in the morning, the line of cars went from the launch ramp back to the red light, okay? I mean, it was a zoo. It was absolute—it was wild. And I guess I understand it. You have a guy that, he's got a huge investment in a boat. He's got, you know, 35, 40,000 dollars. He probably works in a factory in Bay City, Saginaw, or Detroit, and he's looking forward to that seven days or fourteen days he's going to be up in Rogers City just socking them salmon like crazy, but he can't get his boat in the water. [both laugh] And again, we had some very unhappy people—we had a lot of happy people. But it was a challenge. It was a challenge. It really was.

Bruce Grant: They got a harbor expansion. Soon as they got a harbor—and the State put up the money—but you start at Port Huron and you come up the lake—Port Huron, Port Sanilac, Lexington, Harbor Beach, all those—they did the same thing, and they were having a great fishery. But when the charter boats moved in they turned their head because State Waterways [Michigan Department of Natural Resources Waterways Division] told the city, "Well we own the harbor, you own the parking lot. We put up the money for the harbor so you'll follow our rules." They charged the charter boats double dockage. So if you came in and you weren't a charter boat—which a lot of guys come in and left their sticker off and brought their business they had in Port Huron and Oscoda. And there was no policing of the issue other than they knew who the local guys were. And you were licensed—you had to have your license on your boat, so it was displayed. And we're paying 1,600 dollars a year for dockage, and 50¢ to a dollar more for gas because we couldn't get our own gas. The charter boats moved out of the harbor. The lumberyard fixed up their old commercial fishing harbor and moved us in. All of a sudden all of the activity's over at the lumberyard harbor and not in the city. And then it was a big thing about getting money to build a cleaning station and all of sudden now we've got too much guts to get rid of. Too many fishermen. And then—I mean, this town was so crowded I've seen them lined up all the way out of the harbor all the way back to the streetlight in town at 5 o'clock in the morning to unload boats to come in and go fishing. Three hundred boats was nothing. And this all happened in a five-, six-year period. And oh, the city was upset. Too much—they didn't grow with what was happening. And in doing so, they upset a lot of people. You can tell somebody in a nice way, "I'm sorry, I don't have a slip. Give me your name, I'll call you as soon as it opens up." But if you go out and say, "Get out of here, I don't have any slips left, don't bother us," then those people are going to get mad and go back to Lake Michigan. And those were a lot of the issues that we had.

Carson: What was the typical day for you, when—?

Ken Rasche: For me? It was seven days. It was seven days a week. I would usually get down there—depending on the time of the year, I inevitably was down there by 6 o'clock in the morning, I never went home for lunch, I would usually leave there any time between 5 and 6 at night, and I would usually go back down after, okay? But weekends

I would usually try to be down there by 4 o'clock to do nothing more than try to direct traffic down at the launch ramp. Okay? And it was difficult. It was difficult. When you tell people, "Hey, you've got to move. Come on, man. You've got to keep moving, keep moving," pretty soon you get a reputation of being a horse's ass, but you make one guy mad, you keep four people happy, so it's a balancing act. So it was a long day. It was a long day.

Bruce Grant: We had some really wonderful harbormasters, which I think control the whole thing. It's their personality and how they handle the problem. If you handle a problem—you're not going to please everybody—but if you handle a problem the way you'd like to be handled—kind of the golden rule idea—if you lose a few, they were the ones you didn't want anyways. If you made it right with the people, they came back. And they knew the rules, and they had an understanding. And we had some harbormasters—this happened several times. Two buddies. Two brothers. One leaves Detroit on Thursday night. Comes up, gets a slip. His brother leaves Friday morning. He worked nights. He comes up and there's no slip available. His brother got a slip. But there's empty slips. So the guy leaves. Parks out in the parking lot. Or goes to Presque Isle to try to get, whatever. And an hour later, a local comes along and gets the slip. And that's not—I know that goes on, but that's not right. And those people compare notes. Next week, the two brothers don't come back. So you didn't lose one, you lost two by not being upfront. There's got to be transparency. You've got to be fair with everybody.

Ken Rasche: When I started at the marina, we let people camp overnight in the parking lot. That was fine. But when they started emptying their holding tanks out in the parking lot, then it had to stop, you know? And believe it or not they did. So a few ruin it for everybody. I think—a lot of people like—Carson, in the evenings, the launch ramp was probably the busiest place in Rogers City. There was, literally, almost every night there was probably fifty-sixty people down there just watching these boats come in because, it was funny, there was a lot of them that were good boat-handling people. But some of them, I mean, it was like kamikazes coming in. And there's people falling off the docks. I mean, it was just—we had people back their boat in, and I've seen this happen more than once, mother gets on the tailgate of a truck, and she's supposed to unhook the hook, and he's backing down and he hits the brake and mother—. [*Carson laughs*] And we've fished boats out of the launch ramp. I mean, it was absolutely insane. Crazy. We've had people fallen in. I dove in twice, to get kids that fell off the dock. And their parents were standing there. But hey, I was closer, I guess.

CARSON: Did you often take people out?
KEN PARTYKA: All the time.
CARSON: Was that on your twenty-four-foot?
KEN: Yeah. All the time. All the time. [*laughs*] And people—people [*laughs*]—you know, sometimes just people just didn't really like us. Maybe because we were catching fish. Maybe whatever. You'd come in, you'd fish the evening, okay, you're fishing right to dark. But you don't want to wait to dark because things get to be a madhouse. So everybody starts scrambling back to the boat harbor, okay? Now I had like a twenty-four-foot boat. I only had like a 175-horse, a 175-horse Johnson on it. But this boat came from Florida. It was a Florida flats boat. Shallow draft. Scooting right along the top. And everybody wants to get in ahead of the next guy, you know? Everybody wants to get ahead of the next guy. [*laughs*] So I remember I was out there, I was out there with Tom Kelly, Steve Kelly, Todd Kelly, Bob Kelly, whatever. They're standing in back. Mandy and I are in the seat. And we're going. And we're going. And I'm going like, three-quarter throttle. I've got a couple of boats over here that are just catching me. Catching me. Catching me. Catch[ing]—we got the *Salmon Slayer*. We're going to, we're going to beat them in. We're going to beat them in. [*laughs*] I'm like, "Okay, boys, hang on because here we go." [*Carson laughs*] Brr-VOOM! [*laughs*]
MANDY PARTYKA: And he wonders why they called us assholes.
KEN: Cut the buoys, two buoys short and slip in ahead of them and—. "[Look] at him, fucking assholes." [*laughs*]

CARSON: So when the marina expanded in '96, did that make your job easier or harder, having to deal with more—?
KEN RASCHE: It was more responsibility, but it was easier because you could keep more people happy. You really could. We've had—I think there's 129 boat slips down there right now. We had, Carson, at one time, we had the Great Lakes Cruising Club come through. And these

are big pleasure boats. We had 179 boats in there. Every one of them had power and water. They were drawing so much power that we had to run a garden hose on the transformer to keep it from blowing up. That's how hot it was. But we could put a lot of boats in there. We really could. And it turned out to be a great marina. I think it's one of the nicer ones on the lake. I really do. So I'm damn proud of it. Lot of sweat equity went into that one.

JOE HEFELE: —my younger brother, actually, in his youth was one of the dockhands, and that was actually a pretty in-demand job. It's not because it paid better than anything else; it didn't. I think it paid minimum wage, which pretty much all the jobs for high school or early college youth paid. But again, it was just the energy and the fun. It was just the—again, it was not only the locals having fun but it was the different groups of people coming in all the time and the ability to meet people, and even other young people that were in with their families, for the fishing and marina. And so I know as those jobs every year were advertised they were in high demand because of that.

CARSON: Oh, okay. Did he work with Ken Rasche, then?

JOE: My younger brother had worked with Ken Rasche, he did, yeah.

CARSON: I was curious, because I think it was the 1997 tournament, I read—and it maybe had been other years, too—the headline was literally, "More Than 20,000 Pounds of Salmon Caught," and I'm trying to get a picture of, how long does it take to fillet all those fish?[3] And what is that like? [laughs]

KEN RASCHE: The—Carson, the line of people—. We had, at that time we had an IGA store that was right down by the four-way stop sign. They had a terrific business with boaters, and they would let boaters take grocery carts—the cruising boater didn't have a car when he came to town, so he had to get groceries back to the marina, so they would take grocery carts and fill them up at the store and take them down to their boat, and leave them there and the grocery store would go and pick them up, take them back to the store. But the fishermen got in between and they loaded these up with salmon [Carson laughs] to take them over to the fish-cleaning station. I mean, there was literally thousands of pounds of salmon. And thousands of pounds of waste. It was crazy. It was nuts. And you had guys arguing and fighting in line, and some guy's too slow, and—it's funny there was no knife fights over there. It was nuts. And then, you take hot weather, a lot of drinking, late at night everybody's tired—it was an interesting place. [*both laugh*] I stayed away. I tried to stay away as much as I possibly could because—from the fish-cleaning end of it. It was my responsibility to keep it clean and policed and get—but while they were cleaning fish, man, no, I'm—

CARSON: Stay away.

KEN: Or else I'm going to look from a distance, I'm telling you. [*Carson laughs*] It's no place to be. Yeah, it was amazing. What we needed, what we needed, and we had a few, we had a couple of Filipinos, families, and I don't know what they do with fish guts, but they were down there every day getting fish carcasses. I was hoping we would have had [*laughs*] quite a few hundred more of them. I mean, they helped us clean up the waste. Crazy. We had guys hauling salmon waste out for bear bait. We had people burying it in their gardens, which, hey, I encouraged it. Go for it, man. Get rid of it someway. What bothers me, and the DNR, God bless them, they know what a fish-cleaning station is, so they build a marina down at Presque Isle that has probably almost as many fishermen going out of it, catching as many fish as we do. But all these people are bringing their fish to Rogers City to clean. They don't want any part of it. They're smart. [*both laugh*]

ROB KORTMAN: The fishery here—when they expanded the harbor and everything, they put a fish-cleaning station in, which we never used to have, down at the boat harbor, which basically—you go in and clean your fish, grind it up.[4] The waste came into the sanitary sewer and flowed down here to the wastewater plant, which put a very heavy organic load on the plant, okay. Which at a certain point, you're overloaded. You can't process it and have a good, clean effluent going out back into the lake with a good high DO [dissolved oxygen] because you have so much food. You don't have enough bacteria—or organisms, I should say—to handle it all. And the grinders, you know, they grind it only so small. So what would happen is, when the salmon fishing would pick up it would load the plant—and we have a bar screen which we have got to clean—and we get pails of bones and skin—I mean, it's just too much. And then you start seeing—I mean we smelled like a fishery down here. I mean, it gets to the point where it's just—whoa! So then what we'd have to do is they would—they got permits from DEQ [Department of Environmental Quality] and Department of

Ag[riculture] and they would bury the fish waste. They would haul it. And they would clean them—they'd shut the grinders down and then they—carcasses would go in twenty-gallon pails—and then they would haul them out and dump them in a pit and bury it up so even the animals wouldn't get at it. But it was just a load. It's an organic load on the plant. And when I started here in '97 there was still a decent fishery going on. It wasn't like it used to be even back when I—but we didn't have the fish-cleaning station then—and we would haul—we would actually shut them down in July. And they would have to dump all the way into September because we couldn't handle it here at the plant. It's just the organic load. And they would haul—I—somewhere we have records of that—but they would haul twice a day. They would go in the morning. Take out. And before they'd go home from work they'd dump it again. Because there's so much fish coming in. And the majority of it was all salmon at that time. And then as the salmon peaked down we were—in fact last year is the first year in ten—take that back, thirteen years that we made them haul again.

CARSON: Oh really?

ROB: Yeah. So it got to the point where we could handle it. There wasn't enough fish coming in anymore that the plant was able to absorb the extra organic load because they weren't catching. It was just basically the lake trout and the other—you know, browns, steelies. I mean, there was salmon, but it was—never got to the point where we were getting overloaded. But last year was, like I said, the first year in I want to say ten, eleven years because the new superintendent started thirteen years ago, and I don't think we were hauling then. We were already to the point where we could handle it.

CARSON: So you started in 1997, you said?

ROB: '97. I started here at the wastewater plant.

CARSON: Okay.

KEN RASCHE: Fish-cleaning station was just a—it was terrible. Absolutely terrible. We were fortunate, we've had two different guys, and if there is such a thing as a professional fish cleaner, we had two different guys that came in and they lived right on-site. And, because if you didn't—first of all, we had a four-place fish-cleaning station with a grinder. You take—a guy comes in with five fish, it's going to take him—some guys'll do it in fifteen minutes, sometimes some guys are going to do it in an hour and a half. So you've got a line halfway down the parking lot of guys with coolers, and this is 11:30 at night. So we got the guys—and we didn't force people to use the fish cleaners, but a lot of people did, and those fish cleaners could clean fish faster—they could clean five fish faster than the fastest fisherman could clean one, okay? And they were a big asset. But then it got to the point—what do we do with the entrails? Well, wastewater treatment plant couldn't handle them anymore. It was overloaded, okay? So we ended up going down to the U.S. Steel plant—which it was then—we made a deal with them that we would haul them down to their location—we went down with city equipment in the spring of the year and we would dig trenches, in the middle of the quarry up on some hills where they had hauled all this overburden, the junk rock. And then we would haul, in dumpsters, all the fish waste down there. Well, it all takes manpower. And it takes machinery. And it costs money to do it. And it's all coming out of the marina revenue. Well, then we decided—and it was kind of interesting, if you look at the lay of the land here—and it's hard to understand until you look at a map real close—we get a lot of northwest wind. When we get a northwest wind, this area is not real fishable, okay? But if you go down beyond Calcite, beyond Adams Point, beyond Presque Isle, Michigan turns south and that's pretty decent fishing with a northwest wind. Well, we're looking at our parking lot one day and we don't have any really—there's not enough fishermen to worry about having to haul fish waste. And pretty soon this guy comes over who I had never met before, and he says, "Hey. Your dumpster is full." I said, "What do you mean it's full?" "Yeah, it's full." Everybody that was fishing out of Presque Isle Harbor is bringing their fish up to Rogers City. The DNR's smart enough, they won't put a cleaning station in at Presque Isle because those people are coming up here and cleaning their fish, and they're not benefiting our marina one penny. But it is costing us a ton of money to get rid of their waste. So you go to the city and say, "Now look, this is what's happening. What do you want to do?" "Well, we don't know." And I said, "Well, how about this? We charge people—," I think back then it was like, "—4 dollars to launch a boat. Put up a sign that says, 'If you did not fish in Rogers City, go down and buy a 4-dollar launch fee. Come and clean your fish. If you don't want to buy that, then take your fish someplace else.'" Well, you know what, you would have thought that I was the nastiest person in the world. I mean, even our city fathers, You can't do that. Now all of a sudden the marina is broke, and they wonder why.

Mary Ann Heidemann: So meanwhile, before the harbor got enlarged, and before that project really was going full tilt, people were catching a lot of fish, and they needed a place to clean them. Okay? So now the idea is—did anybody else talk to you about the fish-cleaning station?

Carson: Ken Rasche, and I asked Rob Kortman about it too at the wastewater treatment plant because, well, because the—

Mary Ann: Wait, wait, wait—

Carson: Okay, yeah.

Mary Ann: —they may have had a different point of view, but on the other hand they're very informed gentlemen. But I have a particular ax to grind. Speaking of grinding [*Carson laughs*], you know, the location where the fish-cleaning station is was previously the city band shell. They didn't tell you that.

Carson: No. I read about the tearing down of the band shell—I read back through the newspapers—but I didn't know that that's where that was. Yeah.

Mary Ann: The fish-cleaning station is why the band shell fell down, so rather than fix it, they just tore it down and built a state-of-the art, *beautiful* fish-cleaning station, with pulldown nozzles and all stainless steel, big grinders, and all of the top of the top—. The only problem is, which I'm sure they did tell you, when the salmon season got going, the fish harvest that was cleaned in the station was the biological oxygen equivalent to a town of ten thousand, and it made the sewage-treatment plant violate its permit. So nobody had thought about that. So the beauty of it was, as soon as people started catching fish and wanting to clean them, they locked the fish-cleaning station. And what they built as a substitute was a couple of wooden tables out behind the station where people would clean their fish surrounded by scenic fencing, chain-link fence—how lovely is that?—and buckets to throw the guts in. So it would be hot, and they would clean lots of fish, and the buckets would sit around reeking. I mean reeking. And of course it was right by the basketball courts. Now, the young guys didn't seem to care one way or the other. But to replace the band shell, the city had purchased a used, what was fondly referred to by band members, Tin Can. It was like a travel trailer with a side that opened up and you could fold out the flat floor and set up your chairs. But you can imagine the acoustics compared to this beautiful semi-circular, vintage band shell that they were accustomed to. So needless to say the band people weren't too thrilled about that. Furthermore, you'd have the fish cleaners going on, and when there'd be a band concert the aroma of fish guts would envelop the audience and it was not the best experience. Now, you say, "Oh, well, it's a band," but this town has had a band for 120 years. And the band is supported by a tax millage—a quarter mil. And you've got to understand the cultural thing, that bands are really just part of the German heritage, the oompah bands, so people were deeply invested. Initially it was all men, but by the time we got here it was gender-mixed, age-mixed, you have guys in their nineties, you have kids in high school. It really brought the whole community together, and every Thursday night you'd have a free concert in the park, in the Tin Can. Well, eventually my daughter was very interested in music and she was in the band when she was in high school, in the summers, and she went to music school, and when she came back in summers, and after college she became the band director. And by that time the Tin Can was really bad. It was leaking, it was dangerous because there was no railing or anything, people—it's very crowded. They have a big band and people were literally close to falling off the edge. So she went to city council with the proposal to start a fund to replace the Tin Can with a real band shell. And ultimately, my firm wrote a pro bono grant application, and my husband, who was in a barbershop quartet locally, ran around singing songs and getting donations that way, and we ended up building the beautiful band shell that's there now. So the band shell's there because of the fish. [*Carson laughs*] It's really interesting how things work out in a small town. There's so many interconnections. And I have to say that I had to call people, and again, we aren't from here, and we were still relatively new at this time, but you had a facility and a history of band interaction, participation, that was very deep in this town, so it was the easiest fundraising I ever did. You'd call somebody and you'd find out, Oh, my uncle was in the band, or, My grandkid's in the band. And the money just poured in. So we had no problem making the match for that because it was so important to the community. And now, of course [*laughs*], the circle comes round, they use the band shell for the weigh station for all the fish tournaments. [*laughs*] It's not just music. Which is a great location. And there's all kind of events. And actually, when my daughter got married, she got married in the band shell because it meant so much to her. So that was a lot of fun. I think it was absolutely the first wedding in the band shell. [*laughs*] Oh, wow.

KEN RASCHE: But anyway, it was interesting. I enjoyed it. Especially working with the young kids. We had twelve people down there, easily, every year. I had some fantastic workers. Fantastic. And we're pretty close to a lot of them right to this day. And a lot of them have been very successful. Matter of fact, one of the kids that worked for me my first year down there, he's my doctor right now.

CARSON: [*laughs*] Oh, really?

KEN: [*laughs*] So I get darn good care.

"A MILLSTONE AROUND THE CITY'S NECK"

Ultimately, the harbor upgrade was expensive. While it's no small feat that Rogers City was able to secure $1.944 million in grant funds from the State of Michigan to pay for the marina expansion, the grant was a matching grant, meaning Rogers City had to pay the remainder of the $3.78 million endeavor.[5] The city financed its end of the bill by taking out bonds, but paying it all back would depend upon years and years of marina revenue. Reassuring the community of the financial undertaking's reasonability, City Manager Rob Fairbanks stated on December 4, 1995, at a city council meeting, "Unless there is a major change in the boating industry, we will have no problem retiring the debt incurred."[6] The sentiment of his statement suggests the likelihood of such a "major change" was dismissible—unforeseeable. The sentiment also suggests that paying back the debt depended, to some extent, upon no major changes to the salmon fishery.

You might recall from chapter 2 the concern that resident Ed Smith raised at a city council meeting in 1984, when the idea of expanding the marina was first being vetted: "What if this thing [the Chinook salmon fishery] fizzles out in four or five years? We're stuck with another dead horse." Well, given that the marina expansion finished in 1996 and the alewife population had crashed by 2004, it seems in hindsight that Mr. Smith was off only by a matter of three or four years.

As current city manager Joe Hefele would tell me, the city would still be paying those bonds in 2021, a quarter-century after the project's completion and nearly two decades after the Chinook salmon fishery crash. Mary Ann Heidemann called those payments a "millstone around the community's neck." Taking into account all the good that the salmon fishery brought with it, but acknowledging this persistent cost to which it is linked, it raises the question: *Would the degree of economic hardship experienced by Rogers City from the mid-2000s to the present have been relatively less without the financial burden imposed by (1) the marina upgrade debt, and (2) the added operational costs of a now excessively large marina?*

It's impossible to answer. For example, if the marina had remained small, Ken Rasche may not have lasted in his position. The fish-cleaning station would never have been built, so maybe Presque Isle Harbor would have attracted anglers who otherwise chose to fish in Rogers City because they could process their fish on the spot. And just maybe the beautiful Rogers City band shell wouldn't be what it is today without the marina expansion—how do you put a value on that?

DAVE NADOLSKY: —the Vogelheim family had been very influential in this town—number of mayors and a successful business enterprise down at the harbor, so they owned beach frontage and everything else. And for a long time it was assumed that the harbor would expand to the north, rather than the south. And with that mindset, which in no small way was set by the Vogelheim family because they would benefit by it, the city explored that avenue. Well, we were all set to do a deal to acquire the Vogelheim property and expand the harbor to the north, and a local politician at that time was named John Pridnia. And he was from Harrisville, but he'd been working with Presque Isle and with Rogers City, and favored Rogers City because it had the rest of the infrastructure to support it. And due to the internecine squabbling of the Vogelheim family—first with themselves, who they liked to squabble with, but also with anybody else—over the price of the property, we lost that deal, and Presque Isle got the harbor expansion, and that just pissed people off to no end.[7] And that's why that commission was formed. And the Vogelheims were taken out of the equation. And eventually the older members of the family died off and the next generation were not as astute businessmen and they lost the whole damn thing to bankruptcy. I mean, it was five or six hardware stores, and do-it-yourself centers, and, you know, he had a finger in the fishing enterprises along with [Gary] Lamb. So that was quite a deal. And it was a big stink.

MARY ANN HEIDEMANN: Now, meanwhile the project, there was a harbor to build. The Vogelheims are wonderful people, but they really were tough negotiators, and they could not come to terms with the city about purchasing their property. And that was frustrating for all concerned, because the idea had been that the hardware store would move out to the highway and then the condominium development would be here but they couldn't find a developer who was willing to work with the Vogelheims as active participants in the project, not just as selling the thing. So that dragged on for years, literally, and finally came to nothing. So then the whole plans had to be redone without the condominiums, and instead of expanding north it had to expand south. So it just took forever. And sad to say, by the time the harbor was actually finished, the fishing had peaked and was already kind of on the downslope. It wasn't bad, but it wasn't like it had been. And once the harbor was finished—of course it was frustrating for me as a planner because we had worked so hard to put the deal together and it came to nothing, but eventually time goes on and the harbor was built and it got lots of State [of Michigan] support, and they got it from Department of Natural Resources and from Michigan Waterways Commission, because Waterways has a series of harbors up and down the lakes and they want a harbor every so often for safety's sake, harbor of refuge, which this also was. So a lot of public money went into the harbor and it was fantastic. It's a wonderful harbor. But it more than doubled the size. And once it got built, my husband and I, who now lived half a block from here, would walk over in the evenings and walk up and down the docks and count the boats because we wanted the harbor to fill. [*laughs*] And it really—it would fill on Fourth of July weekend and it would fill for the salmon tournament and for the Nautical [Festival], but as a regular matter it wasn't *full* full. That becomes really important later because it wasn't all grants, it was a lot of loans. The city had to put up a lot of money and finance it. And without boat slips being rented, and gas being sold, you can't make your payments. And that became a millstone around the city's neck. And the payments—it's not paid off yet. That's a real problem, because then the city literally borrowed from other organizations like the Downtown Development Authority, because the idea was you'd be connecting this harbor with the downtown, and it would be good for both entities, which of course it is. So Downtown Development money went into the harbor, which limited then what the Downtown Development Authority could do downtown. So the people got mad and things were not great because of—financially stressed. Really a problem. And there were other issues too with the blockheaded approach the State took to charter fishing, because if you were a charter fisherman and you wanted to put your boat in the harbor you had to pay double dockage.

CARSON: Yeah, I heard that from Bruce Grant.

MARY ANN: And that was really on some different reality than what worked here because the fishing season is a couple, three months at the most, and so that couldn't be your only job so these charter guys were part-timers, and—

CARSON: Was that a DNR or a Waterways Commission thing?

MARY ANN: Waterways. And I think that's different now, but for all the time it mattered it was a real obstacle. So what you had is guys that just launched their boat here, and pick up their clients on the dock. So there was a lot of cheating going on—everybody knew it, but that was the only way they could make it work. So that was kind of a—you know, you go to a lot of fishing ports in Florida or something and there's charter guys up and down, and it's a major business. But five hours from Detroit, it's a long way to go to catch a fish. So that was always an issue. And [there are still] one or two people that do chartering, but I have no idea what the current regs are; I'm pretty sure they're not the same. But that was very shortsighted. The idea was public money shouldn't be used to support a private business. Well, the concept sounds like it makes sense, but again, this is not a going concern. This is a guy who's got a boat that picks up some charters on the side. And it could never be worth it to that kind of a situation. There goes all your profit, if you ever—and, you know, the weather doesn't always cooperate.

KEN RASCHE: One of the things for years that bothered me, Carson, being in business for myself—I've got to be careful how I say this—we made a lot of money for the city. A lot of money. The city borrowed, it was a matching grant, to rebuild the marina, and the bond payments were structured in such a manner that when we started off repaying the bonds we made very small payments. But as you got into the bond payments more long-term, your bond payments went up. Well, that was good because we had tons of money after we made our yearly bond payment. And this is where the problem comes in. What our city had decided to do in their—and John Bruning was part of it—they balanced their budget for the city on money that the marina made. And I kept telling them, "Guys, there's going to come a time, you're going to need that money in reserve to pay these—." That's one of the reasons I got out, because the marina was supposed to be self-sustaining. Okay? For the last ten years our streets in Rogers City have gone to hell because the city is subsidizing the marina, which should have never happened. If—[laughs] I probably shouldn't say too much more—but this is what happened. Oh, hey, the marina's got money. We need that. We need that. We—. Like I say, that's one of the reasons I got out, okay. Yeah. It's just—you could see, it didn't matter how much money you made, they could spend it faster than you could make it. And then with the downturn with the fishing, I could see awful dark days coming. I always said, "My mother raised short kids, not stupid kids."[8]

CARSON: I was just wondering, maybe even with respect to your role as city manager and other government types of positions you had, what proportion or how much of your time or things that you were working on had to do with things concerning the fishery or the marina?
JOHN BRUNING: Well—.
CARSON: And you kind of already touched on the marina a little bit.
JOHN: Yeah. That would be—from an economic development standpoint and attracting either new businesses or supporting the businesses that were here, since it had been an important component, the fishery really drove parts of that industry, you know, in the heyday, in the '80s. It was still important, but it was hard to get a hold—you know, it wasn't there. So we were trying to figure out alternative ways while still trying to figure out what to do, or what kind of new approaches maybe could help us with the fishery and help strengthen it and bolster it. I wouldn't say—from my perspective, it was hard to say, because as city manager you're responsible for everything. And we had a harbormaster that dealt with the day-to-day harbor issues. DPW [Department of Public Works] took care of DPW. There was some periodic or regular concern, I guess, with it. Again, trying to figure out from the marina standpoint what kind of impact, financially, is the reduced revenue? You're not having as many people paying daily launches. You're not having as many fuel sales. You're not having as many slip sales for the transient fishermen, people that might trailer up, park their boat in the harbor for a few days, and then head back home. So there were struggles associated with that that we were dealing with. I was—I worked for the city from 2001 to August of 2006, first as assistant city manager and then as city manager, and during that time period, the marina bonds, paying for that stuff, was important. And it was becoming increasingly more challenging because the revenue that had been there wasn't. Or it was greatly diminished. And so it was certainly a challenge. And I'm sure that that challenge extended beyond when I left because conditions really didn't change

much, and you still have obligations. And so we thought about it. We have a harbor advisory committee that would make some recommendations and try to figure out how to market, how to promote Rogers City as a good place to come and fish, and bring with it all the economic benefits that that traffic does. But working with the chamber of commerce and the tourism groups and so forth, but it was challenging. I don't know beyond that how much more detail I can give you, I guess.

MARY ANN HEIDEMANN: You come right up the shore—it's great to have these things, but to some extent it's like a millstone around the community's neck, because somebody has to take care of it. So that's very impractical. But all of the designs and all of the number crunching about how big something should be and size of the slips and rates and all that, the community has very little control because all of that has to be approved. It's silly. It's just not practical. And yet here they are, still paying off the debt. Taking a huge chunk—so, again, a city with fifteen hundred fewer people than when the harbor was built, but the debt doesn't disappear.

CARSON: I talked with Joe Hefele—

MARY ANN: Yeah, city manager.

CARSON: —and I think, *I think* what he said is it's on track this year to finally be able to be paid off. I think that's what he told me.

MARY ANN: I'd like to go to that party when that mortgage is burned. [*Carson laughs*] Yeah. Yeah. So these communities run on a shoestring. They're very fiscally modest. And they have to be. The tax rates here are pretty low, nobody wants them higher, so there's no public support for anything more. And I mean, you read the statistics, this is not a wealthy community. And it's loosened up a lot since we first came, in terms of, Are you from here or not? And richer versus poorer. It's a little bit more open and welcoming than it had been. But I wouldn't say the economy has gotten any better.

7

THE FINAL ANALYSIS

Overall, what role did the recreational Chinook salmon fishery play in shaping the culture, identity, and legacy of Rogers City? I believe an answer to this lies within the stories that I heard, but those stories are not distillable to numerical interpretation in a meaningful way, nor would it be appropriate to treat them as something like replicates or samples in a scientific manner. They are not something for which there is a meaningful average. After all, at any one time, there's only one mayor of Rogers City, a single harbormaster, and a single city manager. There's only ever going to be one Bruce Grant, one Frank Krist, one Jim Johnson. What matters is the uniqueness of those individual experiences, without which the human dimension of a fishery cannot be properly understood.

Beliefs, attitudes, and values depend on who you are, who you were, and how the passing of time influences your thoughts of the past and your considerations for the future. It's hard to argue that without the fishery the harbor would have been expanded—but was it worth it to upgrade the marina and thus incur that debt? That's a worthwhile question. But the marina—and the fishery, to a large degree—gave people something to be proud of, to be excited about, in the midst of the otherwise bleak products of progress—losses of jobs at Calcite, which caused people to move away, and which then led to impacts on other commercial entities. In so many ways, the fishery breathed life and energy into a struggling boomtown of yesteryear.

As the saying goes, you tend to regret the things you *didn't* do more than the things you did. As far as I can tell, the protagonists of the Rogers City salmon story are largely without regret. They *did it*, in Rogers City. It could be argued that it probably couldn't have been done any bigger. And they probably got as much good out of it as they could, although there was resistance. But the resistance was well founded. As Mary Ann Heidemann said, these are practical people. They're not going to make personally risky choices. Their hopes were tempered, and rightfully so. Yet the fishery declines—which so many people said were not foreseeable—happened. But perhaps things could have been a lot worse *without* the salmon fishery.

With respect to living in Rogers City, the reduced state of the salmon fishery after the crash was noticeable—but in a good or bad way? It's hard to ascertain, ultimately. It could be argued that fewer salmon, and fewer anglers, makes Rogers City more attractive as a place to live and fish. Jayme Warwick, Bruce Grant, Frank Krist, and Matt Hollabaugh, all anglers, hinted at this point at various times. While the boon of the fishing heyday had its benefits and was exciting, there's definitely something desirable about having the fishery, and the outdoors experience, more to oneself.

In my final analysis, the fishery was a positive cultural presence in the community. Economically, it provided a windfall. But the town was not built up around the recreational fishery to anywhere near the degree that it was built up, decades earlier, around the consumptive natural resource industries of the early to mid-twentieth century (commercial fishing, forestry, and limestone mining).

If there was a worst-case scenario regarding the community effects of the Lake Huron Chinook salmon fishery collapse, it would most likely be revealed seventy miles southeast down the shoreline in Harrisville. As Frank Krist said, Harrisville had "a thriving, bouncing fishery there and it just came to a complete end." Retired biologist Jim Johnson told me that there's "nothing left" in Harrisville. The parking lot, he described, used to be so full that, right before the salmon crash, they built a new tier of parking spaces (an "upper lot"). He said the upper lot has never been used and often the lower lot is empty. They went from twelve charters to zero. And Harrisville, like most of the other Lake Huron former salmon-fishing ports (besides Alpena), has a relatively small population size—it's hovered around about five hundred people for the past seventy years.

I bring up Harrisville to caution against any interpretation that the Lake Huron Chinook salmon fishery crash was "not that bad" in terms of its effect on Michigan's coastal communities. What I've discovered is that, if Harrisville might represent a worst-case scenario, then Rogers City must represent a best-case scenario (at least in terms of the Michigan waters of Lake Huron). They still have a solid fall Chinook salmon fishery and perhaps the best lake trout fishing between Lakes Huron and Michigan. And

I suspect that a relatively smaller segment of the population in Rogers City was professionally and financially dependent upon the salmon fishery. Like Harrisville and Rogers City, about a dozen Michigan ports used to be the major gateways for salmon fishing in Lake Huron, and they each have their own stories within the overarching narrative of Lake Huron alewife and salmon population dynamics.

Some of the stories from previous chapters reveal surprising ways in which the Chinook salmon fishery in Rogers City left its mark on the town (the band shell, for instance), as well as the reverberations it had throughout Great Lakes fisheries management (for example, the formation of the Lake Huron Citizens Fishery Advisory Committee and the negotiations of the 1985 and 2000 Consent Decrees). This chapter highlights many more of those personal reflections that the community members themselves had about the salmon fishery. Often the effects of the fishery, and how its legacy is thought about, point toward a shared narrative among several people. Yet while it is generally reflected upon favorably, conceptualizations of the salmon fishery's relative importance vary widely. On one hand, charter fishing guide and resort owner Bruce Grant argued that Rogers City should have a big statue of a Chinook salmon in town because, as he remembered, "the salmon brought the people here." In the same vein, retired harbormaster Ken Rasche called it "a big economic boon." But on the other hand, current mayor Scott McLennan had a more tempered perspective. He contended that, in terms of the economic impact, the loss of the salmon fishery has been "somewhat negligible." Of course, each person's views are shaped by their prior, current, and perceived future relationship to the fishery.

Unexpectedly, a couple of the people whom the salmon brought to Rogers City were Mary Ann Heidemann and her husband, Karl, in 1988. I met Mary Ann on a mid-June evening in Rogers City, at a picnic table under the Lakeside Park Pavilion, where I heard of her storied relationship to the salmon fishery—the "Salmon Frenzy" as she called it in our emails. The first of those stories, which she eagerly shared with me, was about her involvement in the planning of the proposed Rogers City marina expansion. Her story represents how the impacts of the fishery extended deep into the community—far beyond anglers. But her story is especially valuable because of the context it provides, which is an outsider's view of Rogers City at the time. And Mary Ann was certainly an outsider in many respects. She was a "big-city girl" in rural Rogers City; she was not an angler; and she was a highly educated, white-collar woman. This part of her interview is a lengthy opener but well worth the read.

MARY ANN HEIDEMANN: Well, I'll relate it immediately to your mission here—the mission is fishing, as a friend of mine likes to say. In
1988 I was working downstate for a large engineering firm. My profession is community planner, and especially environmental planning. So
that firm, Wade Trim and Associates, got a contract with the City of
Rogers City to investigate the possibility of expanding the boat harbor
here, because at the time there was a two- or three- or four-year waiting
list for slips because fishing was so good, everybody wanted a boat in
the harbor. And at that time the harbor was, mm, roughly eighty slips.
So Wade Trim was doing the engineering and I was sent up as a planner to do what they were calling—was an environmental scan, just to
look over the environmental issues of the nearshore environment and
the land part of the project to see if there was any deal-breaking issues
involved in that. And frankly I had never heard of Rogers City at the
time. I knew absolutely nothing about it. I worked in Wade Trim's office
in Taylor, Michigan. And at the time I was living in Orion Township.
But planners like to go to new places so I jumped in the car and came up
and started my research. And, you know, hey, I was a big-city girl, not
at all from a small town. Born and raised in Detroit. Had worked, gone
to school in Philadelphia, and graduate work in Madison, and worked
in New York, and worked in Chicago for a while, actually. So I was
not familiar with small-town environments. But it was kind of love at
first sight, it's such a beautiful little place. And of course the water was
incredible. And it was inhabited by, you know, not the Grosse Pointe
types, but real people, normal houses next to the water, and people
going about their daily lives with the lake in their lap, and I thought,
Wow, is this really interesting.

So I of course had to look at all aspects of the project. One of the
parts of the project that was related to fisheries but not quite was to
build some condominiums by the lake where people could have a boat
slip as well as having a condo or summer place, whatever. So the discussion at that time was expanding the harbor north, and at the time there
was a large hardware store and lumberyard on the shoreline. So that
property owner who was—that family was a very old family here, the
Vogelheims—they were cooperating in the project and he was going to
kind of try to make money off of it, and of course his property was ideal.
In addition to his property—he had the waterfront—but the backside

of the block was a block full of modest homes. But they were right by the lake. So as a good planner does I was investigating the real estate market because under federal law, if you're using federal monies, which this would in part do, you had to make sure if you displaced any persons from their homes—at that time you could in fact take property for a public purpose, which this certainly was a public purpose, so long as you paid fair market value. But you had to find out what fair market value was, so I was looking at prices and I just nearly fell off my chair because that whole block of homes, homes were valued at 10, 12, 13,000 dollars.

Now this isn't ancient history—I guess it is now, you're young, 1988—but you wouldn't be buying a house downstate for 12,000 bucks. And the very most expensive property, residential property, was a duplex for 30,000, so you had two units for 15 each. So I just really was amazed. And I went home and said to my husband Karl, "Karl, you've got to see this place. It's a really beautiful little town and they're giving away real estate. Maybe we can pick something up—," famous last words, "—for our retirement, because it's really fun." And my husband, you know Heidemann, not surprisingly he's pretty German, and the Vogelheims were pretty German, and little did I know that half the town was German, and the other half was Polish. So there was a certain cultural affinity, shall we say. So I did my work and there weren't any insurmountable problems, so my husband came up with me when the firm and myself presented the report to the city council. And while I'm presenting, he's standing in the back of the room chatting with the Vogelheims. [*both laugh*] And they're having a good old time, and we got to know that family right away. Well, that was a Thursday night as I recall, and we decided—we had our kids who were high school age at the time, and junior high, we had them stashed with a relative and we were just going to stay for the weekend and explore around because as I said we were not familiar with the area. So talking with John Vogelheim—all these Vogelheims have passed away since then—but John said, "Oh. If you're going to stay the weekend, you should drop by the high school on Friday night. We're having the home and garden show and our store, the hardware store's going to have a booth." So we said, "Oh, that's interesting."

So we went back to the hotel room, and it was slightly after 5, and my husband pulled out the phone book, and I said, "What are you doing, Karl?" Well, at the time he worked for Metropolitan Life Insurance down in Southfield, and he said, "Oh, I'm just looking to see if

Metropolitan Life had an office here." And he said, "Looks like nothing in Rogers City but they have an office down in Alpena. Well, that's too bad that it's after 5 and I can't talk to them." And I thought, *What do you have in your mind?*

So we freshened up and went over to the high school to the home and garden show—and I should back up a little ways, that was Friday, and we had spent Friday morning, after the presentation, tooting around town. And my husband and I, used to urban areas, we were always looking for urban concerns. So where are the slums? Where are the good neighborhoods? The bad neighborhoods? Well, there were no slums. Everything was absolutely—I'm not talking about wealthy homes, but everything was neat as a pin. So when he had been standing with the Vogelheims back at the back of the city council room, they had a big aerial photo of the town with maps, you know, street names impressed on it. And my husband spells Karl with a *K*. You know, the American would be *C*, of course. But Karl Vogelheim to whom he was speaking was also Karl with a *K*, so that was another bonding thing amongst Germans. So my husband's looking at the map and he sees Karl Street, and he said to Karl Vogelheim, "Oh, is that named after you?" He said, "No, that's my son Karl. And here's my daughter Veronica and my—and son John—," you know, all—his whole family were street names there in a subdivision on the north side. It turned out it was not developed, but we found that out because as we were exploring around town my husband sees a signpost that says Karl Street. Well, we had also been up and down Lake Street here and saw a couple houses for sale. And we saw a for-sale sign on a house that's a half a block there, that of course isn't on the water but it's on the park, and has incredible views across to the water.[1] And you've got the beach, absolutely gorgeous. So he says, "Mary Ann, write down that name of that realty company." So I'm beginning to get worried now because I was a professional woman with a good job at a major corporation and he seemed to me to be going nuts.

So alright, we're driving around and he sees this Karl sign. He says, "Oh, look, there's Karl Street, let's see where it goes." And it was a dirt road, not a developed street whatsoever. And as we proceeded, it was sandy and rutty, the vegetation kept getting closer and closer to the point where we couldn't turn around. So we were going forward, there's no way you could get out of there and we didn't know where we were. So finally I see some traffic down there, and it looks like it's U.S. 23. And I said, "Well, maybe we can get through." But to get out to the road we had to drive across somebody's backyard. Now, they had a hole in the back of the fence, which is a little bit strange, so you could get into the yard and out their driveway and out to the road. So you don't like to get arrested in a town where you're working but what could we do? So we're kind of creeping through the yard, and we look to the side, and here it is that home was used also for a commercial purpose, it was a real estate office, and they had their sign out. And my husband said, "Mary Ann, isn't that the name of the real estate company that had this house listed?" And I said, "Yeah, I guess it is." And so he pulled us in, and we go into the real estate firm and look for the house listings. And here on a bulletin board they have all the listings, in money order. So the bottom row is listings in the ten thousands, and the next row is the twenty thousands, and the third row is really expensive houses—thirty and up. And the house we had seen was in the top row so really, really expensive, right? It was unbelievable.

So pretty soon the agent sees my husband's interest, and he [Karl Heidemann] said, "Oh, yeah, we saw this house. [We'd] be interested in knowing about it." So she pulls out a stack of photos of the inside—now, mind you, I said he worked for Metropolitan Life Insurance. He was an attorney for Metropolitan Life, and he handled the higher-end assets and investments and so forth, and the financial insurance tools. So now the lady's showing him the inside: this is a bedroom, here's the kitchen, living room—and here is the office. And, "Mr. Heidemann, what is your profession?" And he said, "Well, I'm an attorney." And she said, "That's interesting because there's a full law office in the house. The gentleman who lived there was an attorney and saw his clients in the home. Didn't you notice there's two front doors?" Well, we just noticed the back side. The front side on First Street has one door to the office and one to the house. Well, my husband is now totally in fantasy land, and he's now got a dream, and he's pursuing it, so hence his looking for Metropolitan Life offices. So I said, "Oh, that's too bad, Karl. That's really too bad. Well, let's go up to the home and garden show."

So we go up to the high school gym, which is where it was, and we go up to the entry door, and who should be standing at the entry door but John Vogelheim, our old friend from yesterday. And he's like, hail fellow well met with my husband and they're chitchatting, and he says, "Well, go on in. We have our booth right here. What have you been doing today?" And Karl tells him about seeing the house. And of course John asks him, "Well, what are they asking for the place?" And Karl tells him and he says, "*Oh*, that's way too much! Yeah, when that guy died his kids didn't want the place, so their uncle bought it. But the uncle's got health problems and he's got a place in Florida. He's got too much real estate. They just really want to unload it. You know, bring your offer down." And so my husband's nodding, thinking about that. So we go into the gym, and we go down the aisle past the hardware booth, turn the corner, and here's a Metropolitan Life booth, and the regional manager of the company is there, and so my husband and he are now exchanging cards and discussing the possibility of Karl coming up and working out of the Alpena office of Metropolitan Life. So I'm seeing my entire [*Carson laughs*] professional career going—and I brought him up here. [*laughs*]

So, alright, we had a great time. We went down to Presque Isle, we met more people. I mean, we just had a fabulous weekend. So then we go back home and reality comes back. And since we had gone up together—you know, lawyers don't have to go to work early, but planners do. Engineers, by god, they start at 8, were going to be there. So we had shared a ride, and I had left my car at my office and he'd picked me up, so now he had to take me at 7 in the morning on Telegraph Road downriver to Taylor, a scene he had never seen. And of course—what do they call it? Bloody Road, or I don't know. It was horrible then, it probably still is. People cutting you off and road rage and, you know, terrible traffic jams and just awful, because it's not that far but it takes a good hour in traffic to get there. And he says, "Mary Ann, is it always like this?" I said, "Yeah, it's pretty much like this." He says, "I don't know what we're doing down here. We should make an offer on that house in Rogers City." [*laughs*] I said, "Sure, Karl." [*laughs*] So he does. He makes an offer ridiculously low, 20 grand less than they were asking. And the real estate agent said, "Oh, I can't present that to the client. That's way too low, they're never going to accept that." And Karl says, "Present it anyway. See what they say." Well they accepted the offer. And a month later we are living here in Rogers City, *because of the salmon*.

DAVE NADOLSKY: For a while the harbor was our front door rather than being the back door, and we got a number of residents here that were retired Flint or Detroit executives that came up and purchased houses, they got big bang for their buck. They could leave their boat in the harbor. They might have fished, they might have just recreational boated. And they were excellent citizens for the community because they came from that post–World War II generation where they believed strongly in civic involvement so they became chairman of this, and the chairman of that, and even though they weren't working because they were retired, they had a lot of spare time on their hands and they were valuable members of the community, to churches, you know, everything else.

BRUCE GRANT: I think that one of the biggest assets that's buried and is unforeseen in our community was the real estate companies. And we just about had—we only had one real estate company—individual that owned the real estate company was Real Estate One, Bill Petz—he would do anything that he could to back the fishermen that were raising money. But the people were coming here fishing, staying, buying property. And they weren't building cabins. Their second homes were better than the homes they lived in downstate in metropolitan Detroit or Lansing or whatever. And I could right now take you from the city limits of Rogers City out to the Ocqueoc River, which is about a fourteen-mile stretch, and show you millions of dollars in homes and real estate that are here only because of the fishery. And other than the one real estate guy, they were the hardest people to convince but profited the most. Or they just kept their mouths shut and reaped in the benefits. But I mean, we've got housing here now that's totally different than it used to be. And shoreline footage on Lake Huron right here—when I came here it was about 175 to 200 dollars a running foot. Today it's—even after the 2008 recession and what we're going through now—and it's at a low scale right now—it's low at 15, and average about 1,700 dollars a foot. That's because of the fishery. It isn't because somebody drove over here and said, "Oh, what a beautiful sunrise." The fishery brought them here. And I think our community—me, I'd have a big statue in town of a Chinook salmon, not a—alongside the propeller—the propeller down there. The big brass propeller is important. But I feel like Kalkaska [Michigan] did. They knew their trout brought their people there. A lot of us know the salmon brought the people here. And it provided a lot of jobs. A lot of jobs. And we had some county commissioners and some city people that were on top of it, but they still fought a balance issue of, Oh, we don't want to go that far, or, We can't put out that much money for next year. But the people were coming.

FRANK KRIST: Well, yeah, I had a unique situation because I was communicating with people throughout the county and sometimes beyond because we're a four-county health department. And so I got out and met a lot of these people. Of course some people knew me just because of my involvement and stuff like that. People like to talk about, "Yeah, we were up here—." And then of course through our association we got members from the different communities, they know the people that live in their communities, and you begin to realize this is a lot bigger than what you normally hear: Well, yeah, it only helps the bait shop, the motel room, and that's it, maybe a restaurant or two. But it went way beyond that. And just like construction business—people come up here and if the fishing's good, they might come up four or five times a year and their cabin, well, the first thing they want is, Hey, that needs to be fixed. We've got to get a new roof on there. We want it more convenient. Next thing you know some of them are building a new home. And if that's your goal is to keep your community up—it's one nice thing about Rogers City, we've been all over the country and I can't find a place that I would rather live than here just because—and people have different attitudes—but it's quiet, there's very little crime, and it's nice and clean. People keep up with stuff. And you like to see it maintained. You don't want it to go so far backwards that you're not a city anymore. So we felt this would be real helpful and it was.

KEN RASCHE: So it's too bad. It really helped, well, like the motels, the restaurants, stuff like that, it helped dramatically. Growing up where I did, Rogers City was—when Barb and I got married, which was fifty-six years ago tomorrow, okay—
CARSON: Oh. Congrats. [*laughs*]
KEN: —it was about forty-two hundred people. When I started working down at Calcite—I started two days after graduation—there was about six hundred people working there, okay? Now there's about a hundred. I don't know if the salmon industry would have—or, the salmon would have stayed in Lake Huron, would that have made the business in Rogers City better? I think we're now down to like twenty-eight hundred people. There's no more big families. It's changing dramatically.

JAYME WARWICK: You know, I had another thought with how it—the king salmon–fishing brought people from other places. I know people that would come up in their boats and live in their boats for the whole salmon season. They wouldn't get a motel or anything, they had a big enough boat they'd sleep in their little cuddy cabin. There's a couple friends of mine that did it. And they're from downstate—different states. And they lived in their boat. Retired guys, they come up—and there's still a couple that do it—but they would just live in their boat. They call their wives up, "Yeah, maybe I'll come down next weekend, but it looks like the weather's good." Next thing you know, they're up [the wives]. And they buy a house in Rogers City for the salmon fishing. There was a lot of people that did that. And Hammond Bay, we talk about Hammond Bay harbor, up through there there's cabins all along the shoreline up there. People were buying them. Couple friends I'm thinking of down in the thumb area, they had cabins up here because they would come up in the later fall and stay here for weeks. They sold them and moved on out. But there's people that would move here just for the salmon fishery. And now it isn't as good, and some are a little older now, and different priorities, but they had sold and left. Now if that fishery was still good and like the heyday or better, whatever, I don't know, would they still be here, you wonder. That was just another afterthought that I had.

CARSON: Yeah. Yeah, I've never heard of that. People just sleeping on their boats.

JAYME: These guys, some of them—

CARSON: What'd they do with all their fish? [*laughs*]

JAYME: They'd clean them at the harbor. They'd clean them and they had freezers for them, or have friends that would freeze the fish. And when they'd go down back home to the wife they'd take a bunch of fish down. But yeah, these guys were sixty, seventy years old sleeping in their boats, getting up in the morning while I'm going to work, and they're going out fishing. Some of them by their selves. Three of them that I know would mostly fish by themselves. And come in. If they want to go out in the evening, they would. But usually they'd fish the mornings. But yeah, they had the showers right there. The restaurants around. And they had their vehicles here if they wanted to go on a little tour. And they had a place to sleep. And they had fishing. [*both laugh*] Yeah. It's kind of unique. But it goes to show you—and some of them, there's only a couple left that do it, but—and years ago in the heyday there was more of them people that would live right in their boat all summer. It's kind of neat.

TOM ALLUM: Interesting, there's—a guy came up from Ohio, some part of Ohio, I don't know exactly where—about a ten-hour drive from here, maybe, you know, ten-hour—and he comes up every year, name of his boat is *Buckeye Bill*, and he rents a slip for a whole summer. And he lives on his twenty-six-foot boat. Uses the shower, and the—. He eats his breakfast on his boat and then he goes to the restaurant for lunch and dinner and he does that for six or eight weeks every summer. His brother-in-law came at the same time ten, fifteen years ago, and he and his wife bought a house in town. Turleys. Do you know who—I, you know, the Turleys. Bob Turley. And there was another guy, Joe, who came up from Indiana or somewhere and bought a house. But those are really the exceptions, and you know they were single guys that live on a boat, in a small fishing boat, in a sleeping bag for six weeks in a summer. That's kind of an unusual situation. But the guy, the one, Turley, doesn't hardly fish anymore. He doesn't take a slip anymore because there's no more salmon. He hates to catch lake trout. He remembers what it was like in the old days when you could catch big salmon.

DAVE SMRCHEK: We had a few people that, during the heyday, came and they bought property, built houses. Young retirees from downstate that came up here. A lot of them are still here. They're not fishing nearly as much as they used to be. They're my age or older. But they—it's just too late for them to move on.

FRANK KRIST: Then a lot of the businesses—it's too bad—oh, I forget his name. The guy up there at the motel.
CARSON: Rich?
FRANK: Yeah, Rich Hamp. He would have been a good one. [*laughs*] He didn't want to talk to you.
CARSON: Well, I called him a few times. And he would talk to me. And then you'd try to nail him down for an interview and he'd, "Oh, I don't have time," or, "Oh, I don't want to—." He was—
FRANK: Colorful. Very outspoken.
CARSON: He was very outspoken. [*laughs*] Yeah.
FRANK: He had a swimming pool and I was up there inspecting it at least once a year—
CARSON: Yeah, he told me that.
FRANK: —and he was always talking about the fishery and stuff. Things like that.
CARSON: Well, it really influenced him. I mean, that's why—
FRANK: You can see—
CARSON: —he left. Yeah.

FRANK: —yeah. Yeah. And the motels, we had North Star went out of business. And some of the other motels haven't done nearly as well. Like I say, it did impact building. For a while I worked with the health department. Our building permits went down even more. And yeah, it had an impact that way.

BRUCE GRANT: It's very easy—you've got to have discipline—it's very easy to sort your crowd. When we were in our peak they were letting rooms go for 13 bucks a night. Why the heck do you want to let a room go for 13 bucks? It cost me—we put a girl, when I had the motel—we put two girls in there for forty-five minutes [to clean a room], I've got 20 bucks spent. And 13 bucks a night you can't clean a room. You can't make it healthy for the next person. But all a guy would have to do is say, "He just gave me 15 bucks across the street. You want 29?" "Okay, I'll do it for—." "Well, I like this place better for 15." "Okay, I'll do it for 13." This happened all the time. It's not good. I mean, it's not good.
CARSON: I spoke with Rich Hamp. I haven't done an interview with him.
BRUCE: Well, he's in Colorado now.
CARSON: Yeah. But he kind of had a different approach it sounds like, because—
BRUCE: He was a 13-dollars-a-night guy.
CARSON: Yeah, yeah. So his business would be booming July, August, September, and then that was 60 percent of his—
BRUCE: And that's who he had is that guy that'd come up here to fish—his wife didn't want him to go in the first place—he spent the weekend, bought a lot of beer, and went home and argued all week. We were just as busy all through deer season. All through snowmobile season. We've got a lot of cross-country ski trails here. We have the same people in January, February. The only time we shut down is in March when the frost comes out of the ground and the big high snowbanks melt because it's just a muddy mess. And I never wanted asphalt because I want people to come up and have the northern experience—that's what we went on. We weren't short of people because they didn't mind—and if they only stayed for a weekend in the wintertime when a lot of them wouldn't take a full week—we charged a couple hundred bucks a night. They only got a break when they took a full week. We'd have a waiting list. But we had different clientele. Most of the people that stayed with us paid a high price, and if they drive by, now that we're shut down, they

stop by to visit. He doesn't even know who his customers were. Price separates—I'm not saying the good from the bad—you need a place for the guy that can't afford to pay 100 bucks a night—but the part that gets me about the guys like Rich—he's a wonderful guy, too, don't get me wrong—they need to go to Alpena, Oscoda, Traverse City, Charlevoix, or Petoskey—you can't get a room for—on the weekend price goes up, through the week the price goes down because they rely on businesspeople. Or, I mean, yeah, through the week the price goes up, weekend it goes down. But you're not going to get a room over there for less than 79, 89 dollars a night.[2] Another thing you might put in that—I'm against what the communities do—you have a lodging group that bring people—and they're the people that go out and advertise and draw the people. A big problem we had here in Rogers City, and in the county—and right now it's infestive, it's cancer—letting people rent their cottages out. I'm not against somebody renting their cottage out. But I'm against making me put up with Frank Krists at the health department. "How's your water? How's your room?" We've had people leave here, go down the street, rent a cottage for the next summer for a week, come back and say, "Can we get our date—," because if you stayed the first week of August for the [Nautical] Festival, you were the first one—if you told us by January 1st, you got next year, the same week. If you lost it, you started back over in May to get back up to your week. They rent a cottage that, "Oh, the silverware's full of mouse turds. The linens have got spots all over them." And the people are renting their cottages and their homes out to make the payments on them. No health department checks. And here's what'd kill us. They'd pull in here. Somebody would buy a cottage down the beach. I used to snowplow. They go, "Would you snowplow for us?" Because I did all these cottages. When the people would come up, "Yeah, I'll snowplow for you." "Oh, by the way, we might rent our cottage out. If you get overflow, would you give it to us?" I will if you go register at the chamber of commerce and pay their dues. I will if you show me a certificate of insurance, that you got insurance other than homeowners'. And you charge 6 percent sales tax. And 2 percent bed tax that we had. Now we're competitive, right? But don't come get my price list at 12–1,500 bucks a week and then drop yours down 200 bucks, and you don't have to live to any of these standards that I do, and we're bringing the people here, and you're stealing our customers. And then we went through the thing of they'd sit in the driveway out here at 5 o'clock in the afternoon and stop our girls wanting to know if they'd clean the cabin for cash. That's cancer.

CARSON: Was that more of a problem when there were more people coming for fishing?

BRUCE: It started then. I would go in the cleaning station to clean my fish and all on the bulletin board is a sticker up there. Rip this tag off with this phone number. We have an apartment that we rent for the weekend. Right along by the harbor there. Then it was the whole house for the summer. I mean, it's crazy. But they didn't charge sales tax, didn't have to charge the bed tax—that's 8 percent right there that puts us out of the ballpark. But what made me mad, really mad—back then it was 1,200 bucks a week, they'd rent a place for 400 bucks a week. They're leaving a lot under the table. But what made my wife and I stick to it is, everybody that left came back. And it's so foolish. We're right here—especially my wife—and the people that stayed here for three or four years are walking by the beach. You know, walking the—don't want you to know they're staying down the road. And then pretty soon they'd come back and, "Can we get—can we book again?" Oh, this happened time after time. Other thing you have to be careful of—I go back to the same thing with real estate. Somebody would ask you about a piece of property. You knew somebody in real estate who was fairly honest, and you give them their name and they go into the office, maybe that person wasn't there. They picked the people up here and show them a piece of property and say, "Hey, I've got some other—if you can't get in there or don't like it there, I've got a list of other cottages." They got a percentage of renting out some of these cottages. We went to the county and tried to get them to do an ordinance. Went to the city and tried to do the ordinance. They wouldn't talk to us. When I really got into it I found out that half the people on the county commission were renting their cottages out, and the people on the city boards were doing it. It's a cancer.

CARSON: How much of a part of the culture of Rogers City was fishing and salmon fishing, maybe going from the late '80s, '90s, and then how that might have changed until more recent years?

JOHN BRUNING: Well, I think it was more a part of the culture then, when it was booming, than it is now. Just on proportion of mass and activity, I guess. I don't know, because I was so immersed in it, at least in that late '80s period, that it was definitely a part of me and what I did. How far that reached into the community, I'm not really certain.

Certainly there were others that benefited from it and recognized that—the hotel industry, the restaurants, and so forth—so certainly it had influence. But I don't know, I really don't know how—. It's difficult for me to say, I guess, from my perspective because I was so close to it. If I didn't step back and say, "Well, how did this affect somebody else?" I'd say, "Well, this was everything," because at that point I was really involved with it. It was important, I think, and I think people beyond the fishermen recognized it and felt it and maybe depended on it a little bit, but I don't know to what degree it was.

CARSON: With respect to the economic impact of the fishery, and then the marina that was built there in 1996—or I should say expanded in 1996—how important is the fishery and the marina and the water resources there for the local economy?

SCOTT MCLENNAN: So at the moment, the fishery part of it is really minimal. There's not—so in the '90s, as an example, all through the '90s, some of the '80s and into the '90s, all through the '90s, people would travel from the west side of the state to Rogers City to fish. And they'd shop here. They would fish. They would stay overnight. So that had quite an economic impact. That doesn't happen now because the fishing hasn't come back to the degree that it would warrant them driving from, say, Boyne City, Petoskey, Gaylord. You don't see too much of that. Little bit is starting, but not much. So that—we're not seeing that just yet. Now, the harbor itself, though, is a hugely important piece of infrastructure for the city of Rogers City, and here's why: not only does it have its inherent beauty—I mean, you just love going down there and walking, and as you said, it was reconstructed and added on in the '90s and it's a great little marina—but it also attracts boats coming up and down the Lake Huron shoreline that pull in. They come in. They spend money. They fuel up. And fuel is a good way for us to pick up some money that supports the harbor. This particular year is projected to be our best year in the last ten or more years. We already have—I checked with the harbormaster yesterday and he said we have fifteen new boaters this year that—already, that—they just are coming in. They've never stayed here with us before, they've never slipped here. But they're renting a slip for the season and they will boat out of Rogers City. Well, that's a big deal, and it means that our marina is making a bit of a comeback. Now, some of those people will be fishermen, but the majority of them will be pleasure boaters and sailboats.

Mary Ann Heidemann: Now, you have to remember that the tournament is not an economy, so the town didn't rely, for all its daily bread, on the tournament, but it was a huge boost to local businesses. Meanwhile, there were lots of other economic problems in this community. You know that we have the largest limestone mine in the world, but it had been, when we moved, just sold by its longtime owner of U.S. Steel. And U.S. Steel was quite a sugar daddy. They were very generous to the town. The wages were phenomenal. All kind of benefits, for instance—well I guess it relates to fishing too—the woods and waters of the quarry property could be used by employees, so a lot of guys deer-hunted—

Carson: Oh, I didn't know that.

Mary Ann: —on the quarry property. That stopped at some point after they sold it, but it really meant a lot to people here. And also, the quarry company built housing for its employees because when they started, there really wasn't much here as a town. So if you wanted to have a guy come up, a mining engineer or something, and bring his family, they needed someplace to live, so the firm built a lot of housing and that housing stayed owned by the quarry company until well into the '60s. And then it was sold—if the people who were living in it wanted to buy it they could, otherwise it went on the market. So a good third of the housing stock here is left from that heritage. So why am I even bringing this up? At the time when the salmon was a big deal, the town was really afraid because U.S. Steel had just dumped them, and they had no idea what would happen in the future and whether there would be jobs, or there would be an economy. So in a lot of ways they were grabbing at the salmon straw as something that could bring a future.

Scott McLennan: So I was gone for ten or eleven years and then did come back in the mid-'90s. That's exactly right. And I was very excited about being able to come back to Rogers City. I was very excited about that because I loved Rogers City. I found in traveling other places that the natural resources—that's really what drew me back to my hometown. Everything is so relative. You grow up here thinking this is the way it is out there in the world. Well, no, it's not. This is a very special and unique environment here in Rogers City. So I excitedly built a home in Rogers City. Moved my family back. But as we—as I came back to my hometown I noticed that things were actually very different. The amount of traffic was way down. The amount of young people on the streets and up and around were—just, the numbers were just so down. I grew up here at a time when my graduating class was about 180 students. The class ahead of me was a little bit larger than that. The classes behind me were also large classes. And in recent years, I know the classes are about forty-five students—the graduating classes—compared to our one-eighty. So the population from 1970 here in Rogers City had steadily declined from a high of about forty-eight hundred people down to today's twenty-seven hundred people. And what we're seeing is the majority of those people—in that decline—is younger people. So all of the homes today in Rogers City are sold. As soon as a home comes on the market, it's sold. But it's sold to either a single individual or a couple who are retiring here—they love the area, they love going for walks and spending time on the bike trail and the beach. So when I came back to Rogers City in the mid-'90s, it was very noticeable that there wasn't the vibrancy that there once was. There wasn't the activity and the excitement. Back when I grew up, Thursday evenings meant the stores were open. That was the time that—Thursday nights you cash your check and everyone would be downtown, buying groceries and going in and out of the stores. Well, no more Thursday nights now. They stopped that. There just wasn't enough traffic. So in terms of the fishing industry, when I came back in the mid-'90s it was still going on. In fact, a fun part of that is that I have a very good friend—one of my best friends—and he has a great boat for salmon fishing, for the Great Lakes, and we would start going out again. So that was fun. And we would do fairly well. But I would say, "Wow, we're catching quite a few lake trout." Yeah. It had changed. It used to be all salmon. I don't even recall—I don't recall, honestly, catching lake trout back in the day. But we did catch lots of salmon. Now it was kind of a mix, when I got back in the '90s, of salmon and lake trout.

JOE HEFELE: So our goals, really, are just getting as many people to come within our city as possible to see what we're all about. And we hope that they will fall in love with us and we hope that they not only will come back for a second or third vacation but they'll choose at some point to say, "You know, I'd like to be in Rogers City or near Rogers City." The fishery has always been a giant part of that because the lake has always been a giant part of that. We're well off of any major interstate, but we are on Lake Huron and we have as much shoreline and—public shoreline in Rogers City and Presque Isle County as about anybody in the state of Michigan. And this community, in terms of taking advantage of that asset, that shoreline, it's always been fisheries first. But from my youth, like a lot of people, I have fond memories of, not only the marina itself being full, and basically full of fishing boats, but of various tournaments including the large salmon tournament that just brought so many people including professional fishermen with all of the stickers all over the boats, into our community. And it just created an energy. It just created an energy that right now we're quite honestly in the process of determining how to get back. So the fishery brought the energy, and that's always how it was, and just, again, both locally and with visitors, just brought a vibrancy that we don't quite have since the fishery has become more diminished.

DAVE SMRCHEK: So then when things started to go away, with the mussels and every—the fishery just started to decline—they didn't really, well, they didn't really seem to care if it went away or not. There was people that were almost glad you didn't have all these boat trailers up and down the streets and everything.

SCOTT McLENNAN: Yeah, I would say that the loss of the salmon fisheries is something that is very important to the group that loves to go out and sportfish. But in terms of the economic impact, I think it's—it might be an exaggeration to say "negligible," but it's somewhat negligible, I would say. The sportsfishing—so if you think about sportsfishermen as a whole, so when they're coming into Rogers City, they already have a full tank of gas that they've—you know, because they've prepared—let's say they're coming from Gaylord, which was not uncommon back in the day. So they—"Joe, we're heading out after work tonight. I'll have the boat ready to go. All we have to do is back up and away we go." Their tank is full. Their fuel tank—their gas tank is full. Their boat is full of gas. They drive over to Rogers City. They already have their sandwiches in their coolers, and maybe even some brown bottles of some substance to drink while they're out there out on the lake. They pull in, they go out, they fish. They take some pictures afterwards by the Rogers City harbor sign. They laugh a little bit. They toast each other. They get in their vehicle and away they go. So in terms of the economic impact on the community, as it relates to the fishing industry, no, I don't think that there was ever any real—when the fishing industry, the sportsfishing industry, dropped—I don't think that it had a significant impact on the other losses in the community. Our losses in Rogers City are more related to the automation, mechanization, of the limestone quarry that provided many hundreds of jobs. There was that. The loss of our local hospital, which also then lost lots of jobs. A number of professional people that were gone due to that. Then kind of that domino effect of then losing some retail businesses as a result of declining population. So it was more that. But is sportsfishing and—was sportsfishing and is sportsfishing important to the residents of this area? Yes. It is. Not so much on an economic level, though.

CARSON: Okay.

JOE HEFELE: I can just tell you that the numbers alone—I mean, obviously I wasn't the city manager at the time, but during my late high school and early college years I actually worked for the city in the public works department pulling graphs and doing that type of thing, and my brother was working at the marina, and having now been the manager I can see the sheer numbers of fuel sales, and boat slip sales, and all of those things versus what they are now, and it's night and day. Again, a lot of the folks that are still around today are here specifically because of that marina. They're not all here specifically because of the Chinook salmon sportsfishery, but a lot of them that are not native here, that are not generational from Rogers City, have come specifically because of that facility.

CARSON: I'm wondering if you can say how true what I'm about to put out there is. It seems to me like without the history of the recreational fishery starting in the mid-'80s and in the early '90s, you wouldn't have exactly the same marina situation that you have now. It seems like the fishery contributed greatly to the marina expansion in 1996. Would you say that's true?

JOE: I think there's absolutely no question about it. So the marina's the harbor of refuge. But I would say, in Michigan, or in northern Michigan, the west side of the state has a lot of sailboats. The powerboaters kind of come and go and there are some powerboaters and a few sailboaters over here, but by and large that marina has thrived and expanded, without any question, on the fishery and on the fishermen. It's been that way, I think, as long as it's existed. And it's actually gone through two expansions since it was originally built, including the one that you just mentioned, and there's just no question in my mind that just absolutely was not going to happen without the fishery. Again, when you have waiting lists, and work in that type of command, and that thing, again, was making so much revenue that I understand now that the city was actually siphoning money out and using that to help do sidewalks and streets and everything else because it was such a surplus. And so it made sense to continue to expand and at that point it looked like the party was never going to end, the Chinook were thriving and from year to year there was no real change in it. But yeah, Carson, I just think it's absolutely, absolutely the truth without any question whatsoever.

KEN RASCHE: But I did enjoy it, you know, fished. We had friends from down below, we had friends from out west, we had—everybody came to Rogers City. And it was probably the hotspot on the Great Lakes for ten years. It was.

CARSON: So much so that that was a big driver in the marina upgrade and—? Yeah.

KEN: Definitely. Definitely. And it was very financially beneficial to the marina, okay? Yes, you don't sell as much gasoline to a fishing boat quite simply because they fill it up on their trailer on their way in. They fill it up at a gas station because it's cheaper. I understand that. But you still get the dockage. The town gets a spinoff. They go up the street, they buy alcohol, they buy food, restaurants, things like that. And so everybody benefited from it. They really did. So it was a big plus. You know, like Bruce Grant. He's got that resort out there. I don't know if he rents stuff anymore. Is it closed, or what?

CARSON: Not anymore.

KEN: But I mean, I think that he had a waiting list for people trying to rent there to go—and Bruce himself chartered, okay? So I think at one time we had probably four or five charters in the harbor, and a couple that went off their trailers. But they were having, as this thing, the salmon fishing was going down, they were having a rough time making a living too.

SCOTT MCLENNAN: So, back in the '80s, '90s, there was a lot of powerboating. Yachts. [laughs] You know, yachts. And they're big. They consume a lot of fuel. And they would dock in Rogers City. They pump in a couple thousand gallons of fuel. That is a way that it really supported our marina. Back in those days, when we did expand the marina—I don't have the exact numbers, so I would tell you that we currently have something in the area of eighty-five to ninety slips. And that was expanded to that because we needed more dockage for the number of boats we were getting back then.

CARSON: But have you seen a change in the local economy with respect to the Chinook salmon fishery? And whatever demands on the local economy, or different aspects of that that people coming here to fish put on things?

JAYME WARWICK: The big thing I notice is just the motels and hotels in the area, just a lot barer in the time when salmon fishing would start, you know, and really—towards the end of June, first part of July is when the kings would start showing up here. And you'd see the people come in, and they were full through the summer—especially in the fall. The hotel—they were just packed full of vehicles with trailers on them bringing their own boats. There was charter captains back then, charter boats here. Now there isn't one charter boat out of Rogers City. There's other people that will trailer that are from Alpena area, charter boats that will trailer up here if people want to, but for the most part there's nobody running besides maybe one part-time guy out of Rogers City right now. And for, I imagine, the restaurants and everything else—I've never seen any businesses go bankrupt, so to speak, because of the salmon decline, but it had to hurt them. Absolutely.

KEN RASCHE: You know, it was a real economic boom. I—certainly, I don't think you can fault the DNR. I think these exotic species—first of all the alewife was a problem, then you had the zebra mussels. I don't know. I don't think you can—you can't lay the blame on anybody. It's—I know the DNR would have never predicted it. Maybe we should have recognized it sooner, I'm not sure. Had we recognized it sooner and stopped planting as many fish as we did, maybe it would have lasted a little bit—maybe it would have ended up being more like Lake Michigan, where the alewife population is still there to some degree. From what I understand Lake Michigan may be running into the same problem that we are, and a lot of it I think has to do with Wisconsin. They are still planting a lot of fish. So I don't know, Carson. It was fun while it lasted. I'll put it that way. It was a real economic driver for our area. Like anything else there's good parts of it, bad parts of it. I think the good far outweighed the bad. From my standpoint, it made my job tougher. But I didn't have to stay there. I could have walked away anytime I wanted to.

CARSON: The legacy's more—at least, from your perspective, more of something like, That was a really awesome thing to have experienced—

KEN: Yeah, it was.

CARSON: —and it's not so much like, Oh, man, I wish we could go back to that time—not so much?

KEN: Oh, no. No. No. I don't think I would. I don't think I would want to go back to it. Even now. Of course, maybe I'm saying that selfishly, I shouldn't—. I'm living far enough away from it that it wouldn't affect me one way or another. But it would be good for the city if it happened again. I think I would—if I had a wish, I think, I would wish that the DNR would concentrate more on getting like a walleye fishery or something here. It's not as exciting a fish, but it's a nice fun fish to catch too.

CARSON: You wouldn't really—I would say you wouldn't want it to be what it was—

BRUCE GRANT: Never.

CARSON: —in the '80s or '90s.

BRUCE: No, because like I say, look at the problems you have with too many people.

CARSON: So if you put yourself in the perspective of somebody who's not from Rogers City and wasn't here to experience what the fishery was, I'm wondering what you think is the more accurate legacy. Is it the story of a collapse and then thinking about having to recover or wanting to go back toward some previous state? Or is it more like just remembering and feeling like, Oh, that was awesome to take part in this great fishery that was here, and thankful for having had that? Or is it somewhere in between?

JAYME WARWICK: Yeah. I'm thankful for having that memory. We're never going to have that fishery again. Just the way the invasive species are and everything. And I look at it—I'm glad to experience it and have it, and through the years, seeing what happened, I kind of look at it—it is what it is. But I'm really hoping the DNR can focus more on Rogers City than I think they are, but like I say I'm not any type of expert. It's just my own opinion on things. We don't have the people here. We don't have the voices or the money. But I just wish they could at least keep it the way it is. And I'm thankful for what we have, for sure, the type of fishery, because it is a good mixed-bag fishery. We're catching walleyes now, like you said earlier. Atlantic salmon. Lake trout. Steelhead. Then the kings, of course. And you can go out there, right now, you can go out and fish and catch some steelhead and lake trout. We used to have a brown trout fishery, also, that's went to the wayside.

CARSON: I don't know how to say this, but because the salmon fishing went away it's not like it created this void in Rogers City?

TOM ALLUM: I don't think so, because the people that are still here, there's a few of them that fish for salmon. Like I said, maybe forty boats on a good season. That's not a lot of people. I don't think the salmon fishing is—if it were recoverable it would be great for people that like to fish, and it might be, again, great for the economy on a limited basis, but that's not going to do much for the employees at Calcite who don't work anymore, and the other employment situation. Dave [Nadolsky] and I were talking the other day and there's an old analogy of a circus coming to town. And with proper advance notice and so on, and posters on the telephone poles and so on, "Big circus coming to town," everybody gets excited about it. And pretty soon you see the first elephant come, and the circus starts to set up, and it's fantastic. Best thing that the kid had ever seen. But then eventually the circus folds its tent and moves on to the next town, and the circus is gone, okay? So when I think of the salmon fishing, it's kind of that same analogy—it was great while it was here, but it didn't stay. And it would be nice if it could come back, but I don't think it ever will.

8

LAKE TROUT CAPITAL?

By now it's clear that in the absence of alewife, the Lake Huron Chinook salmon fishery largely disappeared. Almost overnight, the collapse of alewife in Lake Huron had a cascade of effects on the ecology of many other fish species as well. Perhaps unexpectedly (since lake trout happily feed on them when they're available), the collapse of alewife was actually hugely beneficial for lake trout in Lake Huron, and this has no doubt contributed to the thriving lake trout–fishing opportunities available in Rogers City in recent years. Before presenting the perspectives of Rogers City community members on lake trout, I'll try first to unfold the complicated ecological backstory of lake trout in Lake Huron—a history lesson that dates back only slightly further than that of the Rogers City salmon story.

Over the years, lake trout in Lake Huron have had a lot of things working against them. For our story's sake, we'll start in the mid-twentieth century, at which point lake trout had been essentially extirpated from all the Great Lakes except Lake Superior. Such were the days during which John Bruning's dad would have said, "The lake wasn't good for anything more than a darn cold swim." In Lake Huron, the downward path to that near-extirpation seems to have started with commercial overfishing in the first half of the 1900s.[1] However, the invasions of Lake Huron by two fish species native to the Atlantic Ocean would ultimately prove to be the primary problems for Lake Huron lake trout.

The two invasive species of note were sea lamprey and alewife, and it would seem they worked in tandem to wreak havoc on lake trout both young and old. As I'll describe, in an ecosystem abundant with sea lamprey and alewife, if a lake trout was fortunate enough to avoid fatal parasitism by sea lamprey and reach sexual maturity, its offspring were almost sure to suffer an early fate due to alewife-imposed ill effects.

I'll start with sea lamprey, whose long snake-like bodies are similar in appearance to those of eels. Their skin is a mottled dark olive-brown on black. But unlike eels, which have top and bottom jaws that they can open and close, allowing them to feed like most other fishes, sea lamprey exhibit a more primitive trait in that they are jawless. Their mouths actually consist of a relatively large, toothy, circular disc, which they use to latch onto larger-bodied host fishes. They ultimately parasitize their hosts by using their sharp tongues to rasp a hole into the host's flesh and subsequently feed on its blood. As sea lamprey proliferated in their new landscape—one to which they'd gained access via man-made canals bypassing Niagara Falls—they found a naïve and vulnerable prey in the soft-skinned lake trout. Presented with this new stressor to which they were not adapted, lake trout succumbed (as did many other native Great Lakes fish species) to the extent that today, sea lamprey are regarded as the primary factor in the near-extirpation of Lake Huron lake trout populations.[2]

And if such a fate wasn't fearful enough, a more insidious predicament would be imposed on lake trout by alewife, that silvery herring species that largely supported the Chinook salmon fishery. The scenes described in earlier chapters portrayed how, in the absence of lake trout as a predator in the 1950s and '60s, non-native alewife populations skyrocketed, prompting the introductions of Pacific salmon that created the recreational sportfishery. And as long as alewife were around, they would have their own two-pronged attack on lake trouts' natural reproduction. First, since lake trout spawn in Lake Huron itself, not upstream in rivers like salmon and steelhead, young, newly hatched lake trout fry, roughly a centimeter long, are vulnerable to predation by adult alewives. To make matters even worse, alewives contain thiaminase, an enzyme that breaks down thiamine (vitamin B1). Adult lake trout whose diets are rich in alewives will convey a thiamine deficiency to their eggs such that, upon hatching, the young fish will not develop properly and die in a matter of weeks—a condition called early mortality syndrome.[3] Indeed, the magnitude of the impediment that alewife imposed on lake trout recovery was hardly comprehendible.

Measures were taken to rescue the lake trout population. Rearing lake trout eggs in hatcheries alleviated the low-thiamine concerns imposed by alewives, and the young lake trout could be raised and then stocked in Lake Huron at lengths long enough to avoid the problem of being eaten by alewives (and other fish too). And after the collapse of alewives, evidence of lake trout natural reproduction became widespread throughout Lake Huron.

But sea lamprey remained a major threat to lake trout as they got older. It wasn't until about the year 2000 that a combination of sea lamprey–alleviation factors finally coalesced such that meaningful numbers of lake trout could even survive to sexual maturity. The first of those factors was sea lamprey control. Each year, the Great Lakes Fishery Commission administers a massive program to kill young sea lamprey, and over the years, it has been a critical component to Great Lakes fisheries management. To understand the "sea lamprey–control" program, as it is called, it's important to know the sea lamprey life cycle. Much like salmon, sea lamprey are an *anadromous* species. The prefix *ana* is Latin for "up," "back," or "again," and the Greek term *drom* means "run" or "running." Together, they form the word used to describe fish species that live their lives in alternating river and sea phases. Specifically, anadromy describes fish that "run" upstream to spawn in rivers and streams that are tributary to large bodies of water such as oceans, seas, and the Great Lakes in which those fish do the bulk of their feeding and growing. In general, anadromy is a life history strategy that (1) supports growth to greater sizes, and in turn greater reproductive capacity, than can be achieved by a completely river-bound life history, and (2) takes advantage of the more stable, sheltered, and relatively predator-scarce spawning habitat of the streams (as compared to the volatile, expansive, featureless, and predator-rich open sea). Throughout the Great Lakes, adult sea lamprey make spawning runs in May and June into many of the same rivers as salmon and steelhead. Their eggs hatch and the young sea lamprey, called ammocoetes (*ammo*-seats), spend several years as small, filter-feeding, harmless little critters in areas of streams where the soft muddy and silty bottom allows them to burrow. At night, an ammocoete will poke its head up from the river bottom and aim its disc mouth into the current to filter feed, like a catcher's mitt awaiting a pitch.

It's that ammocoete phase that is targeted by the sea lamprey–control program. Each year, a coordinated effort is undertaken to apply a chemical called TFM—a sea lamprey–specific lethal poison—by the tanker-load into a comprehensive coverage of streams all around the Great Lakes, in both Canada and the United States. It's a monumental effort, and since the 1950s it continues to be improved. As of September 2021, it's estimated that the sea lamprey–control program has reduced sea lamprey abundance by 81 percent in Lake Huron, as compared to peak pre-control abundances.[4] Coincidentally, TFM was discovered just minutes north of Rogers City at the Hammond Bay Biological Station by a Rogers City resident who worked there as a chemist.[5]

The second sea lamprey–alleviation factor was a result of the continued work of fisheries biologists to approach the lake trout–recovery issue from every conceivable angle. At first, in the 1970s when lake trout had to be reintroduced to Lake Huron, biologists sought to obtain broodstock from populations of lake trout they hoped most resembled those that had been lost. Lake Superior was an obvious choice, and so several genetic strains of lake trout broodstock were obtained from various regions in that lake. But ironically, in the late 1800s, lake trout from Lake Michigan and the Straits of Mackinac had been introduced to a number of places throughout the country so that by the time they were approaching extirpation in their native waters, they were becoming established in new and far-off places. So in addition to the Lake Superior strains, broodstock containing remnant genetic material from Lakes Michigan and Huron were also obtained from Green Lake, Wisconsin, and Lewis Lake, Wyoming (in Yellowstone National Park). This suite of genetic strains was used to stock tens of millions of lake trout in Lake Huron beginning in 1973.

However, it really wasn't until the 1990s when biologists introduced a new, non–Great Lakes origin strain of lake trout that they began observing substantial survival to adult sizes. The new Seneca strain of lake trout, from the Finger Lakes of New York, apparently avoided sea lamprey predation better than the Great Lakes heritage strains. By 2000, thanks to ever-improving sea lamprey control and the new Seneca strain, Lake Huron was finally building up a "spawning stock biomass" of lake trout. The stage was set—a population of adult lake trout once again existed in Lake Huron. When alewife collapsed in 2004, lake trout were able to capitalize on the combined effects of (1) reduced thiamine deficiency in their eggs due to elimination of alewife from their diet, (2) reduced predation by alewife on their newly hatched fry, and (3) reduced harvest by recreational angling due to declines in overall fishing as a result of the Chinook salmon fishery crash.

You might ask, "Well, what are the lake trout eating now that alewives are gone?" First, lake trout are adapted to eating native prey species such as bloater and sculpins that persisted in Lake Huron, but they have also adapted to preferentially eat another invasive species—the round goby. Chinook salmon don't seek out the gobies, which live right on the lake bottom, but lake trout target them. Given the abundance of round goby, there's no shortage of food for lake trout in Lake Huron.

So with the CliffsNotes version of the last seventy years of Lake Huron lake trout history laid out, I'd like to momentarily veer in a different direction before ultimately returning to Rogers City.[6]

Had it not been for the COVID-19 pandemic, I might not have begun this oral history investigation of the Lake Huron Chinook salmon fishery crash. In the early months of 2020, before the country was put under house arrest, I was just beginning my first semester in an anthropology undergraduate degree program at Central Michigan University. True, I already had a BS, MS, and PhD in fisheries biology, but I found myself more interested in the *human dimensions* of fisheries and wildlife concerns rather than the organisms and the ecosystems themselves.[7] So I sought training and accreditation in the social sciences and humanities.

But in the middle of that first semester back in school, all of my classes moved completely online as a result of the pandemic. It was a jarring and unfortunate experience, and at the very least, I felt I was not getting my money's worth. As the semester's end drew nearer, and with no resolution of the pandemic in sight, I lost the desire to enroll in a second semester. At the time, I had also been working nights and weekends as a server at a restaurant to accommodate my class schedule. But COVID put a hold on that as well. The whole scenario made me feel very out of control of the circumstances of my life. I wondered how I might get on with my life in a meaningful way in the midst of the pandemic. And honestly, I felt too old to be back in school again with nineteen- and twenty-year-olds anyway—like I was living in rewind. *If only I could afford to do my own independent research*, I thought.

Fortunately, before the nationwide lockdown, I had met with Michigan DNR fisheries management biologist Mark Tonello and recorded an interview with him as part of an assignment for one of my anthropology classes. The purpose of the assignment was straightforward: get experience preparing for and performing a recorded interview, and then listen back to it and get practice typing up a transcript. But I had some personal motivations in interviewing Mark that extended beyond the scope of the assignment. I hoped our conversation might help me structure my thoughts about potential future research projects—and, as it turns out, it did.

As a fisheries management biologist for the Michigan DNR, Mark Tonello works out of the Cadillac office in Michigan's northwestern Lower Peninsula. He is responsible for *all* the lakes, rivers, and streams within the DNR's Central Lake Michigan Management Unit—a region that encompasses all or parts of nineteen counties. This region includes some of the best cold-water salmon-, steelhead-, and trout-fishing watersheds in the entire Great Lakes region—those of the Manistee, Little Manistee, Pere Marquette, Muskegon, and White Rivers. Mark works with lake associations, watershed councils, local units of government, and angler groups with the goal of improving, protecting, and maintaining the fisheries resources of this large swath. He calls it his "dream job," but it's an immense responsibility, and I have a tremendous amount of respect for him and the handful of other Michigan DNR biologists who hold similar roles throughout the state.

Of course, Mark works on the Lake Michigan side of the state—so why am I bringing all this up? Well, because Lake Michigan, in addition to maintaining a Chinook salmon fishery, now has excellent lake trout–fishing opportunities—approaching those of Lake Huron. I was interested in Mark's perceptions of how well anglers are utilizing that lake trout resource now, and what things might look like for Lake Michigan's lake trout fishery in the future.

CARSON: That's got me thinking about a couple of different things. One is, I guess, we've got lake trout now—well, sea lamprey are being better controlled than ever. In some places you've got natural reproduction of lake trout occurring and fish getting to older ages, [sea lamprey] wounding rates are down, I know that's not the case for more northern Lake Michigan.[8] But maybe in southern Lake Michigan the potential for, maybe ten years from now, thirty-pound lake trout, forty-pound lake trout, I just wonder about that, and connected with that I wonder about, to what degree are angler expectations—anglers who are paying for guided trip services—to what degree are their expectations influenced by the guides themselves? And the guides, if they are really pushing for this king salmon–fishing experience, that they are influencing the expectation of their clients, and maybe if the guides themselves were more—I don't—I don't want to characterize guides because I don't know that many—but if they, if the expectations that they convey to their clients weren't so king salmon–centric, is there a potential for, in the future, like a big lake trout trophy-fishery? I know they have one at like Stannard Rock [in Lake Superior] and different places. I've seen another guide, like especially in the spring, go out and do lake trout–jigging trips and that kind of thing. So maybe like a catch-and-release fishery, or something where you could catch a lot of fish. I'm not advocating either way, I'm just wondering about guide expectations on the angler experience, and maybe the angler experience is not so dependent upon numbers or size of salmon.

MARK TONELLO: Well, what happened on Lake Huron?

CARSON: Eh, that's a good point. [*laughs*]

MARK: You can go on over there and you can catch a lot of lake trout right now. That's not a problem. There's lake trout all—and they're all wild, they're natural fish, they're not stocking like they used to, and yet they can't—again, the charter effort over there is a fraction of what it was twenty years ago.

CARSON: Yeah. And that's not getting better, really.[9]

The point is, while a fisheries success story was gained in the rehabilitation and recovery of a naturally reproducing lake trout population in Lake Huron, it must be emphasized that those same ecological circumstances also led to the loss of the Chinook salmon fishery, which used to inspire vastly greater angler participation. For this reason, as Mark made abundantly clear in our conversation, he points to Lake Huron as a cautionary tale. Lake Michigan still has a viable, yet perhaps precarious, Chinook salmon fishery. To him, the devastation of its loss would almost certainly outweigh concomitant fishery gains of any kind.

So while gaining an appreciation for the social, cultural, and economic impacts of the former Chinook salmon fishery in Rogers City depends upon examining the years during which the fishery was thriving, as well as the years during and immediately following the crash, the value of the former Rogers City Chinook salmon fishery is perhaps best understood in the following terms: essentially in its place, there now exists perhaps the Great Lakes' greatest lake trout–trolling fishery. Fishing for lake trout out of Rogers City utilizes largely the same gear, depends upon very similar tactics, and is logistically just as accessible as Chinook salmon fishing used to be. Yet listen to the accounts of those below and ask yourself, "How does the value of the current Rogers City lake trout fishery actually help further demonstrate the value of the former Rogers City Chinook salmon fishery?"

BRUCE GRANT: Our fishing here is still fantastic. I sold my big boat. I quit chartering. I have a sixteen-foot boat and a four-wheel-drive tractor and I launch off the beach. I go right out here one mile, catch my three fish, and come back.

FRANK KRIST: And it's really a good fishery if you want to go out and catch fish. I mean, I get out there between sixty and eighty trips a year and about the only day you don't catch a fish you go out there and the next thing you know a storm's coming and you're coming back in. I mean, it's amazing. I went out there second week of April, thirty-nine-degree water top to bottom, and I was back in in an hour [with] my limit of lake trout. Gol[ly], fish should be scattered all over the lake that early. But anyway, it's been a real good fishery.

CARSON: I'm kind of curious [about] your perspective on the future prospects of a lake trout tourism-based fishery in Rogers City. And, kind of, your perspectives on why there is some disparaging of lake trout among people, especially those who really glamorize salmon. And what are your thoughts on, just, those kinds of sentiments toward lake trout?

JOHN BRUNING: Well, I think it's—you know, I grew up catching lake trout. I enjoyed them. I like to eat them. Some people just don't like them. I like all kinds of fish. From that standpoint, if I'm going to go and fish, I'm—I'll do catch-and-release, but it's nice to go and catch something, if you're lucky, and be able to have a dinner from it. I enjoy that. And I like all kinds of fish. Salmon isn't my favorite. I would prefer—I guess if somebody said, "Here's lake trout, or here's salmon," I would probably gravitate towards the lake trout. So that sort of drives my preferences. Some people just don't like them. I don't know why. But people have different preferences. I think the glamorizing of the salmon isn't necessarily unfounded because they're fighters. They can be big. They can be theatrical. They can rip across the water. You just don't see that with lake trout in particular. Steelhead, you can't keep them in the water—you can't keep them on the hook as easy, either, because they're out of the—you know. They're fun. And a lot of the other—you know, brown trout, Atlantic salmon, and so forth are more fun, I think. It's more exhilarating. And if you have people that—from a charter standpoint, or from even a recreational standpoint, the thrill of that fish, you know, zz-ss, zipping across the surface and peeling line off—it's thrilling, quite frankly, and people enjoy that. I've caught hundreds of salmon, and it's fun. But I don't always need that to entertain me. Some people, that's just their thing. So I don't know. The popularity of lake trout is—it is what it is, I guess. Some people like them, some people don't. For some, it's something better than nothing. They're not that difficult to catch, I don't think. Back in the day they were maybe a little bit more challenging than the salmon. It was a little bit different fishery, though, and so I don't know if that really played into it much, that the salmon weren't necessarily easier to catch, I think they're just more exciting. And people like that. And they're bigger. I mean, even when you get into a big-lake trout, we're not catching twenty-five- and thirty-pound lake trout regularly, where when the salmon fishery is good, twenty-five-pounders, twenty-pounders, and—way more scrap, per pound, way more scrap. And people like that.

CARSON: Another thing, because you talked about walleye and lake trout, is there's still really good fishing and a good fishery out of Rogers City—[10]

MATT HOLLABAUGH: There is. Excellent. Yeah.

CARSON: —and—

MATT: It's different, very different than what we were used to.

CARSON: —my impression is that it's underappreciated, probably from like a tourism aspect, drawing people in that are interested in good fishing. One of the things I talked about with Bruce Grant and that was a concern to him was that the publicity that was associated with Rogers City in the salmon-fishing heyday left and went to Lake Michigan, and part of that was because the narrative of Lake Huron was that salmon fishing collapsed in Lake Huron, and then it would be like, Well, why would we go to Lake Huron to fish? Well, you still have a good fall salmon fishery in Rogers City. And you've got, depending on who you ask, the best lake trout fishery between Lakes Michigan and Huron, out of Rogers City. And so I've tried to ask people about, Well, how important could the fishery that still exists be today for Rogers City from a tourism aspect? And from your perspective, would you like to see more fishing tourism and more promotion of the fishery that exists here and try to draw more people?

MATT: Well, it doesn't really bother—you know, being a local, it's like, I enjoy being out there by myself but it doesn't really bother me, I think it's great that more people come here. But I think a lot of it is that the salmon—especially the Chinook—are the glamour fish. And if you're not getting these big huge fish, you're not going to get the high-rollers or whatever, people coming in. You're just not going to get it. And you're not going to get a lot of tourism just to fish for the lake trout, even though they're a great fish. The lake trout we have now is a hundred times better than the old lake trout. Those old things, they were like a real fatty-type fish. They were just—you'd have to trim them all down. You didn't know what the heck was in their belly, probably, what, maybe some kind of a heavy metal or something. But the ones we have now, they'll eat on the bottom, but they seem to live up higher in the water column all the time. It's not so—they just are nicer-looking fish too, just beautiful-looking. They look like the ones in Canada we'd get. So that part is great, but people don't gravitate toward that. Even like the walleye here too. There is walleye here but you just don't get—they have Saginaw Bay. So I don't know if that would ever—I mean, it would be great to advertise it, but I don't know if it would ever catch on real big because it just seems everybody is after Chinook. They want the great big fish.

CARSON: Or piles of walleye.

MATT: Yeah. Well, yeah. You can't blame them there. Yeah. [*laughs*]

BRUCE GRANT: But our—when the crowd left, the media left. And our people didn't pick up on that. And now—and you check out what I'm saying, I bet nobody pays any attention—you take all the—*Michigan Out-of-Doors Magazine*, *Michigan Outdoor* television show, *Mike Avery Show*. They all go to Lake Michigan. We've even had a few outdoor writers stab us in the back. One that we catered to was a heck of a swell person. We catered to him in and out. His last article said, "Last one out of Rogers City, please shut the lights off because the town died." I mean, you can't—and put that in a major magazine—I don't even know why that editor would let that go. But we're still fishing. The locals are still catching fish. You go out there now and you count thirty-five to fifty boats. We're still catching limits. We have a beautiful fishery. But we're running aground. And what I was getting at, you go pick up the *Michigan Fisherman*—um—*Michigan Out-of-Doors Magazine*. These magazines, most of their writers—their column writers, their staff—are charter boat operators in Lake Michigan. And in order to make themselves—and their fishing is good over there yet—and our fishing is still good here, we're not out of fish—but when all your articles come from there, they draw the people. And the thing of it is they draw the new people. We get people come up here and sometimes say, "How come nobody talks about this place? It's hidden all the way from here to Cheboygan," and didn't know. It's a secret. Well, it's not a secret. Most of them are in their twenties and thirties—or late twenties and thirties—just getting established, and for some reason got over here and got out fishing. We don't get the media anymore because they're charter boat operators and they write their articles for the magazine, get their 15, 20 bucks for an article, or 50 bucks, and it's hurt our area. But we have such a livable area maybe it's not so bad either. The retirees hated it because it would be so crowded. They came—a lot of GM [General Motors] and Ford retirees up here. And they like to go out on a sailboat. They like to go out and fish. But this crowd came and now they're kind of put back. Everybody's so happy now, but we still have a good fishery. We're not catching thirty-pound fish. But I've got to tell you this, when I first came here you could hardly catch a lake trout that was legal in length. And a lot of them died because they were brought up too fast. They were hooked, and they bled, you know they were going to die. And same thing—I pick up brown trout and lake trout—most of the lake trout were from recreational fishermen that couldn't keep them. They unhooked them, put them back in the water, they died and floated up on the beach. What a waste. Now these fish—there's lake trout running twelve, fifteen pounds. You go out there and it is a fishery all by itself.

DAVE NADOLSKY: He gives most of the fish away.

TOM ALLUM: And I don't really like to eat fish very much, but it gives you something to do. Like this morning, I woke up at 5 o'clock—well, I'll tell you a story. One day last week, I woke up at 6 o'clock, and that's late for me. I grabbed a cup of coffee, threw on some clothes. I live a mile away, I drove down to the marina. Hopped in the boat. Went out to Calcite, about two miles away. Within a half hour I had my three fish—that's the limit on lake trout. Came back, tied up the boat, went over to the fish-cleaning station, cleaned the fish. By that time it was 8 o'clock. I drove up to the clinic where I have some people that are anxious to get that fish, so I dropped them off, came home, got in the shower, got cleaned up, and I was sitting down at my breakfast table having breakfast at 9 o'clock. So that's my kind of a fishing day, okay?

DAVE: And actually he had taken his bowl of Cheerios with him—

TOM: [*laughs*] That's right.

DAVE: —but he was so damn busy pulling fish out that he never had time to eat his cereal.

Tom: Yeah, I keep my cereal—like this morning I had my breakfast out on the boat. So anyway, I really like to fish. I enjoy the culture of the fishermen down there, which is a different culture than sailboats. And I just enjoy it. My wife doesn't enjoy it, she won't go. My grandkids will occasionally go. But the way that boat's set up I can do everything myself and it's an escape, you know?

Carson: When you started getting more back into recreational fishing for your own, like, personal enjoyment, sometime in the '90s, I guess, were you still targeting salmon at all? Or were you really going after lake trout by that point?

John Bruning: I liked the lake trout. They were a little bit more suited to my schedule to a point. They were there when you were. If you could find them you could usually catch them. It didn't matter if it was noon or 6 o'clock in the morning. And in the salmon, especially as it got tougher, I remember it, and even today, it seems like the bite is best first and last light. And especially when I started to get back into it and I was working more, I had other obligations. I had bought a house. I was working on the house and things like that. I didn't always want to get up before daylight and head out on the lake for the chance of catching a salmon. And quite frankly I preferred eating the lake trout, which I did. And so I fished primarily lake trout. I did fish some salmon. Depending on the day, maybe if it was a particularly hot bite and I wanted some additional—a little change, or a little additional excitement—I would certainly go after them. But I would say most of my effort was on the lake trout. And at that point they weren't even, they weren't very large lake trout. As I was a kid we could catch lots of them but they were relatively small. Now they get—they're getting to where there's a few big ones once in a while, which is kind of cool. They used to—you know, when I was younger, I can remember one trip in particular—well, I don't remember all the details because I can't remember if it was a five-fish limit or if it had already changed to three—but we had a cooler, you know, whatever size cooler we had, and usually the fish were a very small part of the volume when you had your limit. And one day we had fish that were probably in the four- to six-pound range, and that was a large average catch because a lot of them were two, two and a half pounds. But they were, for us, relatively easy to catch. Good eaters. And so we enjoyed that. I enjoyed that. Now they're a little bit bigger. Little different—it's just different than it was.

But I still—even now, most of the time when I fish I get up, I get some work done, and then I head to the lake about the time everybody else is coming off. And there's nobody—you know, the parking lot's not as busy—not that it's busy anymore like it used to be, but it just works well into my schedule. And the lake trout, if I can find them I can catch them in the middle of the day. So just kind of personal preference there.

CARSON: But you were okay transitioning, switching to just focusing on lake trout?

IVAN WIRGAU: Oh, yeah. Yeah, I mean, what else are you going to do? I mean, if you're going to fish out there, I've got the equipment to do it, and these lake trout taste better, I think, since they went to the gobies. They're not as fat. The alewives provide a lot more energy for a forage base, but they provide a lot more fat too. And I think that—and the growth rate's so much faster with the alewives. These gobies, they're not growing as fast, but I think the quality of the flesh is so much better. They taste really good.[11] I mean, grilled lake trout's nice. Salmon, yeah, it's nice to catch them, if you can catch them, if you're going to focus on catching them. It's like Ken Partyka, that's what they do, they're focused on a little window of time at the end of the season and then they go get what they want for canning and that's enough. But some years they do well and other years they don't do so well. It's all about timing. And then if you go look at the weir down there where they collect them, where the State collects them, it looks like a lot of fish in the river but it really isn't that many fish when you go and scatter them out here in Lake Huron. It's just not that many.

KEN PARTYKA: I don't fish lake trout. I mean, I don't—I give a shit less about a lake—. I would take one for the grill.

TOM ALLUM: And there's quite a difference between catching a salmon and catching a lake trout.

DAVE NADOLSKY: Is it more of a fight?

TOM: Oh, heavens, yeah. When you catch a lake—if you're looking for lake trout you've got to watch the pole because a lot of times—like yesterday, I was out for two hours I never had bite. I pulled in my line, there's a [Carson laughs] ten-pound salmon just hooked, swimming along—

CARSON: Lake trout, you mean?

Toм: Or, lake trout, yeah. They do that all the time. Whereas a salmon, if you catch a salmon you hear this hundred feet of line go off *zzz* like that. Sound like a buzz saw. And then you've got this big fish on and he's jumping around, as opposed to a lake trout that you have to just reel him up from the bottom. So that's a dynamic that comes in from what you're talking about. What is salmon fishing and why is it attractive? We don't have salmon anymore, so—.

Ken Rasche: And there's really, I think this fishing out there now—I don't go fishing much anymore; usually my grandson or somebody takes me out—but the fishing out there now is still pretty darn good, but it's not for salmon. The lake trout seems to be doing extremely well, but a lot of people don't like to catch lake trout compared to salmon because it's like a Volkswagen or a Cadillac, the difference.

Dave Smrchek: And they don't really want to catch lake trout. There's a big difference, which—. I'm fishing lake trout. That's fine. I just go fish lake trout. A lot of these people, Nope. I'm not going to go fish. Their boats are setting in the barn, or they've sold them, or whatever. They're just not interested. And we've had a great lake trout fishery the last four or five years. People won't come. They just—lake trout are not that fun to catch. They're big fish. But they don't make those runs and so forth. It's a whole cultural—or whatever. But the dyed-in-the-wool salmon fishermen do not want lake trout. And there's some of them still around. They haven't put the boat in the water in two or three years. We're going out and catching limits of lake trout every day, and it's, Nope, we don't want them. And these fish are better fish to eat than the other—the lake trout years ago that were eating the alewives were real fatty and greasy, and these fish are eating gobies and are much better table fare. Probably better than the salmon. We still have a salmon fishery out here in the fall. It's not tremendous, but it's there. And there's steelhead. Last fall was a very good fall for steelhead out here. Who knows what the future's going to bring? It's hard to say.

Jayme Warwick: Yeah, back in the day when we were just out there focusing on salmon, you catch a lake trout that was two pounds it was like, no. In the tournament we'd take turns, you know, me and my buddies, catching fish, and you'd lose your turn if you catch a fish, right? So when a guy brings in that lake trout, you were bummed out. You were trying to shake him off the line before you put it in the net so you can get another turn. We didn't want anything to do with a lake trout. And now we're targeting them, we're fishing for them. And now they're better eating than they used to be.

CARSON: I was going to ask about that because people say that. I didn't ever really eat them before the past five or six years. I think they taste pretty good. [*laughs*]

JAYME: Yeah. It's my wife's favorite fish, is a lake trout. And I'm like, "No way," so I tried one. And it was pretty good. And from what everybody says they're eating gobies now instead of the alewife that would have a certain enzyme in them that give them a crumby taste or whatever. We have good lake trout fishing and big lake trout.

FRANK KRIST: I'm just blaming it on people and anglers in general that, Oh, my goodness, lake trout, those greasy things. But you know what's interesting is, I'm in the diet study again at MSU [Michigan State University], and so I'm catching a couple hundred lake trout a year, and I mean, well how many can Theresa and I eat, right?[12] My neighbors, I've got neighbors all over the place I'm giving filleted, skinned—and they love them. "Oh, my goodness, we just love it." I think it's a matter of that just got out there that they're negative. And most people, depending on how you cook them and how you like fish, but generally they're good. We had them last night. We like them. They're on par with salmon. And that's where it gets back to these ports where you have to market what you have. That's what these charter boats are doing in Grand Traverse Bay and Leelanau and up through there. Hey, you want a great day of fishing? We go out and we catch fish. Take the family out. Whatever. So it's—and, I don't know, have you ever fished for salmon?

CARSON: I have gone on a few charters. I do a lot of river steelhead fishing. So I catch salmon that way. But most of those I'm not so interested in eating.

FRANK: Well, if you ever want to go lake trout fishing you let me know. We'll take you out. I'm not a charter captain. I obviously don't charge or anything, be happy to take you out. But one thing, you go out and you catch lake trout, like we were catching them yesterday, they were running from four to nine pounds. And you got it on, you're playing it, it's a nice fight for about five, ten minutes. You get into these salmon—*I mean they're a pain.* They really are. I mean, here you've got a salmon. Maybe it's fifteen pounds. It's underneath the boat. You're just pulling.

It's not coming up, it's not going anywhere, here's forty-five minutes. To me that's, you know, they make a nice run—a good one will run a lot and get tired quicker—but I mean, to me, I'd almost rather catch a lake trout. You know, they're both fine, but anyway. It's just a matter of how you perceive it, and they are good to eat. Of course now they're feeding more on a diverse diet. They don't feed on alewives much, obviously, but [they] eat a lot of gobies. There's still a fair amount of smelt. Right now they're eating quite a few midges. The ones that we caught yesterday were loaded with midge pupa.

Bruce Grant: But again, when I came here there was no lake trout fishery. Commercial fishermen and the tribes destroyed it. Then the State came back—I think it's the—I think it was the Senecas [a genetic strain of lake trout] out of Lake Ontario—and they're completely different fish. They don't live on the bottom.

Carson: They say they avoid sea lamprey better.

Bruce: Exactly. And they grow faster, and they grow bigger. And they're not stuck on the bottom. In fact—you probably never got to meet the guy—there used to be a guy that managed—it was after Dr. [James] Seelye left—they put Roger Bergstedt in charge of the sea lamprey station. I don't know if you've ever run across Roger—

Carson: I've never met him. I've seen his name a million times. Yeah.

Bruce: Okay. Well, Roger—I used to be Roger's lookout for when the carp spawned when they came around the shore, fins out and spawning, because they kept track of that. That told them when the temperature was right to put the lampricide in. And then when they started getting—we got a few people that whenever we'd catch a lake trout, pretty decent one, we'd keep it alive and take it up and give it to Roger. I'd give it to the neighbor right across the road—he was the chemist there—and they take it up. They'd tag them. Well, they start watching these tagged Senecas, and in the wintertime they stayed that far below [just below] any ice cover. And they figured it was more of an oxygen content there. They weren't down in thirty-nine-degree water laying on the bottom, which they thought they would be. And they would stay suspended. Sometimes in—a couple times a day they would leave, and they figured they were going to feed. But they'd come back and suspend. And out here now, in one hundred to two hundred feet of water you're catching lake trout at fifty to fifty-five feet down. Just find the temperature and you're going to catch them.

9

FRANK KRIST IS A FORCE

Across the street from my house in Mount Pleasant, Michigan, lived my neighbor Judy, who hosted a classical music program on the WCMU public radio station. I used to chat with Judy regularly, and given her career in audio programming, she had a natural interest in the oral history project I was working on. Much of the central and northern portions of Michigan's Lower Peninsula receive WCMU radio and television programming, so I was not at all surprised to hear that Judy knew through email someone who had retired from a Michigan DNR fisheries career up at the Alpena Fisheries Research Station. Maybe the retired fisheries guy she'd been emailing with might be someone worth talking to, we mused. I gathered from Judy that this guy hadn't been short on words in their correspondence—something she chuckled about. "Sure, see what he has to say," I told Judy.

A week or two later, Judy eagerly called out to me from across the street. She had heard back from the retired fisheries guy. "He says the person to talk to about fishing in Rogers City is Frank Krist!" she somewhat yelled from outside talking range as we each strode down our respective driveways to meet in the middle.

I took a few more steps before responding. "That's what everyone has said," I called back, smiling. "Yeah, I've actually been talking with him from the very start."

In the many hours of interviews I recorded, I suspect no truer words were spoken. *The person to talk to about fishing in Rogers City is Frank Krist.* For nearly fifty years, Frank has seen his role as an advocate and ambassador for fisheries resources expand from the scope of Rogers City and northeastern Michigan to encompass the rest of Lake Huron, and eventually even Lake Michigan.

Given Frank's involvement in Great Lakes fisheries, it's hard to comprehend that he's not even a fisheries professional—at least, not in the proper sense. From our interview together, I learned that Frank is a U.S. Army veteran with degrees in fisheries biology and chemistry. He grew up four and a half hours south of Rogers City in Jackson, Michigan, and that's where he met his wife, Theresa. The two of them moved up to Rogers City in 1974 after Frank finished his master's degree at Central Michigan University, and they've been there ever since.

Frank was fortunate to find his career job as an environmental health officer at the Presque Isle County Health Department, headquartered in Rogers City, where he worked for thirty-two years. That job ingrained him as a presence in the community. "I've been to, probably, in my thirty-two years, half the houses outside the city, visiting one time or another," he told me. In his varied role, Frank might have overseen sewage system installations, performed environmental health checks and inspections, and responded to any number of environmental complaints and concerns. As far as the recreational fishery's impacts on the surrounding area, Frank knows they reach "way beyond what some people think because they're not in a position to know that."

Certainly, Frank deserves recognition for his undeniable influence regarding the fisheries resources off the shores of Rogers City over the past nearly five decades. And much of that recognition should be easily identifiable throughout the entirety of this book. But far beyond merely paying reverence to Frank's impact on a myriad of Michigan's fisheries resources, the purpose of this chapter is twofold.

First, the case of Frank Krist embodies the aspiration that so many would-be advocates and activists espouse, which is to make a difference—to have an impact. Frank's story, together with the story of the Rogers City Chinook salmon fishery, serves as an example of how well-founded community-enriching goals can be effectively worked toward by combining genuine motives and forthright objectives with diligence and unrelenting persistence *at the level of the individual*. The degree to which the people I interviewed spoke specifically about this one man demonstrates the awesome potential within each of us as a single person.

Second, this chapter is meant to demonstrate what is at risk of being lost in the near future, which is the representation of the northeast Michigan area and its fisheries. During many of my interviews with members of the Rogers City community, I asked whether there was a feeling of a void in the town's culture following the declines in the Chinook salmon fishery. I was somewhat surprised to hear that, no, there largely wasn't a feeling of a void, or of having to recover from a loss. But perhaps that was because Rogers City never lost its *voice* in the fisheries sociopolitical scene, and Rogers City's voice was perhaps chiefly synonymous with that of Frank Krist (and the Hammond Bay Area Anglers Association). As Jim Johnson explains, that voice provided a continued presence in the latest Great Lakes Consent Decree negotiations, and it helped the region retain fisheries resources such as the continued stocking of Chinook salmon in the Swan River.

Small towns need their doers. As Mary Ann Heidemann explained to me, "The interesting thing that I learned about small towns, when you're in a big place and you want something done, you're always saying to someone else, 'Go do it for me. You do it.' In a small town if you want something done you've got to get off your seat and do it yourself. And that allows for a lot of personal growth." There's no doubt that Frank Krist embodied this mindset, and you get the feeling that it was contagious among Frank, Mary Ann, and the other people who found a home in Rogers City in the '70s and '80s. The way I interpret Mary Ann's view is that it references something like the difference between activism (*You* do it) versus action (I'll do it *myself*). As she pointed out, "You can be more multifaceted in a small place because you have to be. You absolutely have to be. But then that's pretty good because you're learning a lot."

So who will there be to carry the torch for the fisheries interests of Rogers City and other such small locales in the future? Who will be the local environmental stewards? Maybe you live in Rogers City, and reading Frank Krist's story will inspire you to contemplate your potential role going forward regarding the area's resources. Or maybe you're from a "big place," as were Mary Ann Heidemann and her husband, Karl, and you'll be inspired toward a small-town life where involvement can perhaps more readily affect change.

I'll close this chapter's introduction with an excerpt from the Presque Isle Sportsmen's Club's letter to the community, published January 1987, that summarized their accomplishments in 1986—the year that saw the inaugural Rogers City Salmon Tournament as well as the first major run of adult, three-year-old Chinook salmon from the massive stocking initiative begun at the Swan River.

One can't say enough about our fish committee head, Frank Krist. Frank has occupied the majority of his free time, all year long, to the pursuit of upgrading the quality of our northern Lake Huron fisheries. His extreme dedication in attending meetings concerning our fish numbers, tribal netting, and things in general affecting our Great Lakes ecological state is very commendable. A special thanks to his understanding and supportive wife Theresa, also.[1]

FRANK KRIST: My goal is to see the best fisheries we can get. Whether it's in Lake Michigan when I'm sitting on a Lake Michigan committee, sitting on this committee. And being a chair of a committee—I chair this one for the DNR for Lake Huron and I also chair this inland one that's the big lakes up here—Burt, Mullett, and Long, Grand—I can't focus on just Rogers City, Hammond Bay Anglers, the City of Rogers City. In fact, that's the most difficult time is when you're talking about your community because you can't be provincial, you've got to look at the whole lake. So my goal is not to represent myself or anything but let's represent the science. What can the science—what can we bring from the science [to] increase our chances?

JIM JOHNSON: He is just a force. Lake Huron would be quite different if it weren't for Frank, Frank Krist. It wouldn't be nearly as cool a place. I don't think we'd have Atlantic salmon. I don't know what the Consent Decree would have been like in 2000, but it wouldn't have been as good [for the resource] as what we got. So they've been very, very effective.

SCOTT MCLENNAN: Frank Krist has done just stellar work in trying to negotiate an agreement with the Native American group, and the federal government, [and] the Canadian government. So Frank is our local ambassador. He's done a lot of work on that and that particular area. Because that's very important to us because the pressure from the netting of salmon, I mean, it really had quite an impact. So the loss of feed for the salmon was one thing—the alewife, the smelt, et cetera—but also the fishing industry did have quite an impact.

DAVE SMRCHEK: I can remember one of the meetings that I went to with Bruce and Frank, it was a huge victory when the U.S. Fish and Wildlife [Service] representatives finally admitted that tribal gillnet fishing was not compatible with lake trout restoration in the Great Lakes. For the longest time, they would say the tribal gillnet fishing effort is insignificant in the restoration process. But that was just a major, major victory for our side when they finally said, "The tribes have got to cut back on the gillnets because we want to restore the lake trout population." So, little victories.

BRUCE GRANT: And God bless Frank Krist. He's one of the ones that, "Oh, I hate them people crowding the place. I just want to—we got this to fish ourselves." But if it wasn't for Frank, we wouldn't have a fishery here because he just—he's into it. And the rest of us go out and raise money so he can pay the lawyers to keep us involved. And that's just a great thing.

CARSON: How much of an effort was it to raise all that money?
FRANK KRIST: Well, back when we raised most of it—the last agreement we were in was the 2000 [Consent Decree], so—we were in the '85 Great Lakes, and then the 2000 Great Lakes. And then the '85 agreement—I went back and checked that. We raised 35,000 just for the 2000 agreement. Of course we got other groups that added to that, like the Grand Traverse Sportfishing Associations and a few others. And it took a lot of effort, but we had a lot more members. And we would raffle boats off, so you had to sell a lot of tickets. And when you've got four or five people that are on the board and active—a lot of our members are older than I am. I'm seventy-four, they're older than I am. You can't expect them to take on all these things. So, just getting people involved.
CARSON: Was it easier when the salmon fishery was bigger here, or did that have anything to do with it?
FRANK: I don't think so because we got organized in '74, and that was way before the salmon fishery. We had good followings because we were concerned about the lake trout, we wanted to keep them coming. It was interesting. They planted splake in '73.[2] And then they switched right away to lake trout in '74. Well, when I got here in '74, the splake, we were already catching them. They weren't very big. We go, "Wow, this is great. We've got to get involved and make sure—see what's going on." And then the '74 lake trout plant, the agencies finally figured let's just stick with lake trout. There wasn't any competition for them because they had all these smelt and alewives and there wasn't any other predators in the lake, and oh, my goodness, they were growing. And so we got all excited. Got our organizations going. And then we started catching these immature Chinook like I told you back there in the very early '80s, maybe as early as '79. "Wow, we've got to push the State to stock

more of these." So we started before the salmon. The salmon wasn't the key to anything. Because we were happy with the lake trout there, then all of a sudden we're catching salmon. Well, this is even more fun, and more diversity. And so, no, it's the times, I guess, more than anything.

IVAN WIRGAU: I mean, they only planted *x* amount of salmon until Frank Krist got involved with it, and he got involved with the heavy salmon plants and then that all really took off.

DAVE SMRCHEK: I knew that people were fishing salmon a little bit, but it wasn't a huge thing in '70 around here. We were getting our token plant of salmon in Rogers City. Of course everything was going to Lake Michigan. It was just nothing that was in my, you know, picture, that I could picture myself wanting to do. I couldn't afford it, first of all. But then as I got acquainted over the next couple of years, there were people fishing salmon, there were lake trout, there were splake, there were brown trout, and there were steelhead that were pretty much a nearshore fishery at certain times of the year. It was a small-boat fishery. The local guys were doing it in their fourteen-, sixteen-footers. But nobody was coming here from very far away. And it took me a while to figure out what was going on. We had Harry Whiteley here who was on the Natural Resources Commission. Could have brought huge numbers of salmon, I think, if he had wanted to. But for some reason it wasn't happening. And it took me a few years to figure out that here was this little group of really good fishermen. They had their private little fishing world in Rogers City and they wanted their hundred thousand salmon, which was enough for them, but not enough to attract a lot of attention. They had the best of both worlds there in the '70s and into the early '80s before we started getting the bigger plants. Well, then the Indian issue came up too, and that's how I got to know Frank [Krist], and the Hammond Bay [Area] Anglers [Association] got started. I was president of the [Presque Isle] Sportsmen's Club when we had one of the first meetings about tribal fishing and Lake Huron, trying to develop community awareness of what we had out here and what we could lose if the negotiations didn't go—. Most of the local guys that I knew didn't care one way or the other. If this fishery went away, out here in Lake Huron, they'd go back into Black Lake and the little lakes and go fishing. They didn't want—they were going to go fish one way or the other. They weren't willing to invest a lot of time or money in that process.

There was just a little—a hardcore group of people that wanted to protect Lake Huron from gillnetters. And I didn't—I still wasn't involved in it to any great extent up into '80, I think. I was busy with getting married and having a family and career and so forth. In the process I got involved with Ducks Unlimited, which is—indirectly got me involved in fishing. After we had—I had been involved with Ducks Unlimited for a while—Frank, and Bruce Grant, and a couple other guys from the Hammond Bay Anglers came—and it was in the, probably in the early '80s, mid-'80s, and they said, "Can you show us how to make some money?"—using my Ducks Unlimited background—"Can you help us make money through the Anglers so that we have money for the courts?" That was how I got involved with the Anglers at that point.

JIM JOHNSON: Well, the Hammond Bay sportfishing association [Hammond Bay Area Anglers Association] has always been an influential force. Through participation of their members on the Lake Huron advisory committee, and by their contribution of funds and people to the coalition to protect Michigan resources, the amici for the Consent Decrees, they've been very closely engaged with the Consent Decree negotiations. Their role being to advise the judge as to whether or not this agreement that's being proposed is going to be—whether you can sell this agreement to the public. What will the backlash be like if you do this? How will the public react if you do that? And that's been the main reason the judge wants the amici there, and the amici wouldn't be there if it weren't for the Hammond Bay Angler Association. They're the ones that stepped forth in the first place. And their advice has gone beyond just public acceptability of agreements, it's also—they've been really good about focusing on resource issues and keeping the parties focused on what's good for resource sustainability. It's weird that you have to push the resource agencies to talk about resources, but they're sometimes so eager to get into allocation and who gets what that they forget that they haven't yet figured out how big the pie is. And the Hammond Bay Anglers have done a really good job of that through the coalition. Of course the Hammond Bay Anglers have contributed to the Lake Huron advisory committee in a big way, especially with Frank's leadership on the advisory committee. And I used to address—every now and then I'd be invited to talk to their annual banquet. And that was always fun. They have an annual banquet to raise funds for the coalition and other things, and just to have fun. It was always a fun banquet and good food, and lots of good stories to be told and usually some good speakers, including yours truly now and then. And I've been a member of the Anglers Association, and I represent the Anglers Association as an advisor to the Lake Huron advisory committee now.

Bruce Grant: Beverly Bodem said, "We're going to meet over at the Mason Building at 1 o'clock, right after lunch." And she said [*laughs*], "I want to get them after they've had their lunch so I can bring a good burp out of them." We go over there and [fisheries chief John Robertson] starts getting heavy on Frank and I about you guys in Rogers City, with the finger pointing. She stepped between us and she said, "Mr. Robertson, you probably don't know who I am, but I'm on the committee that controls your budget, and if you don't understand that, and you don't understand to listen to Rogers City's problem, then you're going to be picking nickels up in the parking lot to get through next year." His whole attitude changed and Frank and I were like the kids in the neighborhood that he liked. That's what you learn about politics. But if you don't have the right person doing it, it doesn't work. And Beverly Bodem and John Pridnia were both real leaders, very aggressive.[3] And they went out honorably. But we sure lost a lot of representation. But by that time they both taught our Hammond Bay Anglers and our local politicians enough to realize you have got to stand your ground. They'd come in to start a big program and then just abandon it because someone on the other side of the state says, "Oh, no, we should have that over here."

Carson: You were here in the '80s, and so did you think that it was fortunate or special to have John Pridnia and Harry Whiteley here and that was kind of something that set Rogers City apart in terms of getting the type of support or interest in the natural resources issues here?

Frank Krist: I think the key is, is to have somebody in your community that's got that attitude and that will make it spread. Simple as that. I think that—I mean, I've been persistent forever. You think about it. How many people's done that for forty-seven years? Believe me, I don't get discouraged. And I've been trying to encourage you to keep going on this because I think there's a lot of potential there. And I'm really fortunate that people jump on it. You get some good information and you get it out there, all of a sudden, yeah, people think it's a good idea. The problem I'm seeing today is not enough people, whether it's—running the city. We're seeing some of that. Younger managers. Kids in their thirties and forties running for city council and other positions. That's what we need. I mean, you can't let these old codgers run it.

JIM JOHNSON: I wanted to hear communities screaming about the resource because that meant we had stewardship. You had partners out there then. And oftentimes it doesn't work out just perfectly for you. It's messy. But when you really need friends, you want to have resource stewards out there. And that's where Rogers City's always been, is they've been there for the resource. Yeah, they'd love to have more salmon for their tournaments and stuff like that, but they are there for the resource more than just the moniker of we're the "Salmon Capital of the World" and that sort of thing. But there was a serendipitous outcome from one of their—I was a little irritated when they insisted on not taking a salmon reduction to zero. They would only take—they only agreed to reducing their salmon stocking to a few hundred thousand. And I was surprised that the DNR management went along with that. I was thinking we were just going to cut stocking except for the Consent Decree requirements, which is Nunns Creek up in the Upper Peninsula. But they did present good evidence, and they made us look at the Swan weir data. Swan weir was still producing eggs. It was as reliable an egg resource as the Little Manistee weir, and it was good. So why cut it when it's a weir? Okay. So they kept stocking salmon there. Well, little did we know that most of those salmon were feeding in Lake Michigan anyway. And now we know it's Lake Michigan's best stocking site in terms of—in terms of return of stocked fish, survival of stocked fish to the sportfishery is best if you stock them at Swan weir.[4]

CARSON: Oh, that's amazing.

JIM: There's not very many walleyes there, I guess. And it must be that beach zone around Swan weir does have some plankton. And [young-of-year Chinook salmon] will eat a lot of insects too, because you see them just feeding on dropping insects that are washing up in the beach zone. So if they're not getting eaten in the beach zone, [the stocked Chinook salmon smolts] probably have a good chance of surviving that [life stage]. Then they move out into Lake Huron where there's not an adult salmon population to speak of, get to a size where they can migrate to Lake Michigan and not get eaten there, and just contribute to that fishery. Something like that's working. But I didn't think that stocking site would continue to be successful the way it has. They were right.

FRANK KRIST: So the goal is to learn what the biologists need. Learn what the public's interested in. Then you take the science and you increase your chances of success by bringing out the information. And I found, too, that if you're involved, the closer you are to the decision makers the better chance you've got of affecting that decision. And then sometimes I sit back and I think, I don't have any spare time [*Carson laughs*], maybe I should just retire and let somebody else take over.

JIM JOHNSON: One of the things that we didn't understand and what the DNR's office here in Alpena now is starting to get ahold of is just how much [lake trout] spawning habitat there is in the Rogers City area. The focus had been on Drummond Island refuge for lake trout spawning, and the thinking was Straits of Mackinac, you know, out west they call them the Mackinaw because that's where the eggs used to be collected for the federal hatchery system is under the Mackinac Bridge—or well before the Mackinac Bridge, of course. But anyway, people had just not thought much about the spawning habitat in the Adams Point–Hammond Bay area and Presque Isle. But Frank has been, with all his mapping of fish, he's been fishing after the season closes, just catch-and-release of spawning fish, and pretty well demonstrated they were actually spawning on some of these reefs there, and [suggested to Michigan DNR biologist Ji He] to go out and do hydroacoustics work, and set some gear and make sure they were wild lake trout. And [Ji] counted them hydroacoustically. And mapped the reefs. And yes, there's a lot of spawning going on in the Rogers City area, and it could be a major source—not just a small spawning population, but these—from Adams Point to Presque Isle those reefs could be major sources of lake trout for all of Lake Huron. Probably bigger than Drummond Island refuge. And we didn't see that coming. And Frank's just keeping his eyes open and being so perceptive. And he's a scientist. He went to Central [Michigan University] too. [*laughs*] And he's a real scientist. And very thoughtful and tireless. He demonstrated to Ji that he had something going there and Ji was convinced, and took the [RV] *Tanner* there, and with all their high-tech stuff they've got on the new boat that, they made ready work of proving that, yeah, it's important habitat. So things like that.

BRUCE GRANT: Get Frank [Krist] to show you his chart for fishing this year—or last year, the year before—of what he caught, because Frank keeps a record—

CARSON: I was going to ask you about, maybe, what the future of the Hammond Bay Area Anglers Association is, do you think?

FRANK KRIST: My guess is we get through with the tribal negotiations, and we're getting close to the end. I mean, it's a shame because this community has so much—they're fortunate. They've got such a tight connection with all these people in the State. And not only from the DNR, but USGS, all those other agencies I mentioned. And how do you get—? I only got so much energy and right now I don't have hardly—as you can see, trying to get things set up.[5] I'm getting to the point where I'd rather monkey around in the garden, doing some fishing and stuff. But the problem is, you walk away, that's the end. And right now, until we can work out an agreement we can all live with on the Great Lakes here, that's my goal. And our organization has already spent over 150,000 on the four decrees we've had so far. And we're just too old. We can't raise money anymore. When you've got a board that's supposed to be [ten members] and you've only got five. So I don't see a lot of a future.

10

FUTURE

I think it's going to build up— . . . It can come back, it's going to come back. . . . I do think the fishery is coming back. It's going to get strong. . . . And so a fishery can come back.

—Bruce Grant

You could say Bruce Grant is an optimist. He feels strongly that the future of Rogers City's recreational fisheries is bright. But you might hesitate to trust Bruce's judgment. You might say he's biased. After all, he lives in Rogers City and has based years of his life on the fishing there. However, it was that same intuition about future fishery prospects that, once upon a time back in 1983, spurred Bruce and his wife, Colleen, to relocate from downstate all the way up to Rogers City to invest in a fixer-upper resort right on the Lake Huron shoreline. For four decades now, the couple and the Manitou Shores Resort that they manage have grown and thrived in Rogers City. Having visited Bruce at the resort property and having listened to his story, I think one can hardly deny the Grants' prudence and vision. So it shouldn't be surprising that among the many people with whom I spoke, it was Bruce who expressed the strongest sentiments regarding how the salmon fishery experience in Rogers City could and should be used to contextualize future considerations for similar small-town locales.

Now, for most with whom I spoke, thoughts on the future of recreational fishing in Rogers City itself focused on ecology: Is the Lake Huron food web and are the salmon still adapting to the invasive species such as quagga mussels and round gobies? All else being equal, is the ecosystem still in flux? And what will be the effects of a potential new invasive species?

For others, fisheries management decisions were perceived to play a larger role: Why can't more Chinook salmon be stocked again in Rogers City? What is the future role of Atlantic salmon here?

For Bruce, however, considerations of the future fisheries in Rogers City seem inextricable from the sociopolitical dynamics of the past several decades. In a nutshell, he asserts that the State of Michigan and outdoors publicists came to the area and built up a fishery and then, in a similarly hasty swoop, the publicists and the State largely left the area. All said and done, outside agencies had an outsized influence on Rogers City. While Bruce all along felt that local government and area contingents should work together to hold a greater degree of sway over the city's portrayal among, and integration with, outside entities such as business organizations and tourism initiatives, perhaps it is only with hindsight that such a belief can be properly appreciated.

And hindsight tells us that salmon fishing was not the silver bullet that could resolve Rogers City's population declines, as Mary Ann Heidemann described. But the State came in and created a fishery that, when it went away, resulted in significant negative effects on a city already facing its share of hardships. Does the State, and should the outdoor writers, bear some responsibility? Were they truly careless or negligent? Actions and words do matter. Of course, nothing can be done now except use that set of experiences to inform future decision making and planning. That's what Bruce wants. And so a primary purpose of this chapter is to share the thoughts of Bruce and others on this topic.

One thing seems certain: tourism is in Rogers City's future because traditional natural resources employment opportunities (for example, limestone mining, forestry, and commercial fishing) will continue to decline. And maybe Rogers City is best suited to remain a small town. Of course, it will continue to have remnants of its bigger past—for example, the marina. Even by the '70s and '80s, what attracted so many people to the area was no longer related to the big employers there; rather, people who retired there, started businesses there, or took jobs there did so after having visited the area (for instance, Rich Hamp, Frank Krist, Bruce Grant, and Mary Ann Heidemann). They were drawn to the beauty.

But I'm left wondering, *Do you want to be such a touristy destination that your popularity drives prices too high for the recent local graduate?* And along similar lines, while a tourism-based economy depends upon people coming, it must not detract from the beauty, cleanliness, and quaintness that make Rogers City so attractive in the first place. Bruce Grant offered the following warning: "I hope it never comes back the way it was because it creates chaos. Creates enemies. And like I say, we go to the outdoors show and out of every ten people, two had a problem. It was a social problem. It wasn't a fishing problem, it was a social problem."

Right now, though, the locals have the recreational Lake Huron fishery largely to themselves. Beyond the fishery, Rogers City's future prospects will depend upon strong, conscientious, and values-based local governance: something that Rogers City usually seems to have. Before beginning the research for this book, I had never been to Rogers City—didn't even know of it. But now, when I call to mind concepts like "Michigan" and "salmon fishing," I can't help but see a collection of partially imagined scenes of the fishery in Rogers City as it developed and thrived for more than three decades—particularly the Rogers City Salmon Tournament—interspersed with newsprint images from the *Presque Isle County Advance* capturing much of the history's essence. I also picture the city council and other meetings at which many of the people with whom I spoke discussed ideas and made decisions that helped create and support the fishery. I remember the many drives I made through rural northern Michigan to get to Rogers City, as well as walking miles of pebbly shoreline along U.S. 23 during my visits. I'd like to someday get a boat ride south of the harbor just to see Swan Bay the same way the Partykas see it each fall. In that way I could better imagine the spectacle there during the first couple salmon tournaments, and also picture the freighters going in and out of the Calcite limestone quarry—the fleet of boats on which Ken Partyka worked as a sailor, allowing him to retire at the early age of fifty-three.

Unfortunately, as expressed to me in a somber, almost doomsday-feeling email from Jim Johnson nearly two years after my interview with him, the most recent (and ongoing, as of this writing) renegotiations of the 1836 Treaty of Washington pose dire threats to the fisheries of northern Lake Huron. In an editorial published April 1, 2023, Johnson contends that the Michigan Department of Natural Resources Fisheries Division, for which he worked for twenty-five years, acted in secrecy and is bowing primarily to the short-term interests of the tribal fisheries.[1] At risk is the perpetuity of the strong and still recovering lake trout population of northern Lake Huron, as well as populations of all other species, because the proposed new regulations would (1) greatly expand the use of gillnets, and (2) expand the legally harvestable species to include lake trout, walleye, and yellow perch. The new terms would also shrink the lake trout refuge in northern Lake Huron—an expanse over which commercial fishing is currently prohibited—by more than half, and also open the remaining part of the refuge to commercial fishing for most of the year. The proposed greatly reduced commercial fishing regulations are not without impetus; lake whitefish populations, which up until now have supported the commercial fishery, are collapsing. But the core of the proposed new regulations, as Jim describes, *does not promote stewardship and rehabilitation*. Both Tom Allum and Bruce Grant expressed serious concern over the proposed new commercial fishing regulations, noting that the new rules would allow gillnets to be used throughout Hammond Bay, including the mouth of the Ocqueoc River. "It's a shame," Bruce repeatedly lamented regarding the potential undoing of all the hard work by "many good people" to negotiate the Consent Decrees of 1985 and 2000. Those negotiations undoubtedly bolstered the recreational salmon fishery in its day, as well as the recovery of lake trout and the expansion of other recent recreational fishery opportunities such as the development of an Atlantic salmon program. Jim Johnson now represents the Coalition to Protect Michigan Resources, a group that is urging the state government to stop expansion of gillnets in the proposed new Great Lakes Consent Decree. I can't help but feel that given a set of imagined hypothetical circumstances in which whitefish were similarly collapsing but in which Chinook salmon still supported a viable fishery, there would have been a difference in the character of civic involvement in these negotiations such that so harrowing an outlook would have been precluded.

At last, as I close my introduction to this final chapter, I want to discuss the title "Salmon Capital of Michigan" because I find it to be a peculiar concept. To some, Rogers City was once the Salmon Capital of Michigan. But unlike political capitals, which might be supplanted or relocated, the title describing Michigan's premier salmon fishery has been neither assumed by nor bestowed upon another Michigan coastal community. There's been no heir to the throne. From what I can tell, the experience in Rogers City was a somewhat unique phenomenon that represented an exaggerated version of a similar salmon-fishing scenario experienced throughout many Great Lakes port towns. But being the Salmon Capital was not an achievement or status that the people in Rogers City with whom I spoke paraded around or even seemed to care much about. While the term originated in the mid-1980s as a publicity tool to draw tourism to Rogers City, it wasn't an identity that was held onto by the people there. And so I think my use of the term as a title for this book should not be interpreted as how the people who shared their stories with me actually feel about the history of salmon fishing in Rogers

City. However, to be a capital of anything depends upon the so-called capital's relation to other places, and many of the Rogers City residents who fished Lake Huron never really fished the Great Lakes anywhere else. My point is that the perception of Rogers City as a salmon-fishing capital is best left to an outsider. I feel that Rogers City truly must have been the Salmon Capital of Michigan, and I hope that the stories told within this oral history project preserve the best of which that title represented.

BRUCE GRANT: I do think the fishery is coming back. It's going to get strong. I'll be gone and out of here probably, but I do hope that the city gets more adjusted for it and they work to get it because it makes the businesses go. It makes the local business healthier and it provides work. You know, a kid up here gets out of school, he hasn't got a car to drive to Detroit to go get a—or Saginaw or Bay City—and he doesn't want to leave anyways. If they—and it's getting better. You've got Moran [Iron Works]. You've got Cadillac Products. When I came here, a good friend of mine worked at Calcite. He'd been here for about ten years. He worked there ten years. His annual wage was about 17,000 dollars a year. Now it's up—these guys are making 40, 50. Actually they're doing better than that. What changed, it was the sailors were making 50 grand a year and his brother that worked in the quarry was making 30 grand a year. So you've had these ownership changes in the quarry. Now they're making real money. I mean, they're making a standard that you can live on. And it's keeping more people here. It wouldn't hurt to have a few more. And then a town would get established. Not have to go through these roller coasters. You know, good now—this town had it. Boy, I tell you, I couldn't believe. And then they started stealing from the harbor fund to pay bills. Now they don't have enough money to pay their harbor payment and they're crying. And the people in town are bitching because, "Why do we have to make more taxes to pay for the harbor?" They had that money there. They didn't have a rainy day fund. That's common sense. That's gone on since—eons. If the squirrels don't store nuts they ain't got anything to eat all winter. They haven't learned that yet in a lot of cases. And so a fishery can come back. They're going to have to get people to go out and get the writers to come make an issue out of it. It's free advertising, and it's better advertising. An ad in one of those magazines doesn't produce hardly anything. But an article in one of those magazines keeps you busy.

CARSON: One of the things that I hadn't really thought of before speaking with Bruce [Grant] earlier today was he wondered, or thought maybe the fishery here got so big in the '80s and '90s that when it became less than that, it got so written off that—and maybe framed in too negative of a light—and now the focus and the writing and the publicity and the attention is on Lake Michigan. And he was advocating a sentiment that was like, attention just needs to be—if you want to revitalize interest in fishing Lake Huron, it's not a matter of the fishery not being here, it's a matter of how the thing was framed and the attention that is all going to the Lake Michigan side of things. And I was wondering if you had any thoughts on that?

JAYME WARWICK: Yeah, I agree with that 100 percent. Yeah, that's spot on, for sure. Like you said, it's got such a bad rap that, you know, I hear people saying, "There's no salmon in Lake Huron," which is not true at all. And we never totally lost our salmon population. There's less fish, and at times not as big fish, and you just—I think people were so used to going out there and just throwing lines over the side with any color lure, and not paying attention to the currents and weather condition, and where the salmon will migrate in the different areas. Maybe they've given up on that because maybe they're not that good of a fisherman, you know? That could be it. But from what Bruce said, yeah, I agree with that. It just gets a bad rap. And all through this we've always had—anywhere you'd go, people would say this is good fishing. We were spoiled on what we had where it was phenomenal fishing.

BRUCE GRANT: I think it's going to build up. A lot of twenty-, twenty-five-pound fish were caught last year. That's not because of anything other than the fish learning to eat the forage base that's out there now. They're not, Oh, I'm not eating unless I have alewives. Or, you know, they're raised in a trough in a hatchery. I think our fishery here has held up because of the Canadian fish—the ones that learned to eat whatever they could find early on because once they get in the spawning mode they ain't going to eat anyways. So it can come back, it's going to come back.

JIM JOHNSON: —if they want to select for successful salmon they should be selecting for fish that have the best body condition at the egg-taking station which might, in a way, start selecting for fish that will feed benthically instead of pelagically.[2] Because the food's there. Successful salmon are probably those few that are eating gobies in Lake Huron. If they live in Lake Huron, they probably are eating gobies or doing something interesting. But we keep taking eggs from Lake Michigan and fish that eat alewives. And Swan Bay fish, they're coming from Lake Michigan. So you're selecting for Lake Michigan fish, and we're not selecting for something that works in Lake Huron.

CARSON: Now, I hadn't thought about asking this, but do we know about the wild fish that are coming out of eastern Lake Huron? Are they going to Lake Michigan too? Is that the working assumption?

JIM: I think it's just that, just a working assumption. I spend a lot of time on Puget Sound, and just for shits and giggles I looked at—you know, we took the eggs from a tributary to Lake Washington way back in the '60s.[3] And [young salmon of that stock] would migrate through Lake Washington, through the Union Canal and down into Puget Sound, and then from Puget Sound up through Straits of Juan de Fuca and then [west] into the Pacific. That distance is only slightly longer than the distance from Georgian Bay to the Mackinac Bridge. Why not? There may be an eastward migratory tendency in young Chinooks too. We don't know that. But, they sure like to migrate from Swan Bay to Lake Michigan. How do they know to go to Lake Michigan unless there's an eastward—

CARSON: Or westward.

JIM: —tendency? Or *westward* tendency, excuse me. Go west, young Chinook. [*Carson laughs*] But it's all speculative.

CARSON: Well, that's interesting.

IVAN WIRGAU: And then as the invasives come in, you don't know what they're going to do. You don't know how they're going to affect that lake. The gobies, by chance, have really done well for the fishery out here. You know, that's a sustainable forage base right now. But I remember when those zebra mussels were cleaning it up out here. You'd go out in thirty, forty feet of water you'd see right to the bottom, you could see the lake trout swimming down there while you were trolling for them. It was unbelievable. You don't see that now. The zebra mussels are not around here like they were. Not even close. No, the gobies ate them. Yeah. Yeah, when I used to snorkel out here—I still do some—you don't see the zebra mussels on the rocks anymore. You'll see gobies, scooting around by the rocks, that's what you see. The quaggas are out deep. And you'll see them washed up on shore but not even a lot of them. You'd see them, but the zebra mussel used to be everywhere. No, the gobies took care of them. So that was a good thing. And there was just an article the other day by Jim Bedford, he's a toxicologist out of [the] Lansing area, I believe.

CARSON: Okay. I just know him as the guy that spinner fishes for steelhead.

IVAN: He spinner fishes for steelhead, yeah, but he's a PhD of toxicology. He thinks that eventually—it's only common sense—well, eventually those salmon are going to find those gobies and they're going to start focusing on them more, and it'll balance out. It'll never be the fishery it was but it will be a sustainable fishery. Because people have always thought—and I don't know, maybe the research and more awareness brought to their attention that the fish always fed in the pelagic zone, you know, those salmon. And they were starting to find salmon out in the ocean that had scratches on their gill plates, well, they were chasing this certain kind of a forage base down on the bottom and scratching them on the rocks. So they can adapt. So, you know, I believe that. And you get a certain—and those gobies, they die. You know, their life cycle's—they got like three or four times where they're spawning and dying. And I got to believe by chance salmon are getting some of those dead ones that are rolling into the upper parts of the wave action and currents, because they're out there to have. These lake trout are full of them. Full of gobies. Just full of them. And I know some people have caught salmon with the gobies in them. Caught some lake trout last time I was out that had salmon in them like this. [Wirgau clarification: salmon about three inches long.] That was a couple weeks ago. Couple different lake trout had like four or five of those salmon like that in them. I don't know if that was a recent plant. I looked in the database but I didn't see anything that had been planted, but they don't always catch up on updating that stuff. Yeah, not sustainable, and they just kept planting them. Then when they backed off it was already too late. They crashed. And I don't know if you'll ever see the alewives back here again. As long as you've got those quagga mussels out there. You need something that's going to get them. [*laughs*] That's what you're going to need. I know they were talking about planting, what, cisco—

CARSON: Yeah, they had stocked—

IVAN: —down in Swan—or the Saginaw Bay.

CARSON: Saginaw, yeah. They have done that. I don't know—

IVAN: What the success or anything—

CARSON: —anything about—yeah.

IVAN: Right. Exactly. And is it good to try and get the alewife back? Then you'll mess the lake trout back up again. So it's a, it's a balancing act. I don't know. The quagga mussels, I think that's what's keeping that at bay. Unless some invasive gets in here and does something to them, or something in that whole system changes to affect them I think it's going to stay the way it is.

BRUCE GRANT: And still to this day—and we don't do it much—I mean, it's not like it used to be—but it starts the last week of July, the first week of August, I can go out here and I can still catch twenty-five-, twenty-seven-pound salmon. They're not fin-clipped. They're Canadian fish. They're truly natural-reproductive fish that—they're making their swing, they're coming through. And they're not fin-clipped. This—I know they don't fin-clip every single fish that they put in—but why do those fish come through here the last week of July and the first week of August and then you never see them again until next year? Before that and after that you're catching 90 percent fin-clipped fish. That's that Canadian strain that's keeping us going. They're tough. They're natural. I mean, they're settled in here and the Canadians are still catching them good. You can go up in Drummond Island and Les Cheneaux [Islands] and still catch good salmon. I think it's the group of fish that were forgotten about and went up on their own and nobody pays any attention. And that's keeping our fishery going good even though—I know the food's down over there like it is here—but I'll bet any money the fish that—the salmon—that start eating gobies and some of the other stuff was that Canadian batch that were naturally reproduced.

CARSON: Do you think the fishing is better or worse depending on how many they stock there at the Swan River?

JAYME WARWICK: You know, my opinion is, I think we could have more fish planted, really. From what I see with the baitfish and different things. Back in the heyday when the alewives were here you'd see them wash up on the shore. And you don't see that anymore. But I am seeing—there's times I'm down on the beach—and the shoreline's only a quarter mile away from here and I'll go watch the shore—and I'm seeing ducks, like diver ducks, school alewives up to the shoreline so they can eat them. I just seen it last year. And there was a swarm of them. They're jumping out of the water, they're getting beached.

And the ducks and the birds are going crazy. But I'm not any type of biologist to see what's really happening out here. I do read up on it and things. But I just hope it isn't a decision that they don't want to plant any more here because of our low population number, or because of the treaty that's going on, they don't want to plant because they don't want them taking the fish or overharvesting. But I think we could see more, to tell you the truth.

BRUCE GRANT: I think in the future when these things happen to places that a community should establish a committee made up of a couple of businesspeople, a person from the city government, a person from the county government, and just some general sportsmen, to sit down and share their experiences and share what they're hearing at the harbor, sharing the rumors they hear—because we go down and do the outdoors shows, and that was a gold mine for us, because people would come up and say, "I'm not coming back because I didn't like this"—what had happened. You went home and you fixed it. And you called the guy back and said, "We fixed your problem and please come back." Or people would come and say, "Man, that was great, that was great." You can do that with a—I know you can do that with a business group because the Hammond Bay Anglers kind of took that role over. But when you have your city people, and your county people—they're people with a job. They're people with a budget. And what you're doing in a business like this is, I'm looking at what I have got to readjust next year by what happened this year. And they're saying, "We've only got this much budget. We don't know what we're going to have for next year, so we're going to be based on this budget." And I think you could take people from in the county and the community—especially big businesses. We've got Cadillac Products here. We're one of the biggest automotive manufacturers in the country. And this was their prime place. Their cottages were here. We've got Moran Iron Works. That guy went from a high school kid doing welding in his dad's logging garage to one of the biggest businesses in northern Michigan right now. And all they want is to make the community better, and to bring people in that they can hire that's got some common sense. I think if our community would have put a group like that together, I think that would have saved—it would have been easier and better, because—besides trying to make things happen, a lot of times you're fighting the community. Like, oh, we'd get a harbormaster he'd get so mad, "I've got so much guts to dump I don't know what to do." Man [*laughs*], this—this is gold. And we've got a quarry here that let us take it down—they didn't have to go buy a piece of ground and—or make compost. Sea Grant would come in and help them make a compost pile with the commercial fishermen. And because of introgression and they're happy with their commercial fishing, that kind of died. But look at the people over on the west side of the state—what do you call, um, oh, where they take cow manure and they make compost and everything [Morgan's Composting and Dairy Doo]? They're going so big now and it could have been the same thing here. And again, when the fishery died they would have went down too, but they'd have still had plenty of stuff for a product.

SCOTT McLENNAN: Currently, the greatest number of people moving into Rogers City and calling Rogers City home are people who have, perhaps, stayed at the local state park, and rode into Rogers City on their bicycles along a beautiful coastline bicycle trail that comes into Rogers City. So they're out at 40 Mile Point lighthouse. The Hoeft State Park. The bike trail connects all of that. They come into Rogers City. They get an ice cream cone in the summer. They see that it's a very clean community. They see that people keep their homes up nicely. They see that there isn't a lot of traffic. It looks pretty safe. And they love the beauty of it. Some of them say—and I've met these people. As mayor I walk around and greet people on a regular basis that I don't know—and they'll tell me, "Yeah. Oh, I love it here. And my husband, he's an avid fisherman. And yep, we just think this is great. We moved here two years ago. Nice to meet you. Yep, he likes to fish. He likes to hunt. We love this place. We stay here all summer. We go to the summer concerts—outdoor concerts that are in town. And then from November 1st through April 1st, we live in Florida." Or, "We live somewhere else." But they—because they're sissies. We like it here [*Carson laughs*] in the winter. We're okay with it. [*laughs*] But they go away to where it's warm. And so you're seeing an influx of those people. So the demographics are changing very much so from the day that I grew up here. When I grew up here, it was large families. Lots of kids. Now it's singles and single—couples. Couples and singles. That's what you're seeing a lot of in terms of moving into Rogers City. Great folks. Nice people. They love the natural resources here, including sportsfishing, absolutely. There's a number of them that are interested in that. So does it have an economic impact? Sure. In a related sort of way, yes.

KEN RASCHE: And this is probably off the subject, but one of the things in the last year that has helped us in Rogers City, Carson, believe it or not, is this virus. Where did you drive here from? Okay. Last year at this time between here and Rogers City—these are ten-acre pieces of land—there was like six of them for sale. Now there's none for sale, and there's home sites on five of them from people who are moving up from down below, working from home. So, this COVID thing has benefited Rogers City, in my opinion. You don't see real estate signs in Rogers City. The real estate people have a—and I know this is getting off the subject—but they've got a waiting list. They don't put signs up. They've got so many people waiting to buy up here. It's crazy. It's one of the places that's still affordable.

BRUCE GRANT: And right now we've got a walleye fishery out here—and I hope things stay quiet for a little while because this walleye fishery out here is building and building. And once it starts coming back—once we get some people here that are writing about the place—they'll go out here and you can target and catch walleye. Only the locals know that. Or that guy that catches an odd fish, he'll say to the local, "I didn't know we had walleyes here." "Oh, you caught an odd one." They don't want anybody to know. But they're—the stock is building. And it's going to happen. We're going to have a targeted walleye fishery here, I'm going to say in another four or five years. Because now you go out there and you can catch walleye.

CARSON: Walleye bring people. Just look at Saginaw Bay or the Detroit River.

BRUCE: And from my understanding, from fish biologists and people like you, that the fishery expanded out of Saginaw Bay. And then it boosted up in Oscoda. I fished in Oscoda thirty-five years ago and caught a few walleyes. And you had the river. Well, that was a big issue because they were planting salmon in the river and the walleyes were eating the salmon before they got out to the lake. So that tells you something. And then that expanded to Alpena. And now Rogers City's getting the benefit. You can go to Presque Isle and target walleye. I can't say I could go out here and catch you a limit of walleye, but I wouldn't be surprised if we went out and fished and we didn't come back with a couple walleye. And the other thing is, I won't say things are changing, I'm saying people are getting more educated. You don't go out in the summertime and fish for walleye in 110 feet of water. You get on the rock structure at forty-five feet and you'll catch some walleye.

CARSON: Yeah, well, does that about cover it for your side of the story?
KEN RASCHE: I think so. I can't think of anything else I can tell you. It's been an interesting ride, it really has been. As you said, I'm glad we experienced it. Would I—if it—it would be good, prob[ably]—it would be good if it came back to Rogers City, for the community. And, would I get involved in it again? Maybe fishing. But that's—not at the marina. [*both laugh*] No, definitely not at the marina.
CARSON: Alright. Well, thank you, Ken.
KEN: You're welcome.

EPILOGUE

On a personal level, the Pacific salmon and steelhead fisheries of the Great Lakes are really important to me. I don't think I would have started down the path of becoming a fisheries scientist and researcher if I hadn't started fishing for salmon and steelhead as a freshman in college in western Michigan. It quickly became my favorite thing in the world, and it may still be today.

It was 2010 when I started my master's degree program at Michigan State University in the Department of Fisheries and Wildlife. At that time in my life I was still probably spending just as much of my energy fishing as I was on my studies. And so right away after beginning my time at Michigan State, I observed something that was pretty surprising to me: many of my contemporaries—current and aspiring fisheries and wildlife professionals—did not actually hunt or fish. And I also felt right away that, because I fished, I was someone whose values and perspectives with respect to the Great Lakes cold-water fisheries were sometimes much different than those of my peers.

It was confusing. I thought that in becoming a fish biologist, most of the people I'd work with would be hardcore anglers, but most were not. Sure, those in my cohort may have gone fishing on occasion; they might have a fond memory or two from those experiences. But I doubt they considered themselves anglers in the way I regarded myself. They weren't thinking about fish and fisheries every waking minute the way I was. It seemed like it wasn't really an intrinsic part of how they defined themselves.

So the *personal* relationship of many biologists, fisheries professors, and researchers to fisheries in general was not obvious to me, let alone the personal relationship to the vast and largely concealed fish populations of the Great Lakes. I mean, those fisheries are immense. And without a personal connection to a fishery, how can one really appreciate it? I think this applies especially to salmon fisheries because, as those who know from personal experience will attest, they are capable of engendering nearly the gamut of human emotion.

Of course, it's not critical to hunt and fish to be an excellent fish or wildlife professional. And I'm sure plenty who hunt and fish are not necessarily the best biologists. I'm not contending that being one thing is favorable to another. But I often wonder about the differences in how the things we call natural resources are valued among the "stakeholders," or resource users, and the fisheries and wildlife professionals who study and make management and research decisions regarding those resources. To what level does having a personal connection to a fishery (for instance, being an angler in that fishery) influence one's understanding and appreciation of it, or one's professional approach to researching or managing it? And how is the presence of such a personal connection, or lack thereof, perceived by others, particularly other stakeholders within that fishery?

For instance, in the absence of a personal connection to something like the former Lake Huron recreational salmon fishery—either as an angler or as a member of a community impacted by the fishery—its collapse could very easily be construed as a fortuitous, net-positive collection of phenomena: a desirable outcome, in other words. Chinook salmon are a non-native species in Lake Huron and the Great Lakes, as are alewives. With the loss of alewife and the subsequent declines of Chinook salmon in Lake Huron, there have been the recoveries of native lake trout and native walleye.

Many people who compete for Great Lakes fisheries biologist jobs with state and federal agencies like the Michigan DNR and the USGS Great Lakes Science Center are not anglers, and many received their training outside the Great Lakes area. They may never have fished, let alone participated in or observed something like Chinook salmon fishing. In fact, several people who have gone on to secure Great Lakes fish biologist jobs are people originally from outside the area and/or people who had never fished for salmon or steelhead until I took them along fishing with me.

So in the face of similar concerns about alewife and Chinook salmon population stability in recent years in Lakes Ontario and Michigan, I believe that Great Lakes Chinook salmon fisheries should be characterized justly and duly. I hope that preconceived *values* are not imposed by Great Lakes fisheries professionals carelessly and unnecessarily in a way that might jeopardize the trust of people with a cultural connection to Chinook salmon. I fear this because I see evidence that it has already happened.[1]

In a 2012 article in perhaps the most prominent fisheries science publication, aptly called *Fisheries*, John Dettmers, Christopher Goddard, and

Kelley Smith present a dichotomy: "Fishery managers face an interesting dilemma: whether to manage in the short term for a popular and economically important [Chinook salmon] sport fishery or to embrace ecosystem change and manage primarily for native fish species that appear to be better suited to ongoing ecosystem changes."[2] In writing for *Fisheries*, a publication produced by the American Fisheries Society, the authors of course knew their article would be consumed by a vast readership far beyond the Great Lakes region. And it would be read by an audience whose values are primarily motivated by conservation and ecosystem concerns rather than economics. Native species management was pitted against non-native species management, and intrinsic value was supposed to speak for itself. If that wasn't convincing enough in its own right, Dettmers and his colleagues actually went so far as to (1) assert that Chinook salmon *cannot be managed for the long term* in Lakes Michigan and Ontario, and (2) posit the idea of stocking so many Chinook salmon in Lake Michigan so as to "nearly eliminate alewife," which they contend could perhaps lead to the rehabilitation of native species such as lake trout.

To the uninitiated, it might seem that they were vetting new concepts that one should embrace logically. But I'm not the uninitiated, and neither are the anglers and coastal community members of Lakes Michigan and Ontario. Logical or not, I perceived the article as a call to the world of fisheries professionals to rally around a moral high-ground route toward Great Lakes fisheries management, non-native species be damned. In terms of logic, though, if I were in the shoes of a Lake Michigan charter fishing guide in Chicago or Ludington, Michigan, or those of a member of the Milwaukee Chamber of Commerce, I'd definitely be questioning the motives of the agencies supposedly representing my interests after reading such an article.

What Dettmers and his coauthors didn't appropriately characterize (among other things) was the cultural impact, the meaning, of the Lake Huron Chinook salmon recreational fishery loss, which was specific to individual people and discrete, actual places—not something as nebulous as the economy.[3] They didn't really even convey what would be the economic impact of similar losses in Lake Michigan and Lake Ontario, let alone the cultural cost. (Not to mention, the Chinook salmon fisheries of both lakes are still viable as of 2023, so what did they mean by relegating them to the "short term" anyway?)[4] Their article seemed to me to unwittingly highlight the discrepancies in values, attitudes, and beliefs between fisheries professionals and the people whose lives and livelihoods are affected by the recreational fisheries of Lakes Michigan and Ontario. I fear it did so in a needlessly caustic and perhaps even sanctimonious, ivory tower–type manner. Regardless, it now exists as the official academic statement on the subject, shaping the understanding of those grad students and prospective Great Lakes fisheries biologists of whom I spoke earlier.

I hope this book's exploration of the real, lived experiences of the people with whom I was so fortunate to speak helps contribute to a fuller understanding and appreciation of the Great Lakes fisheries. I hope this perhaps especially for students in the fisheries field. Exposure to actual people who participate in and are influenced by fisheries is not often a component of the curriculum, where the training is based almost solely on science. When I was coming up, I felt like I had to tamp down whatever subjective, non-science influences—like being an angler and having a personal connection to a fishery—might be extending into my "work." However, I now believe what I felt all along: science reaches only so far—far short of describing all that we as humans value.

NOTES

PROLOGUE

1 J. V. Adams, S. C. Riley, and S. A. Adlerstein, "Development of Fishing Power Corrections for 12-M Yankee and 21-M Wing Bottom Trawls Used in Lake Huron," *Great Lakes Fishery Commission Technical Report* 68 (2009).

2 When such quantities are encountered, it's typical for the crew to count only a subsample of a particularly plentiful species and estimate abundance per kilogram in order to extrapolate the total abundance represented by the full weight.

3 E. F. Roseman, M. A. Chriscinske, D. K. Castle, and C. Prichard, "Status and Trends of the Lake Huron Offshore Demersal Fish Community, 1976–2015," *Annual Report to the Great Lakes Fishery Commission* (2016): 51–63.

4 T. O. Brenden, J. R. Bence, and E. B. Szalai, "An Age-Structured Integrated Assessment of Chinook Salmon Population Dynamics in Lake Huron's Main Basin since 1968," *Transactions of the American Fisheries Society* 141 (2012): 919–33; E. F. Roseman, J. S. Schaeffer, E. Bright, and D. G. Fielder, "Angler-Caught Piscivore Diets Reflect Fish Community Changes in Lake Huron," *Transactions of the American Fisheries Society* 143 (2014): 1419–33.

5 If you want to spot the guy in the room who's never caught a king salmon, it's the one calling them "Chinook"—at least in the swath of Michigan over which I've fished for them. Okay, that's obviously an exaggeration, and I mostly use the name "Chinook salmon" in this book. But it does seem like in Michigan, most people who fish for Chinook salmon seem to call them king salmon. Among the angling circles I've been in and around, using "Chinook" would be unconventional and something like pretentious, or too formal. At the very least, it would be weird to hear. But biologists and academic researchers never use the name "king salmon," at least not in a professional capacity. It may seem unimportant, but little discrepancies like

this might play a role in cases where anglers feel that fisheries biologists, researchers, and managers don't relate to them.

6 M. Tonello, interview with Carson Prichard, Cadillac, Michigan, February 3, 2020.

7 M. Modrzynski, "For Fishermen, This Is Paradise," *Presque Isle County Advance*, July 4, 1991, 1B, 2B.

8 C. G. Prichard, *Oral History of the Rogers City Chinook Salmon Recreational Fishery*, Michiganology (2021), michiganology.org/index.php?name=SO _61851fe2-f6fe-4039-aaa5-48f680a864f0.

9 A. Portelli, *They Say in Harlan County—An Oral History* (New York: Oxford University Press, 2011), 10.

CHAPTER 1

1 M. J. Hansen, "Lake Trout in the Great Lakes: Basin-wide Stock Collapse and Binational Restoration," in *Great Lakes Fishery Policy and Management: A Binational Perspective*, ed. W. W. Taylor and C. P. Ferreri (East Lansing: Michigan State University Press, 1999), 417–53; M. A. Zimmerman and C. C. Krueger, "Ecosystem Perspective on Re-establishing Native Deepwater Fishes in the Laurentian Great Lakes," *North American Journal of Fisheries Management* 29 (2009): 1352–71.

2 To see how severe the impact of sea lamprey was, consider this excerpt from a Michigan DNR fisheries report documenting the history of the fisheries in the Manistee River below Tippy Dam. "In most years from 1924 to 1966, the MDNR trapped and transferred steelhead over Tippy Dam. Numbers ranged from 2,718 in 1924 to just 17 in 1962. Correspondence in MDNR files states that the steelhead runs in the Manistee River began to fall off in the late 1950s due to predation from sea lampreys, which had become established in Lake Michigan. The correspondence indicates that in 1953, only 5 percent of the transferred steelhead showed lamprey scarring. By 1957, 50 percent of the transferred fish were scarred. In 1961, every single one of the 63 steelhead transferred had lamprey scars. Clearly, the sea lamprey had a profound [e]ffect on the steelhead population of the Manistee River." M. A. Tonello, "Manistee River below Tippy Dam," *Michigan Department of Natural Resources Status of the Fishery Resource Report, 2004* (4) (2004).

3 As Tody and Tanner explain (or rather, herald), they had tremendous anticipation for the future of these young coho, although a few unknowns remained:

The coho is aimed at a specific fisheries management problem—namely to elevate the fisheries resource of the Great Lakes to its maximum potential for recreational fishing. The challenge in adapting the coho to the fresh-water environment of the Great Lakes is an intriguing one. Nowhere in the world has the species been permanently established outside its native range in the north Pacific coastal area. Management objectives are even more challenging. The ultimate aim is to convert an estimated annual production of 200 million pounds of low value fishes—mainly alewives—that now teem in the upper Great Lakes into an abundance of sport fishes for the recreational fishermen. Secondly, we hope to restore the depressed commercial fisheries to a productive and economically viable industry.

To accomplish these objectives, intensive management of high value fish species like the lake trout and steelhead and new species like the coho salmon is required. These species are capable of utilizing the superabundant "trash" fish as *forage* to produce sport or food fish of maximum interest and value. (2)

No mention is made of a goal to eradicate alewives, nor is any mention made (as of February 1966) of a plan to introduce Chinook salmon (although this species would be first stocked in 1967). Altogether, *specific* plans were not really articulated. But from the very beginning, it was clear that the goal of introducing Pacific salmon to the Michigan waters of the Great Lakes was to support recreational fisheries, in perpetuity, with alewives as the prey base. W. H. Tody and W. A. Tanner, "Coho Salmon for the Great Lakes," *Michigan Department of Conservation Fish Division Fish Management Report* 1 (1966).

4 D. M. O'Keefe and S. R. Miller, "2009 Michigan Charter Fishing Study," *Michigan Sea Grant, Final Report*, MICHU-11–200 (2011).

5 The recklessness of "salmon fever" culminated on September 23, 1967, when many anglers disregarded weather reports, small-craft advisories, and pleas by area residents who warned people to not venture out onto Lake Michigan that day to fish for the first adult class of coho salmon. Seven people died and hundreds of boats were capsized, beached, or otherwise damaged, as six- to eight-foot waves generated by winds reaching forty miles per hour rolled and crashed mercilessly in Platte Bay and the waters off of Frankfort, Michigan. "Continue Search for Coho Fishermen; Seven Known Dead, 34 Unaccounted For," *Traverse City Record-Eagle*, September 25, 1967, 1, 3.

CHAPTER 2

1 "Population by Area in PI County: 1930–2000," *Presque Isle County Advance*, April 5, 2001, 1A.

2 "To Aid New Restaurant, Motel Expansion: City Will Try for State Grant," *Presque Isle County Advance*, July 5, 1984, 1; F. Krist, E. Modrzynski, and R. Krist, Letters to the Editor: "An Open Letter to Gov. Blanchard: Gill Nets Not Compatible with Sports Fishing," *Presque Isle County Advance*, September 6, 1983; Presque Isle County Sportsmen's Club Fish Committee, Guest editorial: "Do You Want a Sports Fishery?" *Presque Isle County Advance*, December 21, 1982, 6.

3 R. Dashner, Letters to the Editor: "Praises Value of Fishing," *Presque Isle County Advance*, August 31, 1989, 4.

4 Hammond Bay Area Anglers Association, *Who Is the Hammond Bay Area Anglers Association?* February 8, 2015, https://hbanglers.org/who-we-are/.

5 The following excerpt provides a good summary of the 1985 Consent Agreement:

> The 1985 agreement allocated the Great Lakes fishery among the parties by lake, zones, species and catch limits. It was premised on a roughly 50-50 allocation of the fishery between the State of Michigan and the Tribes. The Tribes were principally allocated whitefish stocks and the State of Michigan was principally allocated salmon stocks. Lake trout stocks were shared with the allocation to each party differing based on the area of the Great Lakes at issue. Generally, the Tribes were allocated more lake trout in areas where they were pursuing whitefish and state-licensed fisheries were allocated more in traditional sportfishing areas. Overall, however, the fishery resources were generally shared equally. Further, the zones created for state- and Tribally-licensed fishers reduced gear conflicts between commercial nets, particularly gill nets, and traditional sport fishing gear.
>
> —I. FitzGerald, *Great Lakes Consent Decree:*
> *A Shared Resource Allocation*, February 4, 2021,
> mucc.org/great-lakes-consent-decree-a-shared-resource-allocation/.

6 "Commissioners Want Fish Plants Increased in Area," *Presque Isle County Advance*, January 28, 1982.

7 "Fishermen Not Enthusiastic about Salmon Stock," *Presque Isle County Advance*, December 21, 1982, 1.

8 "City Council Members Support More Fish Plants in Area Waters," *Presque Isle County Advance*, February 4, 1982, 1.

9 "Million Coho and Chinook Salmon in Lake Huron Waters: State's Biggest Fish Plant Made Here," *Presque Isle County Advance*, May 24, 1983, 1; "Salmon Bonanza: Large Coho Plant Made," *Presque Isle County Advance*, May 3, 1983, 1; "Rogers City Salmon Tournament Brings Fishermen to Town," *Presque Isle County Advance, Nautical Festival Tabloid*, July 29–30, 1992, 16.

10 G. Sheppard, "New Marina Planned: Rogers City Readies for Salmon Explosion," *North Woods Call*, February 1, 1984, 3.

11 "Boat Launch Site Sparks More Debate," *Presque Isle County Advance*, April 24, 1984, 1, 2.

12 C. Stevens, "Rogers City Featured in 'Midland Daily News,'" *Presque Isle County Advance*, September 5, 1985, 3.

13 I tend to agree with Smrchek's sentiment on this point—especially with respect to boat anglers on Lakes Huron and Michigan. But the debate about whether incoming anglers would be messy miscreants played out at the city council meetings. People like Rogers City resident Karen Bloom voiced concern: "These people are not tourists. They're men out to have a good time and your community will pay the price because of that." She added, "I'm not so sure that what we're going to gain from this fishing is worth what we're going to lose. I really don't think the majority of people in this community are really thinking about the impact this fishing will have on them." Conversely, angler Gene Modrzynski voiced what he considered was the majority opinion at a subsequent city council meeting. "I've talked to a lot of people in town and they all felt like I do. We have some people criticize what's happening in Rogers City, the fishery and whatever. Some people will criticize the fishery because the fishermen are going to be drunk and do all kinds of damage or whatever to the town. And yet these people who are criticizing don't spend their energy trying to do something for Rogers City. All they do is criticize. I wish they would do something to help Rogers City, bring in another business, bring a company into town instead of just criticizing the town for doing something." D. Hoekman, "Fishery Questioned Again," *Presque Isle County Advance*, June 7, 1984, 1, 2; "Fishery Has Positive Impact," *Presque Isle County Advance*, June 21, 1984, 1.

14 Blair's Bait and Tackle opened its doors for the first time at 7 a.m., Saturday, April 24, 1982. "Blair's Bait and Tackle Opens Saturday," *Presque Isle County Advance*, April 22, 1982.

15 I misspoke during the interview. It was actually Fred Lewis's successor, Mayor James Stewart, who formed this group.

16 The following is the paragraph referred to by Grant, from O. M. Snyder Jr., Editorial, *Great Lakes Fisherman*, November 1986, 3.

> I spend several weeks of a busy travel schedule each season in Michigan on both sides of the state. I enjoy the west side and have caught a lot of fish there. However, the east side does not have to take a backseat. If there is anything missing on that side of the state it would have to be the crowds. Perhaps because they haven't been harried by the masses yet, like their counterparts on the west side, most service providers—charter operators, motel and resort operators, marina operators and even restaurants—still take that extra time to make you feel a sense of old fashioned hospitality. If the fishing continues to improve and things get as hectic on Lake Huron's shoreline some of that will be lost, which is natural. There's nothing wrong with services on the west side, they remian [*sic*] excellent in spite of the volume, but simply cannot continue as personalized as they once were because of the traffic.

CHAPTER 3

1 "Plans Unveiled at City Council Meeting for a Major Salmon Fishing Tournament," *Presque Isle County Advance*, June 5, 1986, 1.

2 T. J. Fitzwater, "Response to Tournament: A Complete Success," *Presque Isle County Advance*, August 28, 1986, 1.

3 Dan O'Keefe and Steven Miller, in their assessment of the Lake Huron charter fishing industry, found that metropolitan Detroit and Flint used to be a huge contingent of the Lake Huron charter fishing customer base. In 1985, roughly 40 percent of Lake Huron charter fishing customers were from the metro Detroit/Flint area. This changed with declines in the automotive industry in southeast Michigan. As recently as 2009, Grand Rapids and other non–Detroit/Flint areas in Michigan's southern Lower Peninsula constituted roughly 40 percent of the Lake Huron charter fishing customer base. In both assessment years (1985 and 2009), about a third of charter fishing customers in Lake Huron were out-of-state residents. D. M. O'Keefe and S. R. Miller, "2009 Michigan Charter Fishing Study," *Michigan Sea Grant, Final Report*, MICHU-11–200 (2011).

4 Richey wrote articles promoting the fishery in Rogers City, and he was actually up on the Calcite property observing the second round of a million salmon being stocked in Swan River in 1984. He served as grand marshal of the Rogers City Salmon Tournament from 1986 to 1988. D. Richey, "Rogers City Pins Hopes on Salmon," *Presque Isle County Advance*, May 31,

1984, 1, 3; "Richey to 'Marshal' Fishing Tournament," *Presque Isle County Advance*, June 19, 1986, 1; "Over 443 Entries: Ken Partyka Wins Salmon Tournament," *Presque Isle County Advance*, August 28, 1986; D. Richey, "Salmon, Lake Huron's Swan Bay Are Inseparable," *Presque Isle County Advance*, September 4, 1986, 2; "Mother Nature Rules: Craig Moser Wins Rogers City Salmon Tournament," *Presque Isle County Advance*, August 27, 1987, 1, 2; K. Du Lac, "Tournament a Winner," *Presque Isle County Advance*, August 18, 1988, 1, 2.

5 "Detroit Steelheaders Here This Weekend: Anglers Already Arriving for Salmon Tournament," *Presque Isle County Advance*, August 13, 1987, 1; "Many Fishermen and Dignitaries Coming for Salmon Tournament," *Presque Isle County Advance*, August 20, 1987, 1.

6 The food "booth" was actually a big tent.

7 In the earlier years of the tournament, all the boats would stage in the harbor, engines off, waiting for the official start. But when the siren was sounded or the gun was fired, the ensuing scramble to exit the marina was dangerous, let alone inefficient (although it made for a memorable spectacle). For example, in 1986, the 155 fishing boats readying for the tournament start all launched and staged in a harbor that had just seventy-nine slips. In later years, boats were allowed to stage outside the harbor in Lake Huron to await the starting signal.

8 Referring back to some of the terminology introduced in chapter 1, Bombers, J-Plugs, and Grizzlys are plug-style fishing lures, while Northport Nailers, Daredevles, Little Cleos, and Krocodiles are lures of the spoon variety. Firetiger is a popular color pattern for any type of fishing lure—the triumvirate hues of fluorescent orange, yellow, and chartreuse overlain with a black tiger-stripe pattern.

9 So often people overstate the size of waves. I think that's why Ken hesitated here. But the weather and waves that he and Ivan Wirgau faced in the '86 and '87 tournaments were corroborated. Consider the quotes below:

"The 443 anglers and 180 boats entered in the tournament were blasted by 35-knot winds and 8–12-foot waves on Saturday afternoon and Sunday. The gusts were so severe that tournament organizers suspended the tournament for three hours on Saturday in order to protect the fishermen." "Over 443 entries."

"Thirty-five knot winds and 10-foot seas forced the suspension of the tournament shortly after it began Saturday morning." "Mother Nature Rules."

"With 30 knot winds and 8–10 foot waves, a good part of the 825 fishermen braved the conditions to have a chance at catching a prize salmon, but all of us must be thankful that we returned to port in one piece. I ask this, how many of these fishermen would have left the dock if they were not entered in the tournament. [*sic*]

"Many things can happen at sea even in the calmest of conditions. I believe it was poor judgment for this tournament to be allowed to function during these weather conditions. It should have been postponed, as suggested." J. Belusar, Letters to the Editor: "Writer Has Suggestions for Salmon Tournament," *Presque Isle County Advance*, October 1, 1987, 4.

10 Bruce Grant elaborates only vaguely on this, but something untoward happened with the original tournament organizers so that by its third iteration, the Hammond Bay Anglers assumed responsibility. Inconspicuously, Fitzwater was no longer appearing in the *Presque Isle County Advance* by 1988. With the changing of hands, Bruce Grant, Don Cothran, and Mike Modrzynski assumed primary roles organizing and directing. In the process, the tournament rules were changed. It seems the goals were to make the tournament safer (no more Le Mans start, for instance), but they were also aimed at, I think, reducing riffraff (strictly my interpretation). Ken Partyka stopped fishing the tournament as a result.

As Allum intimated, there were a "couple of occasions" of foul play. Cothran, who played a major role in running the tournament from 1988 to 1995, would be arrested in 1996 on charges of embezzlement stemming from his involvement in the Rogers City Salmon Tournament. Du Lac, "Tournament a Winner"; E. Gaertner, "Former Salmon Tourney Treasurer Faces Embezzlement Charges," *Presque Isle County Advance*, March 18, 1996, 1A.

CHAPTER 4

1 D. C. Darga, "Clio Man Takes Top Prize in Salmon Tournament," *Presque Isle County Advance*, August 14, 1997, 1A, 2A.

2 University of Michigan professor Jim Diana was concerned as far back as 1984 that the numbers of salmon stocked might exceed what could be supported by the available prey. In the first examination of angler-caught fish diets, Diana reached out to, among other constituencies, Rogers City anglers to retain the stomachs of the fish that they caught in order to assess what they had eaten. A 1984 article in the *Presque Isle County Advance*, less than

a year after the first round of a million salmon were stocked in Swan River, noted, "Today, fishery biologists and managers fear that the widespread stocking of salmon may be threatening the forage, predominantly alewives, and that the growth of salmon, in size and number, may decline." Although Diana's resultant publication didn't speak to the supposed "threat," it was found that Chinook salmon (and all other predator species, for that matter) fed almost exclusively on alewife and rainbow smelt in Lake Huron. In 1990 Jim Johnson expressed concern as well: "We are finding that salmon in Lake Huron have no fat in their viscera, and that is not a good sign. That means, to a biologist, that the forage base being used by the salmon may be at its maximum carrying capacity and we need to stop increasing the plants and stay with what the quota is now." "Anglers Can Help Fish Research Project," *Presque Isle County Advance*, April 24, 1984; J. S. Diana, "Food Habits of Angler-Caught Salmonines in Western Lake Huron," *Journal of Great Lakes Research* 16 (1990): 271–78; M. Modrzynski, "Biologist Claims Fish Are in Lake Huron," *Presque Isle County Advance*, September 6, 1990, 9.

3 M. Modrzynski, "Zebra Mussels Reach Rogers City," *Presque Isle County Advance*, March 4, 1992, 1A.

4 Ken's memory wasn't over-glorifying the past, as so often happens. The average weight of *Salmon Slayer*'s catch on the Sunday of the 1986 Rogers City Salmon Tournament was exactly eighteen pounds. Of course, that was the average weight caught by the winning crew. But you can imagine that, progressing into later August and September, as the salmon continued to grow, the average weights of Chinook salmon caught would very conceivably have been eighteen to twenty pounds. T. Fitzwater, "A Second Look at the Salmon Tournament," *Presque Isle County Advance*, August 28, 1986, 11.

5 As I sat at the picnic table in the Partykas' backyard, the teeny-tiny boat that Ken was referring to was parked just feet away. He never said as much, but I recognized it as the boat that he won in the 1986 Rogers City Salmon Tournament for his twenty-five-pound, eight-ounce winning fish. I found it so cool that he actually launched that boat right off of the beach in his backyard and caught salmon. "Over 443 Entries: Ken Partyka Wins Salmon Tournament," *Presque Isle County Advance*, August 28, 1986, 1.

6 According to personal correspondence with Mary Ann Heidemann, Mike Modrzynski is actually neither Eugene Modrzynski's son nor his brother.

7 Johnson means the caudal peduncle.

8 Johnson clarified: "Doing cage culture and evaluating cage culture" meant evaluating net pen acclimation. He added that adipose fin clips and coded wire tags were used to identify them.

9 Johnson noted that you could call the raceways "pens" too.

10 The study to which Johnson was referring is: J. E. Johnson, S. P. DeWitt, and J. A. Clevenger Jr., "Causes of Variable Survival of Stocked Chinook Salmon in Lake Huron," *Michigan Department of Natural Resources, Fisheries Research Report* 2086 (2007).

11 The predation problem occurred during the Chinook salmon smolts' beach phase.

12 Johnson meant of a size big enough to be caught in the recreational fishery.

CHAPTER 5

1 The years of Joe's youth to which he must have been referring are 1992, 1993, and 1994. In each of those years, the winning salmon broke the thirty-pound mark. Weights dipped a bit through the remainder of the '90s, but 2000 and 2002 each saw winning fish break the thirty-pound mark as well.

2 Joe covered the Rogers City Salmon Tournament for the *Advance* in 1996, 1999, and 2000. And actually, from 1986 to 2007, the nineteen years for which I have participation data, the three years that Joe covered were three of the top five biggest tournaments held. This included 2000, in which a record 360 boats and 1,225 anglers competed, and the winning salmon weighed 32.95 pounds. J. Hefele, "Flint Man Takes Top Prize in Annual Salmon Tournament," *Presque Isle County Advance*, August 15, 1996, 1A, 1B; J. Hefele, "Salmon Tournament Scheduled to Reel into Action Next Week," *Presque Isle County Advance*, August 5, 1999, 1A; J. Hefele, "The Quest for the Big One: RC Salmon Tournament Set for This Weekend," *Presque Isle County Advance*, August 12, 1999, 1A, 3A; J. Hefele, "Room for Entries in Salmon Tourney," *Presque Isle County Advance*, July 27, 2000, 1A, 2A.

3 A commonly held belief among Michigan anglers is that the bigger, mature salmon—for example, those that used to reach thirty-plus pounds—are four-year-olds. However, Chinook salmon can mature at different ages, and the size at age and age at maturity can vary widely. In the Great Lakes, mature Chinook salmon (that is, fish with fully developed gonads that return to their natal streams in the fall) range in age from two to four years old. It's difficult to tell a Chinook salmon's age without killing it, after which age can be assessed by either recovering a coded wire tag embedded in its snout before stocking or counting rings on bony structures removed from a harvested fish. In general, in the Great Lakes

and elsewhere, there is an inverse relationship between growth and age at maturity. In fact, when growth is poor, as it was in the mid-2000s in Lake Huron, a high proportion of the mature fish would have indeed been four-year-olds. But when growth is at its highest, even three-year-old Chinook salmon would have been able to reach weights exceeding thirty pounds, spawn, and die before seeing age four. Higher maturity rates at ages two and three are indicators of better conditions for Chinook salmon growth than are high maturity rates at age four. J. K. Wesley, "Age and Growth of Chinook Salmon in Lake Michigan: Verification, Current Analysis, and Past Trends" (master's thesis, University of Michigan, 1996); M. C. Williams, "Spatial, Temporal, and Cohort-Related Patterns in the Contribution of Wild Chinook Salmon (*Oncorhynchus tshawytscha*) to Total Chinook Harvest in Lake Michigan" (master's thesis, Michigan State University, 2012).

4 After the collapse of alewife in Lake Huron, Chinook salmon that were stocked in the Swan River near Rogers City were able to adapt by migrating into Lake Michigan where the alewife population remained comparatively abundant. Based upon tagged fish that were subsequently caught by recreational anglers, the proportions of Chinook salmon stocked into the Swan River that ended up being caught in Lake Michigan increased from 0.13 pre-collapse (1993–97) to 0.82 after collapse (2008–14). Even Jim Johnson expressed surprise that this phenomenon was occurring—and rightfully so, because Chinook salmon stocked anywhere south of Alpena were not able to similarly adapt. R. D. Clark Jr., J. R. Bence, R. M. Claramunt, J. A. Clevenger, M. A. Kornis, C. R. Bronte, C. P. Madenjian, and E. F. Roseman, "Changes in Movements of Chinook Salmon between Lakes Huron and Michigan after Alewife Population Collapse," *North American Journal of Fisheries Management* 37 (2017): 1311–31.

5 J. E. Johnson, S. P. DeWitt, and J. A. Clevenger Jr., "Causes of Variable Survival of Stocked Chinook Salmon in Lake Huron," *Michigan Department of Natural Resources, Fisheries Research Report* 2086 (2007).

6 It was actually Norine Dobiesz's PhD dissertation that Jim Johnson was helping with, and Norine finished it in 2003—a year before the definitive alewife collapse. I laughed at this point in my interview with Jim because I knew that, based upon research that Jim would complete in the next several years, Norine's estimate of the Chinook salmon population being comprised of 20 percent wild fish was way low. As Jim describes elsewhere herein, the Lake Huron Chinook salmon population in the early 2000s was actually about 90 percent wild-origin, naturally reproduced fish. N. E.

Dobiesz, "An Evaluation of the Role of Top Piscivores in the Fish Community of the Main Basin of Lake Huron" (PhD diss., Michigan State University, 2003).

7 J. X. He, J. R. Bence, C. P. Madenjian, S. A. Pothoven, N. E. Dobiesz, D. G. Fielder, J. E. Johnson, M. P. Ebener, A. Cottrill, L. C. Mohr, and S. R. Koproski, "Coupling Age-Structured Stock Assessment and Fish Bioenergetics Models: A System of Time-Varying Models for Quantifying Piscivory Patterns during the Rapid Trophic Shift in the Main Basin of Lake Huron," *Canadian Journal of Fisheries and Aquatic Sciences* 72 (2015): 7–23.

8 E. F. Roseman, J. S. Schaeffer, E. Bright, and D. G. Fielder, "Angler-Caught Piscivore Diets Reflect Fish Community Changes in Lake Huron," *Transactions of the American Fisheries Society* 143 (2014): 1419–33.

9 Our interview took place on May 18, 2021, in the midst of the COVID-19 pandemic. Frank's mention of masks was in reference to advisories, and in some cases mandates, for people to wear masks as a means to reduce virus transmission.

10 Johnson clarification: "My answer that follows is confined to the way these issues shaped the Michigan DNR Fishery Division's approach, not the interagency, interstate GLFC interactions."

11 For the story on Alpena's brown trout fishery, see 50:36–57:59 of my interview with Jim Johnson, michiganology.org/uncategorized/IO_bda5a655 -eb04-41c3-b253-07f43187c6f8/.

12 MH-1 is a geographical expanse that describes a fishery-management unit in the northwestern-most part of Lake Huron. It originates at the mouth of Swan River, extends at a northeast angle to the Canadian jurisdictional boundary, then reaches northwest to the eastern edge of Michigan's Drummond Island. MH-1 encompasses all water west thereof within Michigan's jurisdiction.

13 E. F. Roseman and S. C. Riley, "Biomass of Deepwater Demersal Forage Fishes in Lake Huron, 1994–2007: Implications for Offshore Predators," *Aquatic Ecosystem Health & Management* 12 (2009): 29–36.

CHAPTER 6

1 The year Ken became harbormaster, 1989, was momentous in other respects as well. That's when Michigan DNR Fisheries director John Robertson set up the Lake Huron Citizens Fishery Advisory Committee and Jim Johnson started as fisheries biologist for the Michigan DNR at the Alpena Fisheries Research Station.

2 "Nautical City Is Home to Fine Harbor," *Presque Isle County Advance, Visitors' Guide Special* (1999): 7, 8.

3 I cited this article earlier in the book. The lines to which I was referring read, "Imagine 1,548 salmon weighing in excess of 20,000 pounds. That is how much fish was pulled out of Presque Isle County waters over the weekend by participants in the 12th annual Rogers City Salmon Tournament." D. C. Darga, "Clio Man Takes Top Prize in Salmon Tournament," *Presque Isle County Advance*, August 14, 1997, 1A, 2A.

4 A fish-cleaning station is a roofed, open-air, permanent structure that houses stainless steel tables, large plastic cutting boards, water hoses, and a garbage disposal "on steroids" capable of grinding up fish carcasses so they can be rinsed away into the city's sewage system. Most major fishing ports on the Great Lakes, especially those with charter operators, have a fish-cleaning station.

5 "City Home to Fine New Boat Harbor," *Presque Isle County Advance, Visitors' Guide Special*, May 22–23, 1997, 4.

6 E. Gaertner, "Rogers City Receives More Marina Grant Funds," *Presque Isle County Advance*, December 7, 1995, 3A.

7 The Vogelheim property to which Dave was referring sits immediately northwest up the lakeshore from the Rogers City marina and contains the "fish docks" that Scott McLennan described in chapter 1. The remnants of this old infrastructure, which used to harbor commercial boats but is now in disrepair, can still be seen from the breakwall of the marina. And as Dave described, Presque Isle Harbor, twenty-one miles east of Rogers City marina, was purchased by the State in the late 1980s and got a multimillion-dollar facelift, transforming it from a "dilapidated wooden dock" to a 120-slip facility with a fishing pier. "Presque Isle Harbor Improvements Nearer," *Presque Isle County Advance*, January 21, 1988, 11; "Presque Isle Harbor Granted $1.4 Million," *Presque Isle County Advance*, August 3, 1989, 1; Pure Michigan (n.d.), *Presque Isle State Harbor*, www .michigan.org/property/presque-isle-state-harbor.

8 To this point, back in 1999 Ken told Gail Maggi of the *Presque Isle County Advance*, "I wish more people understood that our harbor is self supporting, and has been for the last 10 years. I can't speak for before that time, but we pay between $20,000–30,000 every year into the city's general fund. We also pay wages for any DPW [Department of Public Works] employee when that person is working in the harbor area, it costs the city nothing." G. Maggi, "Hot Fishing Season Continues with Last Chance Tourney," *Presque Isle County Advance*, September 9, 1999, 3A.

CHAPTER 7

1 Heidemann meant half a block from the Lakeside Park interview location.

2 Rich Hamp owned Presque Isle's Huron Shores Motel in Rogers City. Frank Krist, in his role as an environmental officer, performed inspections on the motel's pool. I reached out to Rich for an interview, but for various reasons he declined—in no small part because he had moved to Colorado and was facing the difficulties of managing a restaurant there during the COVID-19 pandemic. But I spoke at length with Rich on the phone. He recalled not even being aware of salmon fishing upon moving to Rogers City in 1996. But during the motel's best five-year stretch, he guessed that 60 percent of his annual business came from salmon fishermen. "You couldn't see the motel from the highway because there were so many boats and trailers parked in front of it," he told me. He said that his biggest worry during those years wasn't money but freezer space for holding the anglers' catches.

Rich's motel operation could be described as "no frills." He told me that he charged a mere $60 for a room for two nights. But when the salmon fishery declined, he said, his prospective clients were replaced by people who wanted "amenities"—not the least of which was air-conditioning, which the motel didn't have. When asked by customers if the motel supplied bar soap or hair dryers, he replied, "Absolutely not." Perhaps not surprisingly, his business took a downward turn when the salmon fishery did.

Nevertheless, on a couple of my visits to Rogers City, I actually overnighted at the Huron Shores Motel. Of course now it's under new management, but I had no complaints.

CHAPTER 8

1 R. L. Eshenroder, "Decline of Lake Trout in Lake Huron," *Transactions of the American Fisheries Society* 121 (1992): 548–54.

2 D. W. Coble, R. E. Bruesewitz, T. W. Fratt, and J. W. Schreirer, "Lake Trout, Sea Lampreys, and Overfishing in the Upper Great Lakes: A Review and Reanalysis," *Transactions of the American Fisheries Society* 119 (1990): 985–95.

3 D. C. Honeyfield, J. P. Hinterkopf, J. D. Fitzsimons, D. E. Tillitt, J. L. Zajicek, and S. B. Brown, "Development of Thiamine Deficiencies and Early Mortality Syndrome in Lake Trout by Feeding Experimental and Feral Fish Diets Containing Thiaminase," *Journal of Aquatic Animal Health* 17 (2005): 4–12.

4 Great Lakes Fishery Commission, "Status of Sea Lamprey," September 2021, glfc.org/status.php.

5 That chemist's name was Cliff Kortman, the father of Rob Kortman, whom I interviewed for this project. Before meeting Rob, I had read the story of how Cliff performed trials with hundreds of chemical compounds at the Hammond Bay Biological Station in hopes of identifying a molecule that would specifically kill sea lamprey and only sea lamprey. Cliff's story, for which he was interviewed alongside Rob at his house in Rogers City, is featured in the book *Great Lakes Sea Lamprey: The 70 Year War on a Biological Invader* by Cory Brant. But it didn't occur to me until after my interview with Rob, when he was reminiscing about how his dad used to work at the Hammond Bay Biological Station and was the one who discovered TFM, that I realized Rob's dad was the same man featured in Cory Brant's book. That book, by the way, is a great read for anybody interested in the saga of Great Lakes sea lamprey control.

6 For a fuller treatise on the recovery of lake trout in Lake Huron, I suggest reading the paper by Jim Johnson, co-written with Michigan DNR colleagues Ji He and Dave Fielder: "Rehabilitation Stocking of Walleyes and Lake Trout: Restoration of Reproducing Stocks in Michigan Waters of Lake Huron," *North American Journal of Aquaculture* 77 (2015): 396–408. I relied heavily on the research they present for the introduction to this chapter.

   More recent genetics research by Kim Scribner and several other biologists describes the disproportionately high contributions of Seneca-strain genetic material in the naturally reproduced lake trout in Lake Huron, further substantiating the better relative survival, and subsequently better spawning success, of the Seneca lake trout strain. K. Scribner, I. Tsehaye, T. Brenden, W. Stott, J. Kanefsky, and J. Bence, "Hatchery Strain Contributions to Emerging Wild Lake Trout Populations in Lake Huron," *Journal of Heredity* 109 (2018): 675–88.

7 The term *human dimensions* describes a subfield of fisheries and wildlife management and research. It is concerned with considering and incorporating people's beliefs, attitudes, preferences, and activities as a formal part of fisheries and wildlife management. "Human dimensions" is defined as follows: "how people value wildlife, how they want wildlife to be managed, and how they affect or are affected by wildlife and wildlife management decisions. The *human dimensions* field seeks to understand human traits and looks at ways to incorporate that understanding into wildlife management planning and actions. The term *human dimensions* covers a broad set of ideas and practices, including economic and social values, individual and

social behavior, public involvement in management decision making, and communication." D. J. Decker, T. L. Brown, and W. F. Siemer, "Evolution of People-Wildlife Relations," in *Human Dimensions of Wildlife Management in North America*, ed. D. J. Decker, T. L. Brown, and W. F. Siemer, 3–21 (Bethesda, MD: Wildlife Society, 2001).

8 Fish that survive sea lamprey attacks are left with circular, scale-less, bright red, grotesque open wounds. Over time, the wounds heal and the scales grow back, but often in an irregular pattern so that the fish maintains a visible scar. Fresh wounds are indicative of relatively recent sea lamprey parasitism, so they provide a useful data source regarding the current size of the sea lamprey population. When lake trout are surveyed in any of the Great Lakes, biologists record the presence and number of sea lamprey wounds on each fish, in addition to other data such as the fish's length, weight, and sex, the presence of fin clips and tag numbers, and so on. Depending on whether surveyed fish are released or harvested, various biological samples can also be collected to age the fish (scales, otoliths, vertebrae), test for the presence of disease (liver, kidney, blood), perform genetic analysis, or gather other types of data. Together, the various data types are used in conjunction to create fish-population models that describe their growth, survival and mortality, reproduction, and sometimes even movement in order to assess population status and best inform how management tools such as stocking and harvest regulations can be optimized to achieve desired outcomes.

9 M. Tonello, interview with Carson Prichard, Cadillac, Michigan, February 3, 2020.

10 Walleye also made a monumental recovery in Lake Huron following the collapse of alewife, particularly in Saginaw Bay. Dave Fielder is the premier walleye biologist for Lake Huron, and he, Jim Johnson, and Ji He also described the story of walleye rehabilitation in their 2015 paper mentioned earlier, "Rehabilitation Stocking of Walleyes and Lake Trout."

11 Following my interview with Ivan, we got to chatting about various things: the two giant brown trout that he'd had taxidermied and mounted on his living room walls, stream steelhead fishing, and other assorted fish stories. As I turned away from Ivan's front door to cross his front yard and head back to my car, he asked if I'd like to take home some smoked lake trout. *Gladly*, I confirmed. He went back into the house and then reemerged with a vacuum-sealed fillet. It was delicious.

12 There have been several diet studies to assess the contribution of the different prey fish species to the diets of predator species such as Chinook

salmon. In these studies, the stomachs of fish caught by anglers are excised and given to researchers with the U.S. Fish and Wildlife Service and state departments of natural resources for analysis of the gut contents. Evidence of alewives and rainbow smelt in the diets suggests a good balance between predators and prey because Chinook salmon prefer to eat these species as they are energetically a very worthwhile calorie resource, and they also reside in the water temperatures preferred by Chinook salmon. Chinook salmon and lake trout stomach contents showing a decreased presence of alewives and rainbow smelt indicate that these prey fish abundances may be vulnerable, alerting management agencies that stocking fewer numbers of these predator species may be prudent in order to maintain a favorable balance for the longevity of the prey species. Currently, this is especially important for Lakes Michigan and Ontario, given the recent history of predator and prey dynamics in Lake Huron that led to the collapse of alewives there. Information on the most recent and ongoing diet study can be found at www.facebook.com/huronmichigandietstudy.

CHAPTER 9

1   I. Wirgau, "Sportsmen's Club Proud of 1986 Accomplishment," *Presque Isle County Advance*, January 15, 1987, 2.

2   Splake are a hybrid cross between brook trout and lake trout.

3   John Pridnia and Beverly Bodem were politicians who represented the northeastern portion of Michigan's Lower Peninsula. John Pridnia was a Republican member of the Michigan House of Representatives from 1989 to 1990, and the Michigan Senate from 1991 to 1994. Beverly Bodem was a Republican member of the Michigan House of Representatives from 1991 through 1998, succeeding Pridnia in that role. It is worth noting that before becoming a politician, Pridnia also owned a bait shop in Harrisville, Michigan, during the early years of the Lake Huron Chinook salmon fishery.

4   Johnson clarified, "In terms of return of stocked fish to the sportfishery, it's best if you stock them at Swan weir."

5   Frank and Theresa Krist's home lies in the heart of Rogers City. They live within a ten- to fifteen-minute walk of many of the others whom I interviewed. Yet right there in town, the Krists have converted the entire northwest side of their yard into a homesteading-level gardening endeavor, complete with no-till row crops, berry plants, and fruit trees. Almost no space is spared, and I bet it covers over an eighth of an acre. It was about

an hour before sunset on a mid-May day when Frank took time out of his gardening work to sit with me in that relaxing, Edenic setting and talk about his experiences related to the Rogers City fishery.

CHAPTER 10

1 Maps demonstrating the current and proposed new fishing regulations can be seen at protectmiresources.com/maps/. J. Johnson, "Consent Decree Dangerous for Local Fishing," *Alpena News*, April 1, 2023, www.thealpenanews.com/opinion/editorials-and-columns/2023/04/consent-decree-dangerous-for-local-fishing/.

2 The term *benthic* describes something that relates to the bottom of a body of water, while the term *pelagic* relates to the middle or surface depths.

3 Washington State gave the State of Michigan Chinook salmon eggs from a tributary to Lake Washington.

EPILOGUE

1 I was also treated dismissively by a prominent Great Lakes fisheries biologist (whom I won't name) during a breakaway session at a research symposium in 2017. I was among eight or ten biologists at the table, each of us with expertise and backgrounds in various regions of the Great Lakes. The topic of discussion shifted to Lake Erie, and the biologist to whom I'm referring was describing the major fisheries there. Leaning in, I felt the need to pipe up: "I know we're talking about the *lake*, but steelhead fishing's huge in the rivers in the central and eastern basins—eastern Ohio, Pennsylvania, New York—"

   "Agh, non-natives," the biologist quickly snipped before continuing, cutting me off.

   I casually scanned the faces of the other biologists seated around me and when no one else seemed to have batted an eye, I settled back down in my chair, pulling my elbows off the table. It was his value system (and theirs, I guess) against mine.

2 J. M. Dettmers, C. I. Goddard, and K. D. Smith, "Management of Alewife Using Pacific Salmon in the Great Lakes: Whether to Manage for Economics or the Ecosystem?" *Fisheries* 37 (2012): 495–501.

3 In 2014, Michigan DNR fisheries biologists Randy Claramunt and Dave Clapp rebutted the Dettmers article with an entry of their own in *Fisheries* magazine. In it, Claramunt and Clapp state how Dettmers and his

colleagues presented an "incomplete and possibly misleading perspective on current Great Lakes fisheries management." Claramunt and Clapp highlight the potential negative social implications of "writing off" the management of non-native Pacific salmon species, which would be the loss of stakeholder support in future fisheries-management decision making. R. M. Claramunt and D. F. Clapp, "Response to Dettmers et al. (2012): Great Lakes Fisheries Managers Are Pursuing Appropriate Goals," *Fisheries* 39 (2014): 123–25.

4 In fact, the largest Chinook salmon ever caught in the Great Lakes was reeled in on August 8, 2021, off the shores of Ludington, Michigan, in Lake Michigan. The monster fish weighed in at 47.86 pounds, setting a Michigan state record. D. A. Rose, "Teen's First Salmon Ever Is Michigan's New State Record Chinook, at 47.86 Pounds," *Field & Stream*, August 9, 2021.

ABOUT THE AUTHOR

Carson Prichard is an avid angler and outdoorsman. He received his PhD in earth and ecosystem science from Central Michigan University in 2018. His research in fisheries science, Great Lakes ecology, and the fish populations in Lake Huron and Lake Michigan has been published in several peer-reviewed journals. Raised in Jenison, Michigan, Prichard now resides in Gainesville, Florida.